The Adult University

Etienne Bourgeois
Chris Duke
Jean-Luc Guyot
Barbara Merrill

The Society for Research into Higher Education
& Open University Press

Published by SRHE and
Open University Press
Celtic Court
22 Ballmoor
Buckingham
MK18 1XW

email: enquiries@openup.co.uk
world wide web: http://www.openup.co.uk

and 325 Chestnut Street
Philadelphia, PA 19106, USA

First published 1999

A catalogue record of this book is available from the
British Library

ISBN   0 335 19907 0 (pbk)   0 335 19908 9 (hbk)

Library of Congress Cataloging-in-Publication Data
The adult university / Etienne Bourgeois . . . [et al.].
     p.   cm.
   Includes bibliographical references (p.   ) and index.
   ISBN 0–335–19908–9.   ISBN 0–335–19907–0 (pbk.)
     1. Adult education—Cross-cultural studies.
2. Education, Higher—Cross-cultural studies.
3. Universities and colleges—Administration—Cross-
cultural studies.   4. Educational change—Cross-cultural
studies.   I. Bourgeois, Etienne, 1958–   .
LC5219.A35   1999
378—dc21   98–44936
                                            CIP

Typeset by Graphicraft Limited, Hong Kong
Printed in Great Britain by St Edmundsbury Press,
Bury St Edmunds, Suffolk

Contents

1

Introduction

Objectives and context

This book brings together two large themes of contemporary society and examines the interplay between them. These themes are the future of the university in an era of mass higher education (HE); and social inclusion or exclusion, which has acquired a new salience in many societies for reasons that are considered below.

The very concept of university has become problematic with the transition from highly selective to more open HE systems. In these perhaps as many as a third compared with a previous number of under 5 per cent of young people in the age cohort approaching 18 years go on to university. The term university has come to encompass a wider spectrum of higher institutions, for instance the former polytechnics and central institutes in the United Kingdom or the colleges of advanced education in Australia. System boundaries remain contested, with the larger colleges of higher education in the UK pressing to join the university league, and over 10 per cent of publicly funded HE taking place in the UK further education sector.

Many analyses allude to a crisis in higher education. There is perceived to be a contest between high standards, or quality, and equity, or access. As with school curricula and systems there is an ideological contest crudely characterized as between progressives and conservatives. In HE it is between those favouring still wider access and those, pejoratively labelled elitists, who argue that standards are declining. There are common tendencies for unified mass higher education systems to redivide into categories differentiated by mission and especially by status. Research or research-led universities are contrasted with teaching-only or community-service organizations. Prestigious leading universities define their membership and identity (they benchmark themselves) in an international league. The University of Melbourne for example, geographically remote from the northern hemisphere, has co-created and is a member of the international 'Universitas 21' club. It has also appointed to its governing body the vice-chancellor of the University of

Singapore and Sir Ron Dearing, who chaired the UK review of higher education and produced a report in 1997 (Department for Education and Employment, 1997). The prestige hierarchy of universities is seen to drop from the international through national to regional and local levels. Yet access for 'non-traditional students' is essentially a regional and especially a local phenomenon, since these students are tied by a web of other life-roles to a locality.

Social exclusion is a newly important policy agendum for the European Community in particular, that features in 1990s green and white papers alongside economic concerns. It tends to be presented mainly in economic terms (waste or under-development of human resources) but also as a direct social cost and a threat of alienation from the mainstream society, its mores and its rewards, results in antisocial and destructive behaviour. Though the term may be less familiar outside 'Eurospeak' the same issue is recognized through concern with the long-term unemployed, the 'black economy', the new 'underclass', and recently the anomic loss of identity, especially of young unemployed males. This group is unable to find an established route into effective social and economic participation in the new lower employment economies with shrinking blue-collar sectors. Even casualized low-paid employment of the fast-food chain variety tends to be monopolized by middle-class youngsters working their way towards a secure, educated position in society.

Connecting these two themes is our focusing interest in the accessibility and receptiveness of universities to those who have not traditionally entered them. This includes young people from minority ethnic groups, working-class communities and still, in some subject areas and some societies, young women. Our main focus, however, is on adults. We are interested in the attitude to, treatment of and experience of students other than the traditional archetypal young man or woman who moves with little or no interruption from a successful full-time upper secondary schooling into what is still for them usually full-time HE.

The subject of access to HE is far from new. It has spawned a wealth of sometimes polemical and ephemeral, policy-oriented and more scholarly literature in the UK over the past twenty years. There is a well recognized 'access movement', and access remains a lively matter on the policy agenda of, for instance, the Higher Education Funding Council for England (HEFCE). Access has also become a subject for international comparative study, adopted by the European Society for Research in the Education of Adults (ESREA) as a network theme and documented across parts of Europe and beyond as far as Australia by Davies (1995a, 1995b). Our sense, however, is that descriptive analysis of HE system behaviours and of forms and levels of provision for non-traditional adults has not yet taken us very far into understanding the dynamics of system and institutional change or of resistance to it. Much of the explanation of why change occurs or is frustrated is to be found in zones below the vision of systems analyses.

The students in our sights are commonly referred to as mature, mature-age, or non-traditional. The stereotypical normal student is young, much preoccupied with sport and sex and clad in a college scarf and sweater.

Increasingly, however, he and ever more commonly she, as women come to outnumber male students, is concerned to turn the investment of degree study into subsequent well-rewarded employment. As student numbers rise and competition for well-paid secure employment becomes more severe, the stereotype is shifting towards a more instrumental, less exclusively hedonistic, popular image – and indeed reality. The type nevertheless remains both young and middle-class.

'Non-traditional' is an accurate if uninspiring descriptor. In fact the majority of students in higher education in many societies are now mature adults in the sense of having a significant break with other life- and work-experience prior to entering HE. The term non-traditional may confine such students to the residual also-ran compartment of our minds. It may mask the extent to which large numbers of part-time and mature-age students have inhabited different 'Western' university systems for decades rather than merely for years (Tight, 1991). It can mislead us by assigning such students to a problematic category of the other: those who require different treatment by virtue of their different circumstances, learning styles and needs, their sheer diversity and differences. This labelling may hide the great strengths which such students bring to the university in their attitude to their study, even while they change the institution. To put it more confrontationally, are they members of a new kind of university community, or an instrument of the university's destruction?

We have set out to explore how the newly named phenomenon of 'social exclusion' is or might be connected, now and in the near future, with the HE systems of the Western societies which we know best. Do universities have the social function of giving access to 'cultural capital'? Does this afford the potentially excluded and alienated a sense of membership of society – of civic and political participation? Has the concentration of nations on economic survival and high-level skill formation obscured this latent function of higher education? These issues are universal and readers will be able to translate them in relation to other societies and systems which we do not examine here.

In addressing this large question we find it necessary to examine in fine detail the behaviour of the individual university in respect of its accessibility and receptiveness for prospective students other than 'successful' 18-year-olds coming on direct from school. The answer to equally large questions about the behaviour of universities in contemporary society, and about their capacity to adapt and to survive, may, we suspect, reside less in general theory and grand exhortation than in the detailed behaviour of academic and administrative staff down there in the undergrowth of the university's departments and divisions, beneath the vision of senior managers and policy-makers.

We freely acknowledge our individual and personal commitments to the principles of access and equity. These give purpose to our respective jobs. In confessing to some passion about matters of equity, and serious concern about the price societies are likely to pay if the facts of exclusion and alienation are ignored, we do not here feel bound to write in polemical vein.

We do believe that universities should be open to all who wish to and appear likely to be able to benefit from them, at whatever stages in the individual's life motivation and likely gain promise most. We understand the selection, grading and training functions of universities and the benefits they gain from the widely held belief that HE does somehow – the exact relationship is problematically elusive – contribute to national prosperity and competitiveness. In other words we recognize and identify with both the equity and the economy factors in the modern HE equation.

Less well investigated, and still more elusive than the causal link between HE and economic prosperity, is the socialization and social inclusion on which, in a comparative way, this study concentrates. Is the modern university potentially, and importantly, a vehicle for social integration in fragmented postmodern conditions? To what extent do established interests within the university (the system and its parts have their own class if not caste arrangements) militate against social inclusion and integration? The struggle for admission and acceptance of the non-traditional adult is a microcosm of the broader issue of access to and membership of the dominant society and its culture.

The 'idea of a university' is frequently, and in the late twentieth century indeed almost continuously, up for reclamation and redefinition. That process is becoming evermore international, as universities internationalize in the 'new globalization'. At the same time, and partly in response to globalization, local and regional tendencies and instincts also gain in strength. Our conclusions, following some exploration of the institutional undergrowth while keeping these larger questions in mind, allow us to contribute further to the process of reaffirmation or reconceptualization of the idea of a university. They suggest how and why, in functional and operational rather than merely in aspirational and idealistic senses, the 'adult university' may now be coming of age.

A comparative study

This study has emerged as a by-product of the work of a small international research team. At the core of the research alliance were the four authors. These belonged to two small national work groups in countries on either side of the North Sea, located in what might optimistically be called ideal-seeking departments of prestigious and successful universities.

The British research group was funded initially by the erstwhile Universities Funding Council, from funds dedicated to research in continuing education, to compare access into higher education in Britain and Belgium. Francophone Belgian partners, already identified, in turn won research funds through the Belgian State system and the British Council. This allowed several years of integrated and not merely parallel study during which each team (concentrated on but looser and wider than the two home universities of Warwick and Université Catholique de Louvain (UCL)) came, with patience and difficulty, to know and understand each other's universities and HE systems well.

The study focused on four objectives.

1. As an initial step, it compared the HE systems and their broader social, economic and cultural environment in the two countries. More particularly, it focused on how the issue of adult – and non-traditional adult in particular – access and participation is dealt with in the two systems. Then it concentrated more specifically on the dynamics of adult access and participation in the two home institutions (Warwick and UCL). The comparison focused on three items:
2. the institutional provision and behaviour (policies and practices) towards adult students;
3. the student participation patterns (proportion of adult v. young students, profile of adult students);
4. the organizational dynamics underlying the institutional policies and practices regarding adult access and participation.

We looked at the differences and similarities not only between the two institutions but also across departments and faculties. The results of the study (Bourgeois *et al.* 1994 and 1995) provided the grounds for the theoretical developments and reflections presented in this book.

This longitudinal inquiry was later broadened to include colleagues undertaking access-type research in other European countries: Ireland, Germany, Sweden, Spain, Denmark, France and the Netherlands. Cohorts of students were followed through but so too were the fortunes of the institutions traced as their respective circumstances continued to change with changing economic and political circumstances. This research project (1998–2001) is currently being conducted under the direction of the Louvain and Warwick teams and is funded by the European Commission (through the Targeted Socio-Economic Research programme, TSER). The ESREA network of researchers, referred to above, provided a still wider forum for testing propositions and exchanging perspectives, with opportunities to confer at Strobl in Austria, Bremen in Germany, Stockholm and Barcelona as well as Warwick, Leeds and Louvain in the two home countries.

Because of the Eurocentric character of the project, the influences and policy orientations – and it must be admitted the emergent potential for new sources of research funding – of the European Community became quite salient in our conceptualization and in the way we attempted to discipline our far-reaching and rather unruly inquiry within a socio-economic context. Social exclusion and the role of HE in facilitating participation and membership in the dominant society soon attracted our attention.

Try as we might to limit our outlook, curiosity and calculation thus took us across into areas not only of social and economic policy consideration but also into areas of organization theory, political philosophy and sociology on the face of it quite far removed from the obvious core of educational research. Our methodology proved to be no less eclectic, encompassing philosophical,

T

qualitative and statistical modes of inquiry and the full spectrum of levels from national policy processes and systems (the macro) through institutional studies (the meso) to the micro-politics of intra-departmental and inter-personal behaviour (the micro). This book reflects in part the multi-disciplinarity of our interest and the eclecticism employed in seeking answers, though by no means all the pain and pleasure of learning to work in cross-cultural as well as cross-disciplinary modes. We relearned an old lesson: that genuinely comparative and truly cross-disciplinary study demands much more than concurrence and parallel inquiry. We have no doubt, however, that the enrichment derived from the cosmopolitanism of working together in the new Europe is rewarding. The cost of exclusion or self-exclusion is high indeed, in intellectual as doubtless also in economic terms.

This book is informed not merely by academic scholarship and field research but also by the immediate experience of ensuring survival while effecting change within different HE institutions and systems. Its authority derives above all from this experiential practitioner base. That base is further enriched by the experience of representing and lobbying for the interests of non-traditional adult students, and more loosely for adult or continuing education, at local, national and regional levels of government.

The authors and their institutions

The academic departments from which the authors were drawn in Belgium and Continuing Education at the University of Warwick in England – are dedicated to opening their respective parent universities – FOPA[1] and FOPES[2] at the Université Catholique de Louvain to a wider, more non-traditional clientele. They live in constant, albeit generally creative, tension within their parent organizations. It is impossible to ignore wider issues and simply get on with one's subject-specific research and teaching, leaving changes in the wider environment, and university politics, to university senior management. The departments exist as bridges between university and community. Creating and widening access routes is central to their respective missions. It might plausibly be held, further, that their missions, their *raison d'être*, required them purposefully to seek to change their parent institutions. They are thus in danger of working across, if not against the grain of, the two universities, with their dominant paradigms of internationally measured and recognized research excellence.

Prior to explaining the organization of what follows in this book, let us now sketch succinctly the key features of the two universities from within the experience of which this study is composed: the University of Warwick in the UK and the Catholic University of Louvain in Francophone Belgium.

The University of Warwick was one of the new UK universities of the 1960s, known also as greenfields or plate-glass universities. The term 'new university' was transferred a quarter-century later to the ex-polytechnics, with the merging of the two parts of the UK's binary system of higher education. Warwick was by then recognized as one of the most successful élite institutions in the old university sector, while remaining young chronologically.

By the mid-1990s Warwick was widely acclaimed to be the most outstanding success of the new 60s foundations. In research terms, the dominant single indicator of standing among academic staff and ranking in universities, it rated in four successive national Research Assessment Exercises, conducted by the HEFCE and its predecessors, behind only Oxford, Cambridge and two or three London colleges. In terms of the hierarchy publicly recognized through a leading national newspaper league table, based on a set of performance indicators which included entry standards of school-leavers, it was well up in the top ten. On one occasion it won a prestigious European award (the Bertelsmann prize) as the best administered university in Europe. Its conference facilities are judged the best in the country.

Warwick also wins a high proportion of its total income from sources other than Government grant (these other income streams are called 'earned income'). It is thus able both to insulate itself from part of the impact of policy changes and to transfer net income from these income-generating activities into core academic work, holding down staff–student ratios and funding academic developments. In a time of stress and some distress in UK higher education, Warwick can thus claim strong financial management, relatively good conditions of study and service, and relatively high morale as a successful institution.

Warwick is quite large by the standard of the 'old universities'. After a shaky start and severe difficulties in terms of student activism in the early 1970s, it grew rapidly through the 1980s when other universities were largely static after government cutbacks in 1981, and became twice as large as any of the other 1960s foundations. From the outset it created strong relations with the local community in relation to which it saw itself as both server and partner. This contributed to early difficulties. Close collaboration with industry was viewed with suspicion at that time. With the changed political and social climate of the 1980s and the long reign of Thatcherism, however, Warwick's problem became its great strength. It has a large population base and a strong industrial hinterland, enabling it to win research contracts and consultancy from the industrial West Midlands and increasingly from further afield. Its earned income stream grew through the 1980s, allowing the University to absorb cuts in state grant and diversify its business and income base. Its standing and its recruitment of students grew internationally, making it a truly international university in reputation and reach by the 1990s.

At the same time, and central to the theme of this book, the University of Warwick remained loyal to a local mission of access and community service. Its arts centre grew into the largest in the land after the Barbican in London. Its science park, created in the early 1980s, grew rapidly and created jobs for the region as well as R&D synergy for the University. Two strong academic areas (business and manufacturing systems engineering) became very high income-earners on the basis of business and industrial use (as did the residential accommodation business through the conference trade). Other academic areas, though less dominant entrepreneurially, also created strong links with particular sectors. For some this was through research projects and related links, including high-level training. For others it was in the down-market access areas with which this book is concerned.

The Department of Continuing Education was brought into being in 1985 and charged with carrying forward the University's community mission in all its diverse ways. In practice it adopted a strategy of partnership, encouragement and support within the institution, rather than seeking to take control or serve as a gatekeeper for the high-income areas of professional continuing education and related consultancy and partnership. Its main focus, and charge from the University, was providing access for adults in the region, who were to be encouraged to look to the University as a place of opportunity for them, or, as the language progressively evolved, a resource for their life-long learning.

In its first decade the new department created and nurtured part-time degree opportunities for adults in the region. It later developed, through partnership with local colleges of further education, a wider range of access courses which had begun in the early 1980s, and subsequently the 'two plus two' open access four-year partnership degrees in which it was to become a national leader. Meanwhile, the large non-award-bearing Open Studies Programme of general interest and personal development courses was modified to enhance opportunities for access into degree study, sometimes with some measure of advanced standing. Symbolically, much of this work was focused from the early 1990s in a Community University Board on which nine college principals and two local training and enterprise councils met with the University to plan local provision of HE and to enhance access.

In summary, what this thumbnail sketch reveals is that the University of Warwick, as a highly successful selective and élite university, took itself away from and ahead of the field of other new foundations to become one of the UK's outstanding research universities of international stature. Yet it chose to sustain a dual identity, remaining also a local community-oriented access institution. The mission statements and strategic plans required annually by funding councils reiterated this duality. It is the tensions within this ambitious mission, and its operation at micro-levels within the institution, which this book draws upon in exploring issues of change towards the adult university.

The Catholic University of Louvain (UCL) was founded in 1425 and is therefore one of the oldest universities in Belgium. However, the University split along language lines as a result of political turmoil in the late 1960s. The Flemish-speaking university of Louvain (Katholiek Universiteit te Leuven, KUL) remained in its home town (Leuven) located in Flanders, whereas the French-speaking university (Université Catholique de Louvain, UCL) moved to a new location in Wallonia (Louvain-la-Neuve). UCL is one of the largest universities in Belgium, with a total of nearly 21,000 students and 4800 staff, including 1255 academic staff. It is also one of Belgium's few comprehensive universities, providing teaching and research in most subjects. It has 10 faculties, or schools, including 50 departments and 200 research units in all.

Although there is no established hierarchy of any sort among universities in Belgium, UCL, like Warwick, can be regarded as an élite, research-oriented institution by international standards, with over 1000 research contracts representing about 2.7 bn Belgian francs and 950 researchers on external contracts. Like most Belgian universities its educational provision addresses mainly the traditional 18–22 age-group of students, while adults represent less than 10 per cent of the student clientele. However, as a distinctive feature it has developed a few remarkable programmes catering specifically for non-traditional adult students, such as the previously mentioned FOPES and FOPA programmes, alongside its mainstream educational provision for the young. More detail about UCL is provided in subsequent chapters.

Outline

What follows is organized simply to take the reader through a complex sequence of issues in a clear and logical way.

Chapter 2 examines our ideas about the modern university mainly in Anglophone and European settings but recognizes the homogenization and standardization which increasing globalization and internationalization promise or threaten to bring about. It notes the changing pressures and requirements of the contemporary environment, with its rapid transmission of information as well as mobility of people; the intensification of economic competition; and the contradictory tendencies of massification, regional aggregation of economies and cultures on the one hand, and localization with a quest for diversity and uniqueness on the other.

From here it moves to an analysis of the subject and phenomenon of social exclusion, and to an examination of the possible contribution which HE might make to its reduction, widening the more familiar debate about economic benefit and return on investment to individuals and societies in order to consider alongside these issues the ideas of civic participation and cultural capital. It examines notions about the role of the university and the extent to which this highly contested role may be expanding or contracting to allow or to shut out social and cultural notions.

Next, attention shifts to the 'secret life' of universities: to the behaviour of the key players within the institution, the administrators, academics and students, and especially to the ambiguous and contradictory identities of academic staff. These have professional and disciplinary affiliations and memberships which are national or international. They may have very little indeed to do with the institutions from which their income is derived and where their research and teaching is conducted (Becher, 1989). This entails some consideration of the differences between the 'academic tribes' which inhabit the common space of the physical campus, and the extent to which a university's behaviour, including accessibility and social engagement, is a matter for generalization. The chapter concludes with some illustrations of these issues and propositions from the universities intensively studied in the longitudinal research referred to above.

Chapter 3 takes us deeper into both a theoretical analysis and an empirical account of the way the university actually behaves. Beginning with an exploration of the university as a 'professional bureaucracy' and, drawing on the work of Baldridge, Mintzberg, Pfeffer and others, the chapter leads us into a consideration of formal and actual behaviour of these organizational forms. The next step is to describe institutional and educational arrangements as these are actually observed, and the way these facilitate or hinder access, teasing out the places and ways in which the rhetoric of access may in practice find expression (at meso- and micro-levels) or be thwarted. A gap is found between formal policies and actual practices, which is crucial to understanding, and for that matter promoting, wider access. This analysis is located in the respective policy environments in the different national systems of the institutions studied, drawing on the several years of research conducted into these institutions' behaviour.

In Chapter 4 we turn our attention to the formal and actual behaviour of the university and ask where adult students are found and how they come to be there. Conversely, why are they not found in adjacent departments and faculties? Turning to these adult students, we have to ask who they are. Their different characteristics will enable us to see whether the university is in fact contributing in any way to policies for social inclusion. To use a distinction now familiar in the UK access literature, are we seeing wider or merely more access? Are universities allowing entry and giving support to quite new kinds of student, or merely making it easier for a larger proportion of their natural, familiar, middle-class clientele from the more successful and mainstream families to gain access – albeit a little later in life and through a new side gate rather than the main front door?

As part of this analysis we consider the methodological problems encountered in identifying and categorizing the constituency. We look at students' backgrounds, at their motivations as well as their sociological characteristics, and at the way different kinds of university and department relate and respond to them. We look, too, at those adult constituencies which are not reached by or accessing the university, before drawing out how universities are behaving in respect of social exclusion and integration. To what extent is the process of selection and exclusion one that appears to be forced upon universities by the societal, policy, political and funding context in which they exist? How far, if at all, do they appear able to transcend these forces and make a direct contribution to reducing inequity of access and exclusion from the dominant culture and employment system? Or do the universities, as is traditionally said of the education system as a whole and even of adult education for all its adherence to principles of second-chance opportunity and equity, merely reproduce and even accentuate the divisions within the established social order?

In Chapter 5 our attention shifts from the first question of signalling opportunity to adults and letting or not letting them through the gates via admissions procedures. We now ask how the institution is experienced by those who make it onto the rolls. Here we listen to the voices of the actors themselves: the adult students who are part of the university community. How do they perceive themselves? How do they experience themselves as students, a role which has replaced, or more likely been added to, a frequently complex set of other competing roles as partner, parent, carer for the elderly, sporting or political association or community member, often also full- or part-time employee? What is the relationship between these possibly changing, evolving, perceptions of themselves and their perception of the university's treatment of them? Are they learning, and winning, 'social inclusion', or learning that they are, and are to be and remain, other, different, outsiders?

On the other hand, we also speak and listen to their teachers: those academics who belong to different tribes and have their different wider, often international, affiliations. What do they think of their mature-age students? How do they relate to them? How do they feel with and about them? Do they distinguish in their teaching roles and styles between these and the younger, maybe more familiarly socialized middle-class students straight from a school study environment? Are these different students, in short, a blessing or a curse? Finally, what is their sense and perception of, and their judgement upon, their university's treatment of these different, older students? In this chapter we also ask in turn how the academic administrator perceives these students, and how he or she sees and judges the institution's behaviour towards them.

Chapter 6 builds on this analysis of actors' experiences and perceptions but moves to a more general and a more theoretical level to consider the conditions and strategies for innovation in universities. What deductions can we draw from the studies cited here about the way that universities can be used – led, directed, facilitated, persuaded? – to put into practical effect policies and arrangements which favour wider access and counter social exclusion, initially within HE and consequently in the society and economy at large?

Here we examine structuralist or cultural approaches, making reference to the work of Becher, Bourdieu, Clark and others. We examine the part played by different structural factors. We relate these to organizational cultures and sub-cultures on the one hand and interactions between the organization and its environment on the other. Alongside this we explore a strategic (or political) approach, analysing the differences we have observed in policies, form and practices of adult participation across different institutions, institutional types and subject fields. We identify within this approach the strategies and behaviours of the different actors, especially the processes for decision-making which underlie these policies and practices. Here we draw on earlier work of Bourgeois, along with work by Baldridge, Pfeffer and others. This helps us to understand how change is initiated, by whom, through which strategies and with what results for the different actors as well as for the institution.

In concluding (Chapter 7), we turn from empirical studies and the different ordering and analytical frameworks employed through the main part of the book to reflect upon, and perhaps to make some grounded predictions about, the adult university of the future. A central question here is who and what changes what for whom when it comes to the question of adults' education in universities, and indeed to the education of non-traditional or unconventional students of all kinds and ages – for we have to ask ourselves whether the adults really are different after all. Do we have square pegs being hammered, uncomfortably and remorselessly, into round holes – or are they perhaps round pegs after all, which just need to be tidied up?

Are the universities – the new mass institutions, living under a mixed economy and operating in semi-privatized mode – really fundamentally changing? Or is the transformation little more than skin-deep? Does the process which Abrahamsson has called 'adultification' contribute to changing the university as a whole? Or can new non-traditional clientele somehow be ring-fenced, 'ghettoized' into certain parts of the institution, leaving the heartland untouched? Do these different students gain the same benefits as traditional students, or are they somehow given a different education, or 'product', by segregation within the one institution or even into completely separate institutions?

In the former event, does this mean that we continue to enhance some life-chances more than others but keep the process masked and the position somewhat obfuscated? In the latter event, in the end, do we have two distinct classes of institution: 'real' and 'other' universities that frankly and explicitly offer distinct life-chances and kinds of sociocultural and economic participation and continue a process of social reproduction? The answer may lie not in such stark alternatives, but in identifying and prescribing the conditions under which real change does and can occur, whereby the adult university can indeed contribute to combating social exclusion.

Notes

1. FOPA – Faculté Ouverte Pour Adultes delivers 'licence' degree courses in adult education. It is structured on a similar basis to FOPES.
2. FOPES – The Faculté Ouverte en Politique, Economique et Sociale of the University of Louvain was created in 1972. FOPES offers 'licence' degree courses in economics and social sciences specifically for adults. In many respects the courses are non-traditional as the curriculum, admissions procedures, teaching methods and time of teaching are geared to meet the needs of adults.

2

Changing to Survive: the Modern University in its Environment

The modern university is characterized in many different ways, often for political reasons, whether conservative or radical: to legitimize a particular view of the university or to stake a claim on the future. Hence we hear the research university, the teaching university, the community university or communiversity. This book stakes another claim by virtue of pronouncing 'the adult university'.

Yet other metaphors idealize the university: as a community of scholars or a powerhouse of society; or problematize it: as a tanker or the Titanic, as united only in squabbling over car parking, an emanation of the state, an ivory tower, an assembly of competing tribes, a clutch of baronial fiefdoms.

In this chapter we consider the changing world of the university, the difficulty of attempting to fix the idea of a university, and the pressures of this changing world in terms of new demands. We probe as to whether university and HE are two terms meaning the same thing. Attention then shifts to social exclusion, first its meaning and significance, then its relationship to HE and the contribution universities might make to its reduction. The final sections focus more on the behaviour of the university itself as a complex organization and its capacity for adaptation and survival as a form of learning organization which is able both to absorb and to resist change without breaking. This general discussion prepares the way for the more empirically grounded study of adult access and social exclusion on which the book is centred, and the more theoretical discussion which illuminates and is illuminated by that study.

The changing environment of higher education

The world in which universities operate and which they reflect is rapidly transforming, placing new expectations upon them and promising continuously to redefine their character and role. From quite small numbers and, by contemporary standards, small size of often distinctive, idiosyncratic, institutions, we have been moved to thinking rather of HE *systems* in which the component institutions are collectively managed or steered to meet what are seen as the nation's needs. The change is mostly continuous and gradual. It is easy not to notice how much distance has been travelled in a short time, say in the period since post-Second World War reconstruction. We need also to remember how much the wider world has changed in order to grasp the enormity of change to HE and to the individual institutions which comprise that system.

Change, apparently still accelerating, certainly complex and interactive, encompasses all aspects of life and society from the global and ecological to the microcosmic and intimate; from global markets and mass communications to changing patterns of relating within the changing family. Most of the certainties and the confidence based in a sense of certainty have gone, giving rise to postmodernism as a cultural, intellectual and social phenomenon. Diversity and relativism replace confidence of purpose at least at the intellectual end of the sociocultural spectrum in Western societies. This is the context within which the idea of a university tends to be defended and refashioned.

Among changes significant for universities is the loss of authority and control from the nation state to international corporations, intergovernmental agencies and the world finance market. The good and bad news travels not by horseback from Aix to Ghent but in a nanosecond from Tokyo to London, while processes of political deliberation and decision-making, and of social control and engineering, stumble along much the familiar old paths of interpersonal give and take, trial and error, hunch and charisma. The world of full employment has disappeared.

Whatever politicians feel obliged to say in public, few expect full employment to return in a technologically fuelled cycle of economic growth led by intelligent labour-saving machines. The world of work is thus highly problematic, further complicated by different traditions, codes, laws and political circumstances affecting labour costs from country to country. More and more work can migrate without the moving of people. Local economic management, especially the regulation of the economy and of employment, becomes more and more elusive. The 'end of work' as we have known it is becoming an inescapable fact of life for old post-industrial societies like those in Europe. What takes its place remains shadowy, a source of fear. For young people in particular, there is the loss of old economic and career-path certainties, the experience of high youth unemployment, and the prospect of periodic job change with spells of unemployment from time to time throughout an uncertain adult life.

Demography is also changing inexorably, if less dramatically than technology and work. Populations stabilize in size and even decline. They get progressively older. Ageing places new pressures on the health and welfare budgets, keen competitors against the education budget. All public sector expenditure suffers from the reaction away from Keynesian and welfare economics in favour of 'dry' economics, greater competition, privatization and 'small government'. Depending to some extent on immigration laws, societies further diversify ethnically and thus also culturally. Racism and ethnocentrism have again become more visible in Western societies after a quieter period, fed by economic concerns and uncertainty about the future in a changing world.

There are contradictory political trends: towards larger systems transcending and transforming national governments, as in Europe, reflecting the growth in scale, or globalization, of finance and big corporations; and towards local, smaller, more familiar scale which takes the form of regional self-government, separatism by small national groups in states like the UK and Spain, and also ethnocentrism, Balkanization and ethnic cleansing at the extreme. There has been more convergence in terms of political ideology since 1989 as most Western systems have shifted to the dry right. Along with the decline of Marxism and the fall of the Soviet Union we see the rise of new fundamentalisms, Islamic and Christian, in a quest for moral certainty in the postmodern age.

Rapid change and even globalization are not new, however. Toffler's *Future Shock* and McLuhan's earlier writings (see, for example, McLuhan and Fisra, 1967) are a quarter-century old. Each generation in turn holds that things aren't what they used to be. There is evidence that the first and subsequent industrial revolutions were experienced as traumatic. Reduced fear of catastrophic nuclear holocaust may suggest an easing of the sense of doom, but preoccupation with other forms of ecological disaster may have filled the space. Preoccupation with postmodern uncertainty might be considered an effete intellectual malaise, the sense of uncertainty relating more to the end of a millennium than to objective data. If so, this makes it no less real.

Subjective as much of such debate may be, there is no doubt that HE has greatly changed. It has grown rapidly and recently following a period of post-war optimism which peaked in the 1960s, through and into a period of far greater doubt and uncertainty. In the West this change of mood is customarily dated from the 1973 oil crisis. That time was also the end of a wave of student activism which broke at the end of the 1960s. In some countries the economic change together with student activism marked and, in part, caused a new questioning of the utility and value-for-money of the expanding university system.

The idea of a university and the functions of a mass system of higher education

The *idea of the university* is paddling vigorously to stay afloat in the flood-tide of mass HE systems. Each separate university seeks to be a distinctive institution in a cultural as well as organizational sense, to offer and represent something unique, something for which its graduates will be known and its alumni may feel proud. 'Under the lid' within these competing institutions it is more complicated and untidy, as we will see later in this chapter. Along with distinctive character and high standing, universities, especially in the British tradition, value and try to project 'intimacy': human scale, student-centredness, the idea of an academic community of more senior and junior colleagues drawn together by dimensions of scholarship.

It is no easy matter to retain distinctiveness in the environment of the modern university. HE has been characterized (in the United States but it might be almost anywhere) as a mature industry: one where favourable presumptions about nurture and the funding of growth are replaced by increasing watchfulness to secure quality and standards with efficiency and economy. Benchmarking to compare performance with that of other competitor institutions, and efficiency gains measured on a basis of student load, have become normal. There are increasingly sophisticated forms of accountability for the use of resources as well as the quantity and quality of teaching and research output. Universities are driven to become better at generating a growing proportion of their income privately through the sale of education and other services. Distinctiveness leads to a quest for niche markets. A distinct identity and image is sought to compete better in the market-place. Under these pressures, however, mission statements and strategic plans also tend to converge and to serve more for public profiling than for planning.

In a mass HE system in which each university's performance is increasingly transparent and publicly compared, where resources increasingly have to be earned through entrepreneurial endeavour, there are pressures to converge despite the desire to be different. Institutions tend to gravitate to the easier and more popular student markets rather than sustain costly and unfashionable courses where numbers are low and reputation is esoteric. Curricula also tend to converge within the dominant discipline areas, especially where the market-place is represented by professional bodies with their membership requirements, and new technologies make it possible to use others' courses via study pack, video or compact disc. Economies of scale and new teaching methods tend to tempt institutions down similar paths. Meanwhile, the collegiality and intimacy which goes with more costly face-to-face and small-group teaching is at risk. Education is a labour-intensive industry. The technological innovation which has reduced employment elsewhere now promises to introduce greater efficiencies and to change institutional culture in HE also.

The core functions of HE, whether 'going up to Oxford' to read PPE or Greats, or to College (USA) or Uni (Australia) to do medicine, law or commerce, have changed less than has the expanded and diversified system. For young people it is still a rite of passage to adulthood and seen as the best pathway to a relatively privileged position in society (Scott, 1995). As systems have expanded contact-building and networking may count for less. This remains important, however, in the more élite and selective institutions. Their alumni still join the club of those who run the country: 'The achievement of "mass" levels of participation in a system retaining and rewarding "élite" characteristics has been one of the distinctive features of the rapid

expansion of British higher education in recent years' (Parry, 1997: viii).
Classical curricula notwithstanding, going to university has commonly been
a means of entering rewarding employment. Conversely, HE has served as a
means of selecting for employment, into the economy at a macro level and
for particular organizations and occupations, from an employer perspective.
Grading and selecting, matching to the labour market, remains albeit in an
approximate sense a function of HE as it has expanded.

The phenomenon of graduate unemployment has become familiar to the
Western world with the expansion of the system and the onset of apparently
permanent systemic unemployment. It is nothing new to the Philippines,
India or Sri Lanka. It has been masked in some Third World countries where
government has practised employment of graduates almost as a public responsibility, as well as from political expediency. Despite this, and despite
periodic political, popular and press scepticism about the value of universities, it remains true that prospects of secure and rewarding employment
are enhanced by HE and a degree (Brown and Scase, 1995). As the proportion participating in HE rises, there is a natural tendency to raise the selection
and grading threshold. In the UK, for example, more students look beyond
the three-year undergraduate degree to a higher qualification, usually the
one-year taught master's degree or a graduate-level professional qualification.
Thus grading and selection remain functions of HE, but the hurdle may be
raised as a response to massification of the system.

For young people going to university (and going away from home in some
countries more than others) is a process of socialization as well as a *rite
de passage*. Some of the modern doubt about HE may stem from the much
greater autonomy of university students today. Universities now act only
minimally *in loco parentis* and they get pilloried for the failure. The passage,
however, still is into more autonomous adulthood, away from parents and, for
many, away from the confines of class and culture of origin. The processes of
socialization – some would prefer to say domestication and social reproduction
– are less clear-cut than for the man [*sic*] reading Greats at Oxford a half-
century ago, because the social and economic structures continue to change
rapidly and social reproduction is a more complicated business.

It may be argued, however, with an eye to debates about the modern university curriculum, competencies, transferable skills such as teamwork, and
the capacity to go on learning throughout life, that the system of HE is still
closely articulated to produce the kind of workforce and citizenry that the
society needs in order to survive. It is the nature of the economy, technology
and the workplace that have changed, not this core function of HE. The
classic idea of a university as set out by John Henry Newman and revisited
by countless writers since is none the less under greater pressure.

That pressure is increased by the adultification of the university. More
than half of those in HE in many modern systems are adults in the sense
of having left full-time education for other roles before returning later to
full- or part-time study. Such students commonly combine study with other
major life-roles: work, family and community. Their dedication to the business

of being a student is less exclusive. On the other hand their occupancy of the student role may be more single-minded and purposeful: getting a degree, not living the life of a student who is growing up. Adults are often described for this reason as better students, but they are also less amenable to the direction and the socialization which the traditional, especially the residential, university may value. The functions of social and cultural transmission are muted. It is less easy to turn a mature-age person than a more malleable youngster into an archetypal doctor, research scientist or lawyer.

Another function of mass HE is to hold perhaps a third of young people out of the labour market for several years, reducing the pressure on that market and lowering the level of visible unemployment. This was unimportant when only a small proportion of the age cohort went to university. It is less obviously a social function in respect of those who have been employed, though it does offer one socially legitimate alternative for those who become unemployed in adult life. Larger proportions of older students, however, hold full- or part-time employment while studying.

For many, and without doubt a significant majority of those entering HE as a 'first-time second-chance' adult in the first half of their natural working life-span, this is a means to improve position in the labour market (Pascall and Cox, 1993). It is seen, and experienced, not so much as a holding bay but as a rapid recharge service station. This does not deny the value and reward derived from learning for its own sake. Curiosity and quest for understanding make many adults as good, and as good or better to teach, as the most inquisitive and demanding of bright young people. Nor does it deny all aspects of socialization, especially the opportunity to acquire both confidence and manners which make higher level job-seeking easier.

The adult university can be a more exciting and challenging place in which to teach. Almost inevitably, however, it loses the character of a place apart, that cloister in which young people are separated from the workaday world to immerse themselves in the work and play of the university, that still survives in fiction and popular myth about the university – and was powerfully modified as well as reinforced by student activism around 1970. There persists a tendency to think and talk of universities as if they are populated by the young. Yet they have grown older in their membership – staff as well as students in many instances and countries. The idea of the adult university within a mature mass or even universal HE in postmodern and post-full employment society is yet to be formulated and celebrated in the way that Newman (1983) gave us his original *Idea of a University* in the mid-nineteenth century.

New demands, requirements and expectations of higher education

What new demands are being put upon the university in an age of mass and increasingly, in the different national systems, universal HE? (A universal system is loosely taken to refer to an age participation rate exceeding about one-third. This means that at one time or another in their lives over half of the population will participate in HE in one form or another – a 1996 estimate for the UK was already 60 per cent.) As the idea of a university is contested and changes, different expectations and requirements gain in plausibility and legitimacy. The university and its curriculum, like the school and its curriculum, may become burdened with an impossible range and volume of social expectations. The university like the school may be blamed for failing society in its care and development of the young; for failing to manage stresses manifest in unemployment, delinquency, youth suicide, racism and other forms of antisocial behaviour, at a time when the very idea and nature of 'society' is contested.

This predicament, problematic in itself, is further complicated, but not necessarily exacerbated, by the shift to the adult university. It is more complicated because the adult student carries a set of roles, social expectations and self-expectations which differ from those of the young person entering the passage to adult life and hopefully to full economic and civil participation for the first time. On the other hand, the sometimes unsettling behaviours of the young student are not typically indulged by older students. Their subsequent take-up, or return, into employment is less visible and socially sensitive than are large numbers of young graduates entering the ranks of the youthful unemployed despite a costly HE. A theme which we all address in this book is that adults within the university are a net asset and an element for beneficial cultural change to HE itself in its new post-élite manifestation.

The large single-age institution, such as the modern secondary school, is not a good preparation for diverse, cosmopolitan, multicultural and all-age adult life. Segmentation by age reflects and exacerbates the problems of modern societies with their fragmented family life and ageing dependent populations. Managing the new war of the generations between the affluent retired and the economically active (yet often poor and unemployed) young is not assisted by segregation of the generations. The adult university with its different generations graduating side by side affords a better model and medium for social learning than does the traditional fraternity college.

The same may be said, more obviously, of the cross-gender and cross-class contact and possibly integration which can be facilitated by mass HE. Yet these forms of covert social engineering are also a source of concern in terms of unrealizable expectations put upon the university. They are one reason for the backlash against the modern cosmopolitan university in favour of the smaller and more selective model which is protected and promoted by a conservative discourse about standards and, in Australia, against 'vocationalizing' HE.

We should remember that the larger and more diverse faculty of the modern mass HE system is itself a microcosm, albeit incomplete, of the wider society. As a result much of the controversy and uncertainty about modern society and its future is replicated within the institution. In so far as it is sensible to speak about 'the university' at all as one institution with one mind, the institution does not simply respond to new demands and expectations proposed or imposed from the outside community and by government. It is within itself a maelstrom of competing ideas, values and interests, often elevated as ideology by the special intellectual character and the internal environment of the university. The contest of new demands against old models thus becomes internalized, self-induced within the university. As we see later, to think of the university as a single, integrated institution with a common value system and interest is to misperceive. The adult university, representing a major paradigm shift in demand on and the mission of the university, sits squarely at the centre of this contested redefinition of purpose and angst over identity.

Let us briefly visit in turn some recognized functions of the university from the perspective of adultification, along with other new expectations and demands placed upon it.

Conservation, the preservation and transmission of culture, remains a significant function of the university, though less celebrated of late. The socialization of new generations remains important. It is also ideologically contested, in so far as it is seen as sustaining the hegemony of dominant class and culture, and marginalizing other cultures and communities – or robbing them of their leadership by co-opting successful individuals into the dominant culture. On the other hand, cultural participation is coming to be recognized as crucial to broader civil and economic participation. There is more awareness of and sensitivity to cultural capital. Social inclusion of minorities is recognized as one means of preserving what is valued in society from outside attack. In the process, the boundaries and even the definition of culture and heritage change.

In this process adult students at university play a complex part. They may represent with greater confidence, authority, but also rigidity, the values of their different minority cultures. They may thus enrich the mix and accelerate wider redefinition of culture and heritage by gender and by social class as well as by religion and ethnicity. They may accelerate the process of institutional innovation and cultural diffusion. They are already mature participants in ongoing adult society, occupying many roles beyond those of student and offspring. Transmission through these channels can be rapid and direct. On the other hand, some adult students are experienced by faculty as rigid, less open to creativity and less willing to change than the naively bright and optimistic young. They may thus be a force for conservation, and for conservatism in a less benevolent sense.

There is disputation in many societies over the vocational preparation and skilling tasks of the university as against the general or liberal education celebrated by Newman: education versus training, economic versus civil, functional versus cultural, narrow versus broad. The debate goes beyond these dichotomies in attempting to understand what constitutes good vocational preparation in contemporary technological and economic conditions of rapid change. It includes, fundamentally, the nature of lifelong learning and learning to learn, including the updating, reskilling and lateral movement of older learners into new jobs.

The adult university straddles these dichotomies in an untidy way. As a 'service station for lifelong learning' it attracts, often for thoroughly utilitarian reasons, graduates of initial HE needing to widen their knowledge or update their skills, often through part-time accredited graduate study. As such students become normalized in the minds of the rest of the university their needs and expectations may increasingly influence thought about the initial undergraduate curriculum. Other adults are late-comers to the undergraduate curriculum. Their response represents another possible source of change for the university.

We consider later in this book how far institutions seek to hammer square adult pegs into the round holes of a curriculum, in the wide sense of experience and process as well as content of learning, and how far the recognition of the adult university may be changing perception and behaviour at the undergraduate curriculum level. At a public and political level where perception is blunter and less subtle, but also among established interest groups within universities, the instinctual reaction against change masquerades as a defence of 'standards' against widening the role and the clientele in respect of both older and younger non-traditional students – those from minority ethnic communities and other groups beyond the middle classes.

There is another set of demands on and expectations of HE which come mainly from governments. These arise from the changing context of the post-modern post-Welfare State and the competition for public resources from the welfare and health budgets as well as for public investment in, for example, ecological sustainability, environmental preservation and restoration, and public transport. With the desire to contain public sector expenditure more sharply and the rapid growth of higher education sectors and budgets, the HE system has changed its status, unenviably, from a growth industry to a mature industry. Demands to contain costs and make efficiency gains in the public part of the budget, and pressure for income generation through 'enterprise' (including more teaching for private fees), are changing the status of universities in many systems from public enterprises to partly privatized corporations. As partial privatization moves them closer to private-sector operations, the public interest in quality and standards paradoxically leads to tighter controls and accountability.

This drives all universities to operate more like businesses. Traditional collegial forms of governance are modified, often under government influence if not directive, in the direction of 'managerialism'. Tougher times call for tighter management. Cost-cutting and the language of the corporate sector are commonplace in HE, first as an embarrassment or a joke, then quickly as normal discourse. From markets, clients and customers, university managers have moved into downsizing or rightsizing, outsourcing and business re-engineering. On the management side in this new configuration – formerly staff and students, now management, faculty, other staff and students – there is rising awareness that (higher) education is an unusually labour-intensive industry. The economies of new technologies, as well as economies of scale, may represent ways to remain economically viable, even while 'virtual' universities represent a competitive threat to the more traditional.

The crucial change is that, especially with rising public expenditure now out of fashion with governments generally, the cost of a greatly expanded HE system must be transferred in significant part to the private sector and the consumer. The newer information technologies (IT) for teaching and especially learning hold out hope of labour-saving and cost-cutting. The rationale, however, in the professional and highly political environment of the university must be couched in pedagogic and student rather than business terms. Self-reliance and flexibility through self-directed learning and learning to learn thus acquire an importance well beyond the pedagogical. Naturally, and one might add properly, advocacy of new IT for university teaching, the substitution of learning in place of teaching, is viewed with suspicion by critics of the changing university. At best, a good idea has arrived very late in the day (in terms of often quite old technological know-how) to solve a resource problem: doing the right thing for perhaps the wrong reason.

How does this set of pressures and changes, starting with declining per capita resources in a fast-expanded system and expressed as rising staff–student ratios and the displacement of teachers by learning machines and packages, relate to the adultification of the university? It is held that young people take more easily to the new learning technologies as a generation brought up on new IT in entertainment and quickly bored by lectures. (Early research on attention-span in lectures is surely specific to a particular generation as well as a particular society and time: Chinese students observed in the early 1980s retained concentration in the face of 'talking head' TV university in a way unthinkable in most of Europe then or now.)

Many of the older clientele of the adult university, however, look upon its services more instrumentally and with more calculation than do their younger colleagues. Adults include many for whom the thirst for knowledge is compelling and unquenchable, especially among those second-chance access adults who are central to the story in this book. Many, however, are under great pressure to get on with study, and with the accreditation and exploitation of what they are taught and credited with learning, for purposes of job-seeking or professional advancement. Flexible learning and accessible information freed of the time and baggage of attending college and taking part in campus life may be much more attractive: hence the diversity of adults' modes of study, from distance programmes (correspondence, radio or TV-guided) through self-directed IT packages (videos, CDs, interactive multimedia) to intensive short courses. Study is fitted in at night and weekends around more dominant social roles.

For many the adult university is also the marginal university. Oddly, as the university expands in a mass HE system to become all pervasive and widely accessible, it may also become 'permeatively invisible' in the rich and complex fabric of modern society, a distant remove from the unattainable ivory tower of Thomas Hardy's *Jude the Obscure*.

The effect of new expectations and demands may thus be far-reaching and unexpected. The university, as it has come of age in a more vulgar time of mass HE in a mass and mass-media society, is under pressures unknown before the 1960s. In Australia, where academics and vice-chancellors alike feel newly embattled with the end of publicly funded growth, and where student activism has returned after many quiescent years, there is scarcely a day when HE does not feature prominently in the media, and especially in the broadsheet press. The press (and in Australia particularly the popular tyrants of talk-back radio), the public and politicians are critically interested in the university, its ownership and behaviour. So too are many lobby groups, from the national student union to organized business, commercial and professional, and sometimes also wider 'community' interests.

The voice of the adult student is muted by comparison. Those not at university, the excluded and marginalized, are mostly by definition publicly voiceless. Where equity is thought important, precedence goes to the needs of the young: both from natural instinct, but also from fear of youthful lawlessness and the likely cost of youth unemployment and alienation. Within universities, student unions and their premises are quintessentially the territory of the young. Youthful altruism and generosity towards the disadvantaged, however, manifests itself – for instance at the University of Warwick as featured in this study – in great concern and generosity to the older student who is marginal to most student union activities and interests. The fact remains that excluded adults by definition, and participating adults who are in student roles, are too heterogeneous to be an organized lobby in and on HE.

Universities in most modern societies have an adult majority. Universities need them for business purposes and welcome them often, at least in some faculties, on highly valued equity principles. Within the life, tradition and culture of the institution, they remain more silent, less visible, than the young. Only those who are at university as mature-age second-chance 'disadvantaged' adults are likely to attract campaigning energy from the organized community of young full-time students within the institution. Meanwhile, the needs which society has for professional updating and industry partnership in its various forms are expressed more variously and in more fragmented ways.

Social exclusion and the university in postmodern society

Equality is the central of the three slogan words of the French Revolution. Two optimistic centuries later there has been a loss of confidence in 'the Enlightenment project'. The dominant mood of that period, reconstructed with hindsight, was one of inevitable progress through reason, of enlightened liberalism in which political democratization, individual freedom to express oneself and to grow towards one's full potential, and economic progress, were in apparent natural harmony. If there was poverty – if, even, 'the poor are always with us' – there were ways of mitigating poverty and protecting citizens from its ravages, above all, later, through the post-war welfare state.

The welfare state tilted the balance in favour of a more socialist concern for equity as against that liberal inclination towards individual freedom which has come to be expressed increasingly in economic rather than political terms. Recent years have seen a progressive weakening of the welfare state, especially but not just in the UK. A concern for equality has nevertheless persisted, not only as a counter-cultural force but also within public policy. Within education it is concerned with equality of opportunity rather than the more radical equality of outcomes. In this sense it remains a significant policy consideration.

The collapse of modern enlightenment optimism in the face of economic difficulties, a shift to the political right, and the philosophical and cultural triumph of postmodernism, have encouraged some in the HE equity lobby to take the less provocative ground which avoids head-on conflict with right-wing politicians. Rather than advocating equality the argument is based in economics: the waste of human resources which arises from its under-utilization and the cost of unemployment. Especially in the European Community, however, the discourse has widened somewhat from the strictly economic ground characteristically expected of the OECD to a concern with social exclusion and its social costs. The argument may still be largely economic, the opportunity cost of unemployment, the direct costs of welfare, social security, policing and corrective services, but there is a widening of the scope of debate. Much as the Social Chapter represents a wider view of employment relations than that favoured by national governments of the right, so does concern with social exclusion reflect wider concerns about the social as well as the economic costs of creating an excluded underclass. The fabric of society is on the agenda.

In a negative sense the preoccupation has to do with the weakening and even destruction of this social fabric: the collapse of taken-for-granted security and domestic peace as the horrors of the last great European war recede. First Bosnia and then Albania, albeit only just on the fringe of wealthy EC Europe, suggest that there may be risks inherent in *laissez-faire* social policies. There is recognition of the widening gulf between the richest and the poorest after a period of somewhat reduced differentiation. Fortress Europe is no more able to keep or drive out the poor and the ethnically diverse than was melting-pot USA. The social order is threatened by an outclass or under-class of the culturally marginalized, under- or long-term unemployed, living sometimes in no-go quasi-ghettos and surviving through an illegal informal economy. Dispossessed and unemployed young people in particular, as well as ethnic minorities who are sufficiently different to cause anxiety in the cultural mainstream, make social exclusion a live political issue.

In more positive mode, there survives a vigorous belief in 'active citizenship', in effective, committed membership of and participation in society, politically, socially and culturally as well as economically. Adult education has served in Europe throughout the century as one vehicle for such values and ideas. The wider co-operation which has accompanied political Euro-peanization has also helped this process. It has been inspired by concerns about access and opportunity at least from its nineteenth-century antecedents, its survival assisted by the very moderation which more radical social critics have found offensive. The progressive and still incomplete dissolution into mainstream education of a distinct adult education tradition, preoccupied with equity and second chance, has probably helped to keep equity on the agenda of further and higher education in a number of societies, most obviously in the UK where neo-classical economics and radical conservatism have been especially strong under the name of Thatcherism.

The term 'social exclusion' brings together several distinct lines of thought and concern. In a world where economic migration is virtually at an end, and political refugees less and less acceptable, there are few places to go, less ways for society to let off the steam of political dissent and economic difficulty. It is not surprising that social exclusion has become a policy concern when there is nowhere else for the excluded to go or to be sent. As the European Community and its different member states look inward to find solutions to social stress and distress, the relationship between social exclusion and the new mass HE has come onto the agenda. Scott predicts that: 'Higher education will become a democratic enterprise, part of the lives of ordinary people, not simply of a privileged minority. In Britain this represents a cultural sea change – from exclusion to inclusion as the basis for access to educational opportunities and all they represent in terms of life-chances' (1996: 245). Can participation in HE open the way for incorporation of cultural minorities into the mainstream of society? Does access to the nation's cultural capital, and maybe some simultaneous expanding of what is seen as culturally valuable, open the way to broader social and economic inclusion? How far is there a function for HE in restoring the damaged social fabric – facilitating not just access to the labour market but also a sense of commitment to preserving and building society, possibly extending the base and strengthening the foundations of that society in the meantime?

The interactions between individual student-citizens, the cultural and economic groups from which they come, and the university as custodian and reproducer of privileged dominant society are fundamental to our attempt to answer these questions. Does the university merely pick off successful token individual members from dispossessed minority ethnic communities, and co-opt them into the dominant society, away from, for instance, the Bangladeshi community in Britain, an Aboriginal community in Australia, the Turkish community in Germany or a Bosnian community in France?

Post-war Britain produced novels of the *Lucky Jim* variety: depicting working-class boys (usually) who won scholarships, went to university, and become separated and alienated from their working-class origins, families and communities as they succeeded individually in a still class-ridden society. Co-opting individuals is not the same as ameliorating social exclusion, though it may weaken the leadership of potentially subversive communities.

The question this book addresses is whether the new mass and rapidly emerging universal HE, with its adult majority in one country after another, can transcend its historic mission of social reproduction and create genuinely wider access as a response to the threats posed by social exclusion in new end-of-century conditions. To answer this we need to examine the behaviour of universities and the component parts within them, as well as the experience of those non-traditional adults who manage to enter them.

The same issue should be posed in respect of young as well as adult aspirants to HE from excluded communities, groups and classes. The adult university offers an easier way into addressing these questions, however. Typically, universities are much softer, more at ease, about non-traditional adult entry than they are about the entry of under-performing, minimally qualified youngsters who have not come through the school system well. As systems have moved from the more personalized, cosy and intimate scale of the élite mid-century university to the mass HE systems of the late 1990s they have also come to operate more like mass-production systems – the kind of production systems, indeed, from which advanced industry has moved away in favour of more individualized products tailored to the diverse tastes of more discerning customers.

When a third or more of the upper-secondary school-leaving population has to be decanted into a large number of institutions which together comprise a national HE system, with little time to make the arrangements each year, standardization is well-nigh inevitable. Once the same 18-year-olds, and those who left school earlier, have been out in society and created more distinct profiles and patterns of experience, and especially as they then come to aspire to HE and present themselves in smaller numbers and in many more different ways, individual discriminating judgement becomes as essential as by contrast appears to be the standard batch-processing of school-leavers. Universities, for all their instinctual conservatism, are much more willing to recognize that older applicants may have different ways of learning and preparing themselves for HE. In practice, it is easier for the non-traditional adult to enter many universities without confronting standard bureaucratic forms than it is for the young, in the UK and Australian systems as well as in some of the systems of continental Europe.

The mere fact that there may be a second chance is a possible palliative. If the possibility is there, aspirations may rise in individuals and expectations grow up in marginalized communities that university, as a gateway to social standing and a rewarding job, may not be barred to their sons and daughters. Secondary (if need be, private and fee-paying) and then higher education still appear to be seen as a good investment, maybe the best, for one's children and even, in more traditional communities, for one's own old age.

It is an important question for each society which of its more marginalized, possibly feared, loathed and despised, groups see university as in any direct way relevant to them and their offspring. At what point for instance do newly arrived refugees come to look to and find entry to HE? In which European countries are universities found or felt to be accessible to gypsy communities and travellers? Apparently the New World societies to which Europeans migrated or were sent have proved more accessible in this sense of participation and success via HE than has old Europe, to which refugees from Europe's fringes and from further south have more recently arrived. Who is the new underclass in each society? Which of these have any sense that university might be available for them? For whom is this a relevant, even meaningful, question? Who assumes responsibility for answering it? What does it mean for an individual university and for an HE system to seek to embrace such responsibilities as part of its mission?

We need at this point to probe further into two matters: the nature of the HE system to which access may or may not be granted; and the outcomes of the higher education thereby attained. Who gets access to which parts of HE, given the hierarchies which exist both within and between individual institutions? What happens to the graduates afterwards? Does the enlarged HE system, to which more and more diverse people, young and older, gain access, make for a more open meritocratic society? Or have the hard-to-pass barriers merely been relocated within rather than at the entry to HE? Is the 'new degree' merely a passport to a new form of social marginality and un- or under-employment? We need to know more about access to social and economic life beyond education, especially for the expanded output of young and older students from less privileged backgrounds entering less favoured institutions.

The university system is used to privilege a small minority in an unequal contest for high social and economic status. So long as universities remain largely in the public sector this remains a subtle process of sponsorship and selection of the individual, and of competitive grading between institutions in a generally recognized if informal hierarchy. Prestigious institutions attract outstanding students as well as staff, thus creating and sustaining distinctive high status and offering a potentially vigorous learning environment, though the latter does not automatically follow. The richer flow of research funds, bequests and other donations and contracts is likely to foster a better resourced infrastructure so that a benevolent cycle is created and prestige attracts more success. Some societies, for example the UK, have seen the creation of very public league tables with transparency based on official assessments of quality in teaching and research, and other publicly available statistical data to measure and compare performance.

In formally unified national systems there is pressure to diversify mission and function. Universities tend to be graded according to their research funding and performance. Prestige from research flows across into the market value of degrees. In the most successful institutions lower staff–student ratios, at least in theory, give students more access to senior staff and certainly to degrees which are better known to employers. In a competitive labour market, leading employers may only consider applicants from the older and more prestigious institutions (Brown and Scase, 1995). Access to university and a degree may then not lead to the economic rewards traditionally expected: access to a middle-class profession or to well-paid private-sector employment.

We have noted already that the labour market has changed. It is less predictable, with more rapid job obsolescence and higher, apparently systemic, unemployment. As the proportion of the young population entering university and graduating rises, and more older people also find their way in to first-time HE, the gap between past and future economic outcome for the individual widens. In some countries planners now speak of the society being 'over-educated' – a curious term which betrays economic tunnel vision but also poses a question about social exclusion.

If the one true test of social participation is a good job, an expanded HE system will be unable in modern economic conditions to overcome social exclusion. If one takes a broader and longer view, however, and sees the accumulation of cultural capital as a route to general social and civil participation, and at the least to a sense of belonging, there remains a strong case for seeing HE as a means to overcoming destructive divisions between society's haves and its have-nots. This takes us beyond economics and levels of employment and into what individual students feel about themselves and their education: whether and how they see it transforming their identity, outlook and prospects. We need to consult the players and not just the statistics about their employment.

None the less, divisions within mass HE systems between prestigious 'research universities' and other institutions characterized as 'teaching only' pose questions for the social planner, social engineer and social scientist. If hitherto excluded categories and communities of people, for example, by gender, social class, ethnicity or remoteness, find that the HE to which they win access is by every recognizable indicator inferior and does not result in significantly enhanced life opportunities following graduation, their inclusion in the broader society at least in any economic sense through HE may prove illusory and may feel a deception. If the result is a sense of discontent and dispossession, dissatisfying in itself and without promise of later extrinsic rewards, then extending HE and allowing adults a chance thus to catch up and join in later in life may prove hollow for the student and graduate – a poor response to the problems of social division and exclusion.

To some extent the students who feature in this study provide relevant information. However, this is partly a question that only a prolonged period of wider participation in a diversified mass HE system in the context of a world of fractured, uncertain and sporadic employment, will allow us to begin answering with confidence. If there emerges a meaningful post-full-employment society in which self-worth does not depend essentially on one's paid employment, then an HE system which allows participation in other than employment terms may play a vital role. Even this, however, will not overcome the social desire to be separate, distinguished from and superior to the mass, whether the mass be in HE or not.

In functionalist terms, the university is a means to upward social mobility in a meritocratic system. This sustains a measure of stability by promising rewards to those who strive and succeed. So long as the system is seen as reasonably open and accessible, and as offering real rewards, it may be a means of containing potential social unrest. If the system is seen as rigidly divided into classes of institution offering very significantly different life-chances, its utility in this sense is much reduced.

It seems certain that HE will come to be seen as a right for all who feel the interest to enter it within a few years. It is less clear whether this will be from an expectation to 'get on' or, rather, as part of the normal business of participating in the life and riches of contemporary society. In this more general sense, going to university, whether at age 18 or later, will simply be part of normal life, a right rather than a special privilege. In this event exclusion will be the more bitterly felt, even if the rewards are not obviously economic. In so far as the university continues to be, or once again becomes to a greater extent, a transmitter of common values, social mores and a common culture, its function in terms of social stability and continuity will remain. It may indeed be enhanced as other kinds of institution and organizational form prove more transient.

Later in this book we have the opportunity to explore how particular universities appear to function in respect of admitting as students older people who have not moved 'naturally' on from school, and how far some of those thus admitted experience their higher education as a privilege and a means to social access and personal change. Before this we need to probe a little into the life of the university behind the ivy or sandstone walls.

The persisting secret life of universities: a hundred secret gardens?

Music students celebrating their Australian institution on the occasion of its annual festival characterized it through their theme song as *a university of great diversity*. The master planner for the renovated old campus of the same institution characterizes its latent appeal through its historic buildings and the spaces between them as *a hundred secret gardens* – intimate spaces in which students and staff could interact in the privacy of their own local areas and arenas.

Both phrases are memorable. Both in this context were original creations. Accidentally, they also reflect an abiding phenomenon of the contemporary university: its highly segmented, often deeply divided character. The intimacy celebrated, for example, by Peter Scott (1995) in the UK is often at a very local level within departments still frequently based in academic disciplines, even where the name of the unit has been altered to widen its appeal in a competitive HE market-place. Tony Becher (1989) has analysed this phenomenon by reference to academic tribes: loyalty to the discipline commonly outweighs loyalty to the employing institution.

The university is the employer. The reference group, however, the basis for self-esteem, professional identity and even career advancement within the employing institution, is a different academic community, the world tribe of nuclear physicists or classical scholars, geneticists, sociologists or mathematicians. This is where conference papers are presented and judged, refereed articles passed for career-worthy publication, research grant applications subjected to peer scrutiny, and references for promotion usually written. Ultimately, esteem and advancement for the traditional academic scholar are won in these tribes. Universities rely on them to decide who is to be valued, rewarded, who side-lined into more menial chores or, increasingly nowadays in many systems, out of employment altogether.

Universities are the geographical territory occupied by the tribes in uneasy coexistence with management or administration. They bring in, or at least register, the students and award the degrees. Behind the genial exterior of the glorious ceremonial procession on graduation day, behind the ever-more glossy annual report, back there within the secret gardens of the university there is an all but ceaseless process of negotiation: trading and dealing, invasion and attrition, as different forces wrestle over freedom, accountability and control. We need to understand this constant dynamic, to ask how far it is changing under new pressures, to understand how the adult university is shaping within it. How does the new adult clientele affect the already changing university? How does the university come to terms with the new clientele and the new functions which it represents, in its already complex and often fractious life?

The 'traditional university' (a hazardous term since the tradition is contested to claim contemporary legitimacies and yet used pejoratively) stands somewhat apart from normal life and work. Ideally it is a place for learning and discovery, for the development of individuals and ideas and for somewhat detached critical commentary on the worlds around it. Different disciplines divide up the ways of analysing and understanding that world. They in turn further divide, and occasionally associate or coalesce with one another, the better to study, teach and undertake research; also to survive and prosper in the tribal wars of academe. They share an interest in protecting themselves from intrusion and interference as they go about their professional business, claiming in the name of academic freedom much the same autonomy as is sought by other professions.

Many even of the more independent university systems, on a spectrum from state-run to highly autonomous, have seen a shift towards greater oversight and accountability if not regulation as they moved from élite (and so socially rather exclusive and in public expenditure terms rather marginal) to mass HE: from growth to mature system state. From being detached ivory towers or marginal commentators upon the public scene they have become more like microcosms of the society of which they are increasingly fully a part. The result has been a period of loss of confidence, status and income for academic staff, and generally declining morale and perhaps influence, as A.H. Halsey (1992) has suggested. Much of the blame is directed at government as per capita funding has reduced. University managements, vice-chancellors and others are also blamed by student and staff unions for doing the work of governments for them in administering unwelcome changes: deterioration in student financial circumstances, increasing workload, more intrusive quality assurance systems, more rigorous and numerous forms of accountability.

If management is one kind of enemy within, another could be the adult students who are now the statistical majority in many systems. As the university becomes more representative of the community in terms of age as well as social class composition, so it becomes more of a microcosm, less a place apart.

It may seem fanciful to conceive adult students as agents of subversion, especially as so often they are the most rewarding of students to teach. Yet the complexity of their social and economic character and of their life-roles (whereas for young full-timers the student role is embracing) helps to dissolve what is distinct and, to many, all precious about traditional or college life into a wider stream of activity much closer to the rest of social and cultural life. Adults make the university more normal, more ordinary. They may initially be quite over-awed by the encounter with academics and their disciplines but they are also less likely to remain compliant, less easy to socialize into the different tribal mores. Though written earlier, *Educating Rita* well captures both aspects or phases that are typical of this adult encounter with the university.

In other words, adult students, with their more vulgar understandings and their experience of life beyond school, come to respect less (though often to value even more highly than younger students) the local cultural mysteries and intimacies that make academic tribes and their disciplinarities precious in both the original and the modern uncomplimentary sense. Academic freedom may likewise be highly valued by the enquiring adult who comes to the privilege of university intellectual encounter later and thirstier than the young person; but the pretensions and hypocrisies accompanying it may also be less indulged. Poor, tired and lazy teaching is tolerated less. Students paying their own fees, in part or in full, are seen as more demanding customers, i.e. consumers. Adult students in this circumstance are likely to be more assertive and to know their way around better than either young local or overseas students, especially if these are drawn from more deferential social systems. The scourge of the library staff at the University of Warwick was said to be the full-fee MBA (Master of Business Administration) students who knew and demanded what they wanted as their 'right'. The benign face of 'access' for Jude in *Jude the Obscure* to the 'adult university' looks more threatening, especially when litigation in turn threatens to follow after student complaints in the way of an increasingly litigious commercial world outside.

Caution is required over generalizing across different national systems about the university in the postmodern world. Internally each HE system is formally or informally grouped and ranked hierarchically. Within each there is a widely acknowledged (albeit also resented and contested) hierarchy of academic subjects (Young, 1971; Becher, 1989). Usually mathematics and physics are at the top, with medicine also enjoying high status by virtue of the status of its allied profession and the cost of its research. Emergent fields of study serving quasi-professions and other occupational groups are low in the order. New and recent fields of study and practice are quick to claim the status of a 'discipline'. This term has lost precision and much of its meaning as it has become thus institutionally politicized.

And yet across the diversity and the hierarchies, the dynamics of the warring tribes and the secret gardens are widely recognizable through most universities and HE systems. The parodies of the university, 'united only around its fight over car-parking', for example, are instantly and affectionately familiar. As market-forces are more keenly felt and competition between universities and with private providers increases, the attempt to create a corporate image and 'market' the university as a whole rather than merely its different parts raises bitter hostility as well as mirth from the tribal leadership of deans and professors. Mission statements, corporate plans, logos, videos and the other paraphernalia of promotion and public relations attract instinctual hostility – but more from tribal centrifugalism than from academic purity. All of these threaten to shift the balance from the academic tribe to the institutional employer – to corporatize the university.

These tendencies, patterns of behaviour and conflicts may be muted or strident, but they are essentially common across and within the different categories and classes of HE institutions. One would expect scholarly or tribal resistance to the new managerialism to be stronger in the more traditional and prestigious universities. Yet the private classrooms and the secret gardens are being invaded with scant respect for prestige or antiquity, as the UK quality assessment and audit processes exemplify. In turning, finally, within this chapter to the resistance to change, we may note that no university is immune from the pressures induced by massification and adultification. The adult student, confident MBA or anxious return-to learner, is an important if unwitting agent in the process.

Adapting to survive: a case of dynamic inertia?

Is the university as an institutional form likely to survive far into the third millennium? It is frequently pointed out how long universities have lived, as an institutional form and as particular institutions. The former chairman of the Further Education Funding Council (FEFC), Sir William Stubbs, stressed this in a seminar at the University of Warwick in which he also called for recognition of the increasing social and cultural (rather than merely economic) significance of the maturing further education sector in Britain. Often the university is among the largest employers, if not the largest, in a region and one of the most long-lived as industries rise and decline. Increasingly it is seen as a general community resource and cultural reservoir as well as an economic refuelling station in an era when the rhetoric of lifelong learning has become fashionable. Bold modern talk about virtual universities will do little to remove the preference where it can be afforded for a real, face-to-face campus social learning environment. The difference is that the campus and the institution are used in more fragmented ways as on average the student population ages and, indeed, as even young students increasingly study and work for income part-time, notwithstanding their formal administrative status as full-time students.

The university remains precious as a concept and as an experience, for an increasing proportion of the population. The literature on the idea of a university and about the 'crisis of the modern university' multiplies and will continue to do so, testimony to continuing evaluation. Meanwhile the university and HE as a social system, and as a territory occupied by diverse and warring tribes, still displays remarkable resilience in the face of great expansion and governmental incursions.

The university gives the appearance of changing, expanding and varying what it does – how it teaches and conducts research – to accommodate new demands and new efficiencies. Its public self-presentation, its mission and strategic plans, recruitment literature and annual reports, change more than do the basic relationships and professional technologies within the house. Later in this book we explore in some detail the way that selected universities manage new demands placed on them by an adult population, and how that management, and adaptation, varies at different levels: the formal (or meso-) institutional level of registrar and admissions, and further down (the micro-level) in the secret gardens of the different departments.

A proposition at this point, to be tested through subsequent chapters, is that there are strict limits to what social engineering will achieve in terms of sociocultural change via the universities; and similar restrictions on the extent to which and the rate at which universities change internally, under the pressures brought about by expansion of access and containment of public expenditure. The university is resilient. It is able to absorb change and to shift in the breeze. It can take a long time over transforming itself. Its democratization will continue to be gradual. Indeed there are contrary forces pressing back towards a more exclusive or élite model. For these reasons, its contribution to reducing social exclusion in modern societies, though cumulatively significant, is unlikely to be sudden and dramatic.

In writing this book we hold, scholarly scepticism and a measure of academic detachment notwithstanding, that it *does* matter that universities be seen as relevant to, and engaged with, the serious and important issues of social division and exclusion. It matters also that 'the idea of a university' *does* survive, that a university experience be something moving and memorable for the later life first-time adult student as well as for the young school leaver – and indeed for the older returning student seeking updating and professional continuing education. There will be a continuing debate as to whether modern societies with their high technologies but low employment patterns, and with their changing and ageing demographics, can afford to be generous in terms of HE opportunities for older as well as young students.

Some of these questions of political economy go beyond the scope of this study which focuses now on the observable behaviours of particular universities within this broad framework of issues. In moving on to study the behaviour of particular institutions and to analyse the different perceptions and attitudes of the different actors on the scene, we sustain the view that adults' access to a 'real university' is and remains increasingly important for society as well as for the individual.

3

Are Universities Organized to Facilitate Access and Participation?

Introduction

We turn now to the subject of institutional provision: what does the university actually do, and not do, to facilitate the access of adults, especially non-traditional adults? This chapter addresses the question at two levels.

In the first part we discuss some theoretical contributions which can be used as keys for understanding the university's behaviour in respect of access. First, we examine the characteristics of the university as an organization. We then consider several theoretical approaches which can be used as frames of reference to understand the university's behaviour, and more specifically the differences that can be observed in institutional behaviours affecting adult access across countries, institutions and sub-units within an institution. We present theories which explain organizational behaviour primarily by reference to the actors' behaviour, the so-called 'strategic approach'. Subsequently, we turn to theories which point primarily to the organization's structure and environment to explain its behaviour – the 'structural approach'.

The second part of the chapter is more descriptive. It is intended to provide illustrations of the diversity of actual institutional behaviour in terms of adult access, mainly across countries and sub-units (departments and faculties) within an institution. This section largely draws upon the survey conducted three years ago to compare adult access and participation patterns at Warwick and Louvain. In the conclusion, we draw out the benefits of using these several different theoretical approaches to enable us to interpret and understand the differences observed.

The university as an organization

How can universities be characterized as organizations? What if anything do they have in common that distinguishes them from other types of organization? This question has been dealt with quite widely in the literature over the last twenty years. The central argument developed here is twofold. On the one hand, in reference to Baldridge and his colleagues (Riley and Baldridge, 1977) and to Mintzberg (1979, 1983b, 1989) and followers (such as Nizet and Pichault, 1995) we suggest that the university has most of the features of what the latter authors call a *professional bureaucracy*, which distinguish it from other organizational configurations identified by Mintzberg. On the other hand, the university has additional specific characteristics that distinguish it from other types of professional bureaucracy.

A *professional bureaucracy*

Ambiguity and heterogeneity of goals

Like other *professional* organizations, HE institutions have multiple, ambiguous and highly contested goals. The university could hardly be reduced to any single mission. As Baldridge *et al.* put it: 'What is the goal of a university? This is a difficult question for the list of possible answers is long: teaching, research, service to the local community, administration of scientific installations, support to the arts, solutions to social problems' (1977: 3). The list could go on and include widening or increasing the access of adults to HE among other possible missions for the university.

Goals are not only numerous, they are also ambiguous. Each of those missions may take very different definitions and meanings within a university. How would research, teaching or community service as missions for the university be defined in departments of mathematics, philosophy or education? Because they are multiple and ambiguous, the goals of the university are also most often highly contested and conflictual. People may disagree not only about the definition of each the university's missions but also about priorities.

For Mintzberg (1983a), academic organizations are furthermore characterized by tensions between the 'system goals', which are carried out by top management and by the technostructure (the administration), and 'mission goals', which are carried out by the professionals (the academics). Moreover, conflicts may also occur among the professional themselves, as individuals or sub-groups pursuing their own professional goals.

Problematic technology

The tasks to be performed by the university with regard to its various missions are not only multiple. They are also particularly complex, uncertain and problematic. As emphasized by Pfeffer (1981), the high degree of complexity and uncertainty of technology explains the 'heterogeneity of beliefs about technology' usually found in universities as professional organizations, not only among academics of different disciplines but also within a given discipline. Academics as individuals tend to have their own beliefs and conceptions as to the ways to achieve their research, teaching and all the other missions they are obliged to accomplish.

Professional culture
The characteristics outlined above explain why universities rely so much on *professionals* to fulfil their missions, that is persons with a high level of qualification that has been acquired through a relatively long process of training and socialization. Sociologists have long highlighted the specific traits that characterize the *professional* culture as follows:

Demand for autonomy Professionals demand freedom and autonomy in their work, given the high complexity and uncertainty of the tasks they have to deal with (Mintzberg, 1979) and the considerable expertise they have acquired to perform them (Baldridge *et al.*, 1977).

Moreover, as is shown below, the fact that they have or claim a monopoly over the expertise required to deal with those tasks gives the professionals considerable power to claim that autonomy (Bourgeois, 1990; Bourgeois and Nizet, 1995). In the university context, this demand for autonomy is most often expressed as a claim for academic freedom. It should be noted that such a demand for autonomy is peculiar not only to the professionals as a group in the organizational structure (for example, with regard to other groups such as the administration or the top management) but also as subgroups (for example, between research units within a department), if not as individuals – the individual faculty member also claims maximum autonomy in their work (Bourgeois, 1990).

Another aspect of professionals' demand for autonomy is that they be controlled and evaluated only by their peers. Typically, professionals are reluctant to have their performance evaluated or judged by any other than their peers. In the university context this can be an important source of tension between academic and administrative staff, and sometimes between academics themselves across disciplines. For example, academics in a given discipline may be reluctant to have their research proposals or projects assessed by a board with faculty members from other disciplines.

Divided loyalty As repeatedly emphasized in literature on the academic profession, academics as professionals tend to identify with their profession and their peers first and with their local institution second. A professor or researcher in psychology tends to see themself as a psychologist first and a member of their local institution second. The more excellent the professional measures against the standard of the discipline, the greater their loyalty to their profession over the local institution. The long and intense training and socialization to which professionals are exposed not only during their initial education but also throughout their career, builds up and cultivates this predominant identification with the profession (Mintzberg, 1979). This has important implications when it comes to trying to interest academic staff in the particular local mission of the institution, for example, in respect of access.

Modes of labour division and co-ordination

Division of labour   In professional organizations the division of labour typically combines high-horizontal with low-vertical specialization of tasks (Nizet and Pichault, 1995). This is particularly true in universities. On the horizontal dimension, this strong specialization is shown in the multiplicity of academic disciplines and specialisms which coincides with the multiplicity of academic sub-units devoted to teaching and/or research in those disciplines. On the vertical dimension, the division is very low. Professionals enjoy considerable autonomy, not only in the execution but also in the conception and management of their work. In principle, what Mintzberg calls the technostructure, or analysts, that is to say the administration in the university context, and the top management have little influence in the conduct of the professional's work. Again, the implications for mobilizing the institution around a task such as extending access can be quite profound.

Co-ordination of labour   The co-ordination of labour among operators in professional organizations is ensured mainly by the standardization of qualifications and norms, distinguishing this organizational configuration from others which rely on different forms of co-ordination such as the mutual adjustment among operators, top–down direct supervision, or the standardization of outcomes. Again, the standardization of professional qualifications is ensured outside the local organization, that is, through initial and continuing education and socialization in the profession. In this process professionals acquire a repertoire of standard skills and knowledge which they can apply to both diagnosing and resolving the cases (situations, problems, and so on) which they deal with. This form of co-ordination is, however, somehow restricted by two factors. Mintzberg himself acknowledges that such standardization can never be perfect, given the high complexity of the situation to be resolved by the professional and available technology. Moreover, and more importantly, the standardization of professional qualifications in the universities can operate effectively as a co-ordination mechanism within a given discipline, but it is far less effective across disciplines given the great fragmentation that characterizes the professional body in the university as a type of professional organization.

Professional power
Another characteristic of professional bureaucracies is the decentralization of power to the operators. Professionals have considerable power and influence in this type of organization. They draw it from the combination of two elements. The tasks they are hired to perform are crucial to the organization and they monopolize the specific expertise required to perform those tasks. That is to say, they are irreplaceable. As Mintzberg (1979) argues, the professional's work is too complex to be supervised by a superior or standardized by analysts.

A particular form of professional bureaucracy

So far, we have pointed out some characteristics which the university clearly shares with other professional bureaucracies and which distinguish them from other organizational configurations. However, universities as organizations have some particular features which differentiate them from other types of professional bureaucracy.

Fragmented professionalism

Many years ago, Clark (1977) had already argued that what distinguishes academic organizations from other professional organizations such as hospitals, is that they tend to have highly fragmented professional staffs. For him, and others before (for instance Jencks and Riesman, 1968), there is no such thing as *the* academic profession. Rather, academic professionalism should be regarded as a sort of federation of academic professions. There are as many professions as there are academic disciplines. This fragmentation of the professional body as a specific characteristic of academic organizations is somewhat overlooked by Mintzberg and followers. As a consequence, the argument that the standardization of professional competences is the main source of organizational integration in professional bureaucracies does not quite fit academic organizations (Clark, 1977: 73). Moreover, fragmentation of the professional body in universities results not only from the multiplicity of academic disciplines but also from the number and divergence of functions and goals carried out by the academic organization. We have noted in Chapter 2 the multiple pressures, demands and expectations placed upon universities, including a range of economic and social expectations.

Whereas the professionals in academic organizations are fragmented as groups, they are also fragmented as individuals. We have already mentioned the general tendency of professionals to secure their individual autonomy in their work. This trend toward increased individualization is also typical of academic organizations, according to Clark and others.

Academic governance pattern

For Clark (1977), the combination of high professional influence and fragmented professionalisms produces a peculiar governance pattern in academic organizations that combines a federated form of professional authority with overall bureaucratic co-ordination. On the one hand, because of the fragmentation of the academic profession, faculty authority tends to take a federated form:

> Within an academic federation, a number of departments, divisions, colleges, professional schools, institutes, and the like can coexist, each pushing its own interests and going its own way to a rather considerable extent. Professional authority structured as a federation is a form of authority particularly adaptative to a need for a high degree of autonomous judgement by individuals and subgroups (Clark, 1977: 76).

On the other hand, the major risk of this type of authority structure for the organization as a whole is disintegration. Therefore, the organization needs to generate co-ordination mechanisms for holding the pieces together. For Clark, this trend toward fragmentation has generated a counter-trend toward overall bureaucratic co-ordination superimposed by the administration and top management.

Paradoxically, this may result in increased power of top management and administration to the extent that they come to play a crucial role in the management and arbitration of conflicts among the professionals and, ultimately, the protection of their autonomy. This trend is, however, somewhat restricted by the faculty's effort to exert some control over bureaucratic co-ordination, for instance, by having peers occupy academic management positions (most faculty members take some share of administrative assignments as dean, chairperson or member of committees), including top positions in academic management and sometimes in the administration itself.

Today, as inside observers of the academy, we can certainly state that the peculiar mixture of fragmented faculty authority and overall bureaucratic co-ordination which Clark observed over twenty years ago as a new rising trend has been confirmed. Think of the increasing burden of bureaucratic and management tasks imposed on deans, chairpersons and other academics taking responsibility in the management of their institution; the increasing professionalization of the administration and academic management, and the growing number of bureaucratic regulations and procedures imposed on all faculty members and units in the planning, management and assessment of their work. The need for overall bureaucratic co-ordination has also been increased by the aggravating scarcity of resources which universities in general have faced for the last two decades. As we will further develop below, the scarcer the resources, the larger is the potential for conflict in the organization, everything else being equal, and therefore the more there is a need for overall arbitration and co-ordination. The harder it is, too, to introduce additional responsibilities to institutions and faculty which place further strain on limited resources.

A consequence of that situation is the problematic relationship between faculty members and academic administrators. The former, who strive to keep the greatest possible autonomy, are naturally reluctant to have administrators interfere in their professional work. However, they depend on administrators to secure the institutional and material conditions necessary for their autonomy. A second consequence is that faculty members are submitted to increasing interference of the administration in their work. This is also a potential source of conflicts given the deep differences that exist between the professional culture of the faculty and the bureaucratic culture of the administration.

Environmental vulnerability
In 1977, Baldridge *et al.* noted that academic institutions, specifically, had long been rather insulated from their environment. At that time, however, they also noted a growing trend toward what they called environmental. For

us, the authors, who have examined the evolution of the relationship between the university and its environment in the last two decades (see Guyot, 1998 for a recent review of this literature), one of the reasons explaining growing control of the environment over universities relates to the socio-economic and demographic context which has caused declining revenues for the universities. They have to rely more heavily on external sources of funding. This exposes them to increasing demands and regulations from external agencies. We also emphasize the great diversity among the university sub-units (divisions and departments) from this point of view. Some segments have remained relatively invulnerable to these external demands and pressures, whereas others have been very extensively exposed to them.

This can be a source of internal and external conflicts. Externally, between the university and its environment, the former is increasingly confronted with demands competing with its typical mission and *modus operandi* as a professional organization. Internally, conflict can be twofold for not only is the university faced with an increasing variety of external demands to which it must accommodate, resulting in internal diversification of its goals, our, accordingly, it must undertake further internal differentiation of its structure to cater for those demands. This is likely to increase the potential for conflict even further. It is also likely to increase bureaucratization of the university, and therefore tensions between academic professionals and bureaucracy.

Conclusion

Thus far we have attempted to outline some of the major characteristics of the university as an organization. It has most of the typical features of what Mintzberg (1979) called the professional bureaucracy configuration, but also some peculiar characteristics that distinguish it from other types of professional organization. What emerges from this picture of the academic organization is its high potential for conflict:

- conflict among the multiple and ambiguous goals and missions the university is supposed to carry out in a society that increases its demands, expectations and pressure upon it;
- conflict between the social necessity of those missions and the need to achieve the 'system' goals of survival, competitiveness and growth in a context of continuously declining resources and increasing costs;
- conflict among the academics who do not form a single professional body as in other professional organizations, but look more like a fragmented collection of quasi-autonomous clusters, tribes and territories, with their own goals, technologies, interests and sub-cultures;
- conflict between the professionals doing their job in the classrooms and laboratories on the one hand and an administration and top management, on the other, which grows in size, power and presence in trying to ensure the overall co-ordination needed to overcome the risk of disintegration resulting from faculty fragmentation.

It is with such an organizational context in mind that we can look at the university's behaviour towards adult access and participation. Each of the characteristics of the academic organization examined above can be referred to in order to explain differences observed in the access policies and practices across HE institutions, their departments and other sub-units, and within top management and departmental initiatives in that matter. For example, promoting the access of socially excluded groups to HE may be in the official agenda of most HE institutions but will, of course, compete with other missions. The position of that mission in the actual priority list of the institutions may vary widely between, say, a local further education college and an élite research university. In the same institutions, the specific meanings and operational definitions attached to this mission may also vary significantly across departments, depending on their predominating professional subcultures, goals, interests, power, responsiveness to the environment, and so forth. This heterogeneity may also explain the wide variety of practices and technology that can be used in different places all striving to achieve the same mission.

At this point, however, two missing theoretical links which we really need to understand are: the university's behaviour apropos adult access and participation and the differences in access policies and practices observed across and within institutions. They are presented in the next section.

Understanding the university's behaviour in respect of adult access and participation

A general theoretical framework

When we speak of adult access and participation we refer to the set of policies and practices developed and implemented by institutions in relation to this issue. We call *policy* the set of specific objectives and strategies defined by the institution to achieve its goals and/or solve problems in that area. We call *practice* that which is actually implemented in the institution to achieve these goals and/or solve those problems. Policies and practices can be viewed as the results of *decisions*. Seen thus, understanding access policies and practices of an academic institution or sub-unit and the differences in the policies and practices that can be observed across institutions and/or sub-units implies a two-level analysis.

At the first level, one can look at how decisions producing observed policies and/or practices have been made. This implies closely examining the whole decision-making process, that is, the process through which the decision issue has been initially raised and activated, and the final decision reached and eventually implemented. Who is involved and who not in the different steps of the decision-making process? What are the actors' relationship patterns? What are the goals and preferences supported by the different actors in the decision process? Through which processes are the actors' goals and preferences gradually translated into decisions and, ultimately, policies and practices? How do the actors behave in the process? From this perspective, the organization's behaviour – in this case university policies and practices about adult access and participation – is interpreted and explained primarily by reference to the *actors' behaviours and strategies* (either in or around the organization). This is what will be referred to below as the strategic perspective on organizational behaviour.

At the second level of analysis, one can look at the rationale, or logics, underlying the actors' behaviour in the decision process and try to identify the factors that could explain the actors' stance (goals, interests, preferences, and so on) with respect to the decision issue in the organizational context under study. Why do the actors behave as they do in the decision process? How can their position with regard to the decision issue be explained in that context? Whereas the first level focuses on the actors' behaviours as determinants of the decision underlying the observed policies and practices, the second level focuses more on the organizational structure and context as determinants of the rationale underlying the actors' behaviours in the decision process. From this latter perspective, the organization's behaviour is interpreted and explained primarily by reference to the organization's structure and its environment. This will be referred to as the structural perspective. As is shown below, different factors may be taken into consideration from this perspective. It could be macro-factors which relate to the characteristics of society at large – ideological, economic, political, social, legal and cultural factors – or it could be meso-factors which refer to characteristics of the organization's structure and its immediate environment.

Different, and often competing, theoretical frameworks are available at these two levels of analysis. Some will be briefly presented in this section and discussed from the point of view of their relevance to the specific organizational context of universities described above.

The university's behaviour in relation to actors' behaviour: the 'strategic' approach

The strategic approach to organizational behaviour looks in great detail at decision-making processes in the organization. Five theoretical models can be found to account for decision-making in universities specifically: the *rational-analytic* model, the *bureaucratic* model, the *collegial* model, the *garbage can* model, and the *political* model. Among those (see Bourgeois, 1990 for a detailed discussion of those models), the last appears to be best suited to the specific characteristics of the university as an organization, as outlined above.

The *political model* has been used in several comparative and/or case studies of policy and decision-making in academic organizations (Baldridge, 1971; Riley and Baldridge, 1977; Pfeffer, 1981; Friedberg and Musselin, 1989, and so on). However, very few of them (Bourgeois, 1990, 1991; Bourgeois and

Nizet, 1993, 1995) have used it to study the university's behaviours with respect to adult access and participation specifically. The model is grounded in Cyert and March's (1963) general theory of organization, which considers the organization as a system of interdependent and conflicting coalitions striving to impose their own preferences and interests upon the large system.

In this model, decision-making is viewed primarily as a bargaining process through which various interest groups with conflicting values, goals and preferences attempt to influence the decision outcome through various power strategies (in other words, use of politics) so as to have it reflect and serve their own interests. Influence and power is therefore central in this model. The greater a participant's influence capacity – that is, power – and the more effective the use of this capacity in the decision process, the more likely is the decision outcome to reflect his or her preferences. In short, power, as opposed to consensually shared, over-arching and clear goals, bureaucratic rules and procedures, professional consensus or chance, is the best predictor of the outcome of the decision process.

The political model accounts for most of the distinguishing characteristics of academic organizations. It clearly acknowledges the fragmentation of the academic community into various interest groups with different and conflicting goals and beliefs about technology. It also explicitly deals with these organizations' growing vulnerability to the environment. More fundamentally, it puts major emphasis on the problem of conflict which, as we have pointed out, is a major feature of academic organizations. It appears particularly relevant to describe the decision-making processes that concern the issue of that access for adults and non-traditional students. Indeed, this is a typically controversial issue, hence increases the conflict potential in those decision-making processes. The access issue directly addresses vital questions for the university: questions of quality and standards, priority in its missions, its target student clientele, the relevance of educational and institutional provision, and so on.

From a political perspective, organizations in general are viewed basically as systems of interest groups with conflicting goals, values and beliefs which, at the same time, are interdependent and therefore bound to reach their goals through influence and negotiation. However – and this is an important assumption of the model – this does not imply that all the participants will be involved actively in all decisions all the time, or that they will mobilize influence and power strategies to achieve their interests. In other words, the political model does not assume that every decision will be resolved every time through the use of politics. On the contrary, it suggests that *inactivity* tends to prevail. Getting involved in decision-making is costly, especially when it requires the use of politics to reach the decision. Therefore, so long as it is possible, organizational participants tend to avoid decision-making situations, and when they are involved to avoid the use of politics. Politics will, therefore, be used only when certain conditions are jointly met. Pfeffer (1981) distinguished several necessary conditions for the use of politics in decision-making: participants' interdependence; heterogeneity of goals and beliefs about technology; a context of resource scarcity; participants' perception that the decision issue is important with regard to their own interests; and that power must be distributed among the participants.

It can therefore be argued that the actual use of politics in decision-making is more likely to be observed in academic than in some other organizations, given their specific characteristics of high conflict potential; and it is more likely to be observed in decisions about access than in decisions about some other issues, given the specific highly controversial nature of that issue. From a political point of view, the differences in access policies and practices which are observed across and within academic institutions, and/or over time can be interpreted as the results of different power configurations among the organizational actors, and differing interplay of power strategies in the decision-making process underlying those policies and practices.

Understanding the organizational structure and context: the 'structural' approach

The political model and the others presented above are useful to understand the actors' behaviour in decision-making and to understand how their goals and preferences are translated into decisions, policies and practices. This is, however, only one part of the story. Those models say nothing about why the actors in a given context have those goals and preferences in the first place, and are ready to strive for them. Where do those goals and preferences come from? Why in a given department do we find a majority of faculty members struggling to open access, whereas in another department only a small minority, or even nobody, will mobilize for such a goal? Why may organizational participants differ so much in their goals, values and beliefs across, and sometimes within, departments with regard to an issue like adult access and participation? What 'meso'- and 'macro'-factors could account for those differences?

Again, several competing theoretical models available in the literature address these crucial questions. In a review of the literature, Guyot (1998) identified five models, namely, the *epistemic*, the *personalist*, the *cultural*, the *contingency*, and the *structuro-functionalist* models. The last three of these are presented in more detail in Chapter 6. Each of these models emphasizes a particular set of structural factors that can explain the differences observed in institutional behaviours both across and within institutions, as follows respectively: the intrinsic epistemological characteristics of the subject matter, the individual characteristics of faculty members, the characteristics of institutional sub-cultures, the type of relationship of the institution or sub-unit with its environment, and the legitimation principles which predominate in the institution.

In conclusion let us reiterate the complementarity of this level of analysis with the first one, to the extent that each of them highlights only one part of the whole picture. Ignoring the second level may paint a picture of the university which over-emphasizes the role and power of actors in organizational behaviour. Conversely, ignoring the first level may overstress the role of context and structures as determinants of organizational behaviours.

So far, we have sketched a general theoretical framework which may help us to understand the university's behaviour with regard to adult access and participation and, in particular, the diversity of policies and practices that can be observed across and within academic institutions. The next section provides some illustration of that diversity.

Describing the university's behaviour in respect of adult access and participation

We do not set out to provide an exhaustive typology of the wide range of institutional provision for adult access and participation that can be observed in HE. We want instead to highlight the diversity of this provision at both national and institutional levels. This section draws upon the findings of a comparative study of a UK and a Belgian university – the University of Warwick and the Université Catholique de Louvain, UCL.

The diversity of national HE systems

National patterns of adult access to HE

Based on a review of the descriptive policy literature of international adult higher education, Kasworm (1993) has identified three patterns of national policies for adult access and participation in HE, differentiated in terms of level of integration of adult students into the HE system, as follows: 'The *first of these patterns* reflects a national commitment with entire systems of universities or national higher education policy devoted to adult programs or adult access to university systems' (Kasworm: 416). Sweden is one of the best examples of this pattern. Here there has been a national commitment to restructuring the whole HE system to support adult access and participation. Adult education is embedded in the HE system as a national policy.

> Referred to as the 'adultification' of higher education, Sweden has created a national policy of restructuring higher education to support 'recurrent education', alternating access by adults to learning (higher education), work, and leisure experiences. Several key features of this system include an alternate adult special admissions policy, the 25:4 rule. This 25:4 rule notes that a person must be at least 25 years of age, have 4 years of work or related-life experience, and must have certified prerequisite knowledge and competence in subject areas essential to the study program.
>
> Sweden supports single-subject studies, part-time and evening studies, provisions for distant learning, a stronger integration of vocational and

academic concerns, a consideration of credits for experiential learning, and concern for equity and efficiency in educating their entire population (Abrahamsson, 1986; Abrahamsson, Rubenson and Slowey, 1988; Tuijnman 1990). (Kasworm, 1993: 417)

The *second pattern* 'represents a minimal national commitment, with emphasis on university level policy for the integration of all students. In this pattern, there is integration of adult and young adult within adapted structures and forms of university studies which support adult learner access' (Kasworm: 416). Many countries would fall into this category, including the United States, the UK, Australia and Canada. The pattern has two essential characteristics:

1. Most of the adult access policies and provision tend to be initiated locally by the institutions rather than by national governments. This does not mean that in those countries institutional policies are never supported by regional or national policies. Some initiatives are sometimes taken at that level, for example, in the UK some alternative access schemes (assessment of prior experiential learning, part-time degrees, and so on) are clearly supported by national or regional bodies (see Parry, 1995 on this point).
2. Most of the access policies provided by the HE institutions are aimed at integrating adults into their current academic programmes, resulting in a mixed adult–young student population in most academic programmes.

The *third pattern*, as defined by Kasworm, is quite different in the light of those characteristics: 'The pattern of national or university policy for specialized adult learner or institutions . . . reflects a policy, university structure, or academic programme designed to solely serve adult learners' (1993: 418).

Belgium typically would fall into this category. HE institutions tend to segregate the academic programmes (and sometimes academic and administrative structures) between programmes catering predominantly for the traditional 18–22 student population on the one hand, and specialized programmes for adults only, on the other. In this 'dual' system, most of the adult HE access schemes and provisions are concentrated in such 'adult' programmes whereas very little is generally undertaken to facilitate the access of adults to 'mainstream' academic programmes for the young. These 'adult' programmes generally offer the whole range of alternative provisions specifically designed to serve the needs of adults, whether in terms of admissions schemes (APEL, and others), course scheduling (evening and WEA courses), teaching methods (such as self-directed learning or co-operative learning), delivery systems (open and distant learning), student services, curriculum (for instance modularization). This segregated institutional provision of course results in a rather segregated student population. The adults are concentrated in 'adult' HE programmes and very few can be found in other programmes. Again, in reality the picture is not as clear-cut as it might appear here.

It should also be noted that most of the time this 'segregation' pattern is initiated and developed by institutions, although there are some notable cases in which it can be developed as a national policy. An obvious example is the UK's Open University, a specialized adult HE institution which has clearly been created as part of national policy.

Adult access to HE: the UK and Belgian systems

Structure of the Belgian system

Three major characteristics of the Belgian HE system can be distinguished. The system is differentiated into two sectors: the university sector (*Enseignement supérieur universitaire*) and the non-university sector (*Enseignement supérieur hors-université*). These sectors differ in terms of status, mission and provision, and student clientele. In general, the non-university sector is associated with lower social status, although the situation is currently changing in this respect. It is more vocationally and professionally oriented, with shorter courses. Although data on the social class and socio-economic background of students are not readily available in Belgium, it can be safely assumed that the non-university sector recruits higher proportions of disadvantaged groups. However, paradoxically, non-university institutions have always been quite traditional in terms of non-traditional adult access provision, more indeed than universities. This is a striking difference from the British system.

Binary systems like the Belgian one exist in other European countries, such as France, Germany, the Netherlands and Denmark (Rasmussen, 1992; Gellert, 1993; Davies, 1995b). The differences observed between the two sectors in Belgium can be considered as general trends in those countries with binary systems (Davies 1995a: 280–81). There is virtually no difference in status among the institutions *within* each sector. There is no formal or informal institutional ranking system, no national or regional quality assessment system, and no significant differences in the admission and selection policies. Differentiation within each sector is based rather on philosophical orientation (Catholic v. lay institutions), management structure (public v. private authorities), and provision (vocational, professional or disciplinary fields). A clear divide is established between the secondary education and the HE systems. There is no 'intermediate level' sector, such as further education in the UK. The HE system on the one hand, and the primary and secondary system, on the other, are even run by two distinct Ministries of Education.

Structure of the UK system

The UK system differs significantly from the Belgian with respect to these three characteristics. The binary system inherited from the 1960s, which distinguished between universities and polytechnics, was abolished in 1992 by the Further and Higher Education Act. This permitted the polytechnics to award their own degrees and adopt university titles, and established a common funding structure for HE (Parry, 1995: 103). A similar trend was observed in other countries such as Australia (Davies, 1995a: 280). In reality, however, differences between the university and non-university sectors in binary systems have survived to some extent in the UK between the 'old' universities and the 'new' ones, the former polytechnics. Traditionally, the now 'new' universities have been more open to non-traditional adult students than 'old universities', both in terms of institutional provision and in the actual participation of this clientele.

HE institutions are strongly hierarchized in terms of status, both inform-ally, in terms of prestige, and formally, through a national quality ranking system and admissions policies which objectively differentiate institutions in terms of selectivity (see below). Accordingly, the student population varies strongly across institutions in terms of socio-economic status. This is a theme and issue to which we return periodically throughout this book.

The frontier between secondary and higher education in the UK is far less clear than in Belgium. Post-16 education constitutes an intermediate level between secondary and higher education. Post-16 education provides either academic qualifications, in particular the Advanced Level qualifications required for entry into HE, or vocational qualifications, either the BTEC First Diploma which can directly lead to a job or the BTEC National Diploma which can now also be used for entry into HE, or a mixture of both. Post-16 education is delivered by three distinct types of institution: secondary compre-hensive schools, sixth-form colleges which cater specifically for the 16–18 age-group, and further education colleges which cater for people over the age of 16, including adults. The further education sector has been growing since the 1980s. Alongside the previously mentioned qualifications, it also provides non-vocational adult education, industrial training and retraining opportunities, courses for students with special needs such as English lan-guage courses, Access courses for adult students wanting to enter HE, and HE courses such as 2 + 2 degrees or franchised courses, through particu-lar agreements with local universities. In this respect, further education has become a significant alternative entry route into HE for non-traditional students, either through the standard entry qualifications such as A levels and BTEC provided independently by further education colleges, or by specific HE access opportunities franchised by a university to a local further education college.

Governance and funding of the Belgian system

As in Belgium, UK universities enjoy significant autonomy in their govern-ance, especially in academic matters including admissions policies. None the less, this autonomy is indirectly limited by funding policies for HE. In both countries, university funding is linked to student numbers to a large extent, and the rules that regulate this affect university admissions policies. In the French-speaking part of Belgium, a recent law (*Décret sur les études et les titres universitaires*) has redefined the criteria on the basis of which a student can or cannot be taken into account for funding. One of those criteria con-cerns the prior qualifications of the student. A student who does not comply with the legal entry requirements cannot be taken into account for funding. Moreover, the amount of funding allocated to each university currently has an upper limit fixed at a given level of enrolments. Beyond this no more students can be taken into account even though they comply with the funding criteria. The funding formula can affect the French-speaking Belgian universities' policies towards adults. On the one hand, universities are reluctant to admit students that cannot be taken into account for funding, that is, those who do not have the legal entry qualifications. On the other hand, the fixed upper limit of student-based funding does not encourage universities to cater for new student constituencies, so long as they can reach the quotas with the traditional student clientele aged 18–22.

Governance and funding of the UK system

Funding constraints also affect university adult access policies in the UK. As in Belgium, funding is determined by student quotas. Quotas are fixed not just for the institution as a whole – as in Belgium – but by subject area. This does not leave the university much room for manoeuvre since it cannot compensate student losses in one department by gains in others. Limited by quotas of accountable students on the one hand, but having discretionary power over admissions decisions on the other, departments may tend to admit the 'best' students as a priority over others, including adults without the standard entry qualifications. This mechanism is further reinforced by the fact that the amount of funding per student varies across institutions and departments, according to their position in the hierarchy of acknowledged quality. The amount of funding per student allocated to a prestige international university will usually be significantly higher than that granted to a more local ex-polytechnic.

Furthermore, the abolition of the binary system in 1992 modified the funding system of polytechnics and further education colleges, institutions typically more socially responsive than the older universities. Before 1992, the governance and funding of those institutions were in the hands of the local education authorities, many of them largely controlled by the Labour Party and hence favourable to the socially responsive nature of their mission and provision. The 1992 Act abolished this local control. On the one hand, all universities, including the 'new' ones, now depend on the same unique structure for funding. The power balance has therefore been modified. Ex-polytechnics are more exposed to elitist pressure as they are now directly in competition with the old universities for funding. On the other hand, the abolition of local education authority control has increased the individual autonomy of further education colleges in both governance and funding. This kind of market deregulation in the tertiary sector makes it more difficult for institutions to carry out socially responsive policies, as they are deprived of the necessary local regulation mechanisms formerly provided by the local authorities.

The normal entry route to HE in Belgium

In Belgium, anyone with a secondary school degree has the right to enter any first degree in any HE institution and department of his or her choice, regardless of the grades obtained. With very few exceptions, there is no further restriction at entry level. This means very large student intakes in the first year of study (in university that is the first year of the *first cycle*). However, selection actually operates *during* the first year. The drop-out and failure rate in the first year of *candidature* (first cycle) is usually very high in most subjects (around 55 per cent). Moreover, a student who failed (or dropped out) in the first year in a given subject has only one more chance. He or she can start the first year again, either in the same subject or in another of their choice, but in the case of a second failure they have to quit the system.

The normal entry route to HE in the UK

The situation in the UK differs sharply from the Belgian one where all conventionally qualified students leaving upper secondary education can claim a university place as a right. Most UK candidates are required to seek their higher education through a centralized national application system known as UCAS (Universities and Colleges Admissions Schemes). Traditionally, admission to the university is based on A-level academic, although alternatives do exist. This is the normal route for upper-secondary school-leavers. Institutions make offers to such candidates for places on particular programmes, with or without interview, and usually subject to achieving specified grades at the upper-secondary General Certificate of Education Advanced-Level Examination.

Whereas the government, through the HEFCE and its Scottish and Welsh counterparts, determines the total numbers of students that a university can enrol (full-time undergraduate numbers in the 1990s being tightly controlled, while part-time numbers can be expanded at a university's discretion, as can graduate numbers), the council leaves it to each university to determine whom it will actually accept. Thus, within total funded numbers, universities have great freedom as to whom they will admit. There is diversity of practice between and within institutions, partly from the popularity or market strength of the admitting university and department, partly from philosophical and pedagogical calculations at department level as to who would together comprise a desirable quality and mix of students.

Consequences in terms of selectivity

On the whole, the Belgian system appears far less selective in terms of minimum entry requirements. Having a secondary school degree is the only requirement for entering any first degree course in any university. However, paradoxically, it is much more difficult for someone without the minimum requirements to enter the system, whereas a department in a UK university has discretionary power to decide to admit a candidate who would have none of the standard admissions qualifications. Another paradox lies in the fact that the very high selectivity of the standard route in the UK system has favoured the development over time of various alternative access routes for those who do not have the standard entry qualifications, a point discussed in more detail in the next section.

Likewise, the higher selectivity of the UK system has pushed the issue of equal education opportunity and the accessibility of HE to the forefront of the social debate, more so at least than in Belgium. The visibility of the issue in UK society is obvious to the outside observer. One is struck by the astonishing quantity and quality of the statistics publicly available on the issue – participation rates by age cohorts, transfer and flow rate, socio-demographic profile of students, and so on – as compared to countries like Belgium. We note, too, the abundance of the literature as well as networks, associations and institutions dealing with the topic.

Finally, the higher selectivity of the UK system also results in more efficiency, with comparatively lower dropout and failure rates whereas in the Belgian system, as pointed out above, entry is easier but once in, the chances of dropout or failure are much higher. The selectivity of the Belgian system, therefore, operates within the system rather than at entry level.

Adult access opportunities in the UK

Four main entry routes into the university can be distinguished in the UK in terms of entry qualification requirements: academic (A-level) qualifications, vocational (such as BTEC) qualifications, Access courses, and accreditation of prior experiential learning (APEL).

Admission through Access courses generally implies specific schemes arranged between a university and local further education colleges. Those courses are mostly delivered by the FE colleges and accredited by the university for admission into specified undergraduate programmes. They are targeted at specific groups who lack the traditional qualifications for entry into HE, such as women, working-class and minority ethnic groups. They are normally of one year's length and successful completion provides a route into HE. Their growing importance nationally was recognized in a 1987 White Paper which endorsed Access courses as a third route into HE alongside A levels and vocational qualifications.

APEL takes two forms. One is the accreditation of learning acquired outside the world of traditional qualifications by open college networks. The latter's role is to identify pathways and progression into HE for adult students. They accredit courses in adult, further and higher education institutions enabling students to accumulate and transfer credits. By this procedure, a candidate can claim equivalence of prior learning to formal admissions qualifications. APEL may also be used by an HE institution for admissions. In that case, the department itself assesses the candidates' prior learning through a variety of procedures (portfolio, interview, written test, recommendations, and so on) and makes the admission decision on that basis.

Again, the actual availability of those routes varies widely across and within institutions, given the wide discretionary power of institutions and departments to decide whom they will actually admit within fixed numbers. Some institutions and some departments within institutions may have a more open admissions policy, allowing access to people with 'non-standard' qualifications, whereas other institutions and departments may have a more restrictive policy, giving priority to candidates with traditional A-level academic qualifications. Moreover, some institutions provide alternatives to the traditional full-time three-year honours degree at undergraduate levels, such as part-time and 2 + 2 degrees. The 2 + 2 is a four-year course in which students spend the first two years in a further education college and the last two at the local university. The first year of the course in particular prepares students to work at the level required for a degree. It is designed to enhance the access of non-traditional students in a number of ways. Students do not have to possess qualifications to enter the course, but they do need to show an ability and willingness to learn.

As far as access to graduate education is concerned, the typical admission route to a Master's degree is via a good honours degree (normally a first- or upper second-class degree), although, as at undergraduate level, there is no automatic right of entry in the UK. Departments generally have graduate admissions tutors (often different persons from the undergraduate admissions tutors). They have the power to admit at discretion within established policy guidelines, and departments have different expectations and practices. As at undergraduate level, alternative routes into master's degrees are also available to a varying extent, depending on the institution and subject. Work experience may be considered highly relevant as a matter of policy in some departments, while not at all in others. Likewise, graduate part-time degrees are more or less developed across institutions and subjects.

In conclusion, what strikes the observer of the UK situation is the diversity of alternative access routes available besides the 'normal' route described above. This observation again underlines a paradox of the UK HE system. It is one of the most selective in Europe. At the same time, it is one of those that offers the widest diversity of alternative access routes. We must, however, keep in mind the extreme disparities existing between, and sometimes within, institutions in terms of alternative access provision. Not all the alternative routes mentioned above are available in all institutions or in all departments within a given institution. Some institutions and some fields are definitely more selective than others, and will therefore provide fewer alternatives to the normal access route. Accessibility is often correlated with institutional status. Older universities, especially élite research-oriented universities, are on the whole less accessible than the new.

Adult access opportunities in Belgium

Alternative access routes into HE are less diversified than in the UK. However, let us keep in mind that the normal route is also less selective. Effort to ease the access of non-traditional students to HE concentrates at the entry level of the *second cycle* (*licence*) rather than at the entry level of the undergraduate level (first cycle). Most of the access routes are aimed at facilitating entry into upper levels of the HE system, in particular at the entry of the second-cycle level. Instead of facilitating entry into the undergraduate level, the alternative routes are meant to shorten the duration of the second-cycle (licence) course by allowing credit transfer from non-university final degrees into university licence degree in the relevant subject. In this case, someone with a non-university degree in a given field will be allowed to enter a licence degree in the field, either directly or after completion of additional course requirements, often taken from the corresponding first-cycle degree or after demonstration of relevant experience. APEL provision as an alternative to formal entry qualifications also exists but remains very marginal. It can be found only in a very few licence degrees. So, as a paradox, a candidate without secondary school qualifications has more chances of gaining access to a second-cycle degree than to a first-cycle degree athough, again, this opportunity concerns a tiny minority of programmes. In some cases work experience is required in addition to formal entry requirements.

Disparities in terms of alternative access provision also exist in the Belgian HE system, but they appear more across departments and fields of study than across institutions. It should also be emphasized that the current legal framework allows for more openness than is observed in the field. For example, access to a licence degree through APEL schemes is explicitly allowed by law but is actually used by very few institutions and departments. Finally, as mentioned above, although the non-university sector does in fact cater for more disadvantaged social groups than the university sector, there is generally more adult access provision in the latter institutions than in the former.

Diversity of institutional provision: the Louvain and Warwick cases

Our Warwick–Louvain comparative study (Bourgeois *et al.*, 1995) illustrated the diversity of policies and practices implemented by universities to facilitate access and participation of adults in their award-bearing programmes.

Admissions policies and practices at Louvain

As in all Belgian universities, access to candidature (first-cycle) programmes at Louvain is virtually secured for any candidate who possesses a secondary school degree, regardless of the grades obtained and the subjects taken. However, it is very difficult for an adult without such a qualification to enter a candidature programme. The only opportunity which would exist for that candidate would be to take a secondary degree first in a special school (called *Ecole de promotion sociale*) that caters specifically for that part of the student population. In some fields it is also possible for someone who has previously obtained a non-university degree to reach the candidature degree (usually two years) through a shortened course of study (called *candidature unique*). In this case, the person gets credits for some courses of the candidature programme on the basis of the previous degree.

The standard qualification required for entry into a second-cycle (licence) programme is a candidature degree in the subject. However, access opportunities for non-traditional adult students who do not have the standard entry qualifications at that level are much wider than at the first-cycle level. Some licence programmes, the so-called 'bridging' (*passerelles*) programmes, admit candidates with a specified non-university degree. In some cases, the candidate with the proper non-university qualifications can enter the programme directly. Sometimes admission is conditioned by the grades obtained in the non-university degree. The candidate may also be required to take additional courses in the relevant first-cycle programme, ranging from a very limited number of credits, which can often be taken during the licence course, to a whole year of first-level courses. Relevant work experience can also be required for entry to some programmes.

In some other licence programmes, the so-called open faculty programmes (*facultés ouvertes*) which cater for adult students only, admissions are based on some form of APEL policy. In those cases, candidates are admitted on the basis of their life- and work-experience, regardless of prior formal qualifications. Sometimes, they have to pass an additional admission test.

Admission to *third-cycle* degrees (PhD and other postgraduate degrees) requires the standard qualifications, a licence degree in the field, with very few exceptions. In fact, additional entry requirements are most often imposed, such as relevant work experience, grades obtained in the licence degree, and so on.

Disparities in terms of admissions policies and practices exist not only across degree levels but also across subjects. For example, in examining the entry qualification required for admissions in degree programmes, our study showed that 76 per cent of the surveyed degree programmes specifically designed for non-traditional adult students (open faculties) recognize non-standard qualifications for admissions, against 45 per cent in psychology and education, whereas this proportion falls to 23 per cent in law 25 per cent in engineering, 21 per cent in medicine and a mere 5 per cent in humanities. It should also be emphasized that admissions policies (conditions and procedures) in most cases are regulated by rules and jurisprudence that are fixed by the department, within a framework strictly defined by university and governement regulations.

Admissions policies and practices at Warwick

Most full-time undergraduate degrees, the traditional or normal undergraduate degrees, belong to and are essentially taught within and controlled by a single academic department. All are honours degrees. Most are single but some are joint honours degrees. Most take three years of full-time study, but some special programmes take four years.

For traditional full-time undergraduate degrees, admission is controlled by the department, within University-wide guidelines and under the policy supervision of the Undergraduate Admissions Requirement Committee (UARC), and is administered by department admissions tutors appointed by the department head. Admission to graduate programmes is similarly a matter for department admissions tutors. In this case, however, general policy oversight is exercised centrally by the Board of Graduate Studies (BGS). Within the policy guidelines of UARC and BGS, and within the constraints on total numbers set for each programme centrally according to government policy and financial considerations, admissions are thus controlled and administered at department level.

The system of undergraduate part-time degrees, introduced in 1987, is managed University-wide through a part-time degree office, although particular courses within the broad-based programmes are taught and 'owned' by the different specialized subject departments. Admission is managed by the director of part-time degrees in consultation with the different teaching departments. The system of 2 + 2 degrees is a more recent innovation intended to increase the numbers of non-traditional, older undergraduates entering the university. With a first intake in 1991, this four-year programme is developed and taught in partnership with a group of nine local FE colleges. The first two years of study take place in these colleges which manage the admissions process in consultation with the University and within agreed policy guidelines and numbers. The third and fourth years (the honour years corresponding to years two and three of a conventional full-time three-year honours degree) are taught on the university campus.

At Master's level there is no centralized system. Each department publicizes and recruits to its programme up to the limit of capacity and/or demand, subject always to general university strategy and policy. At Warwick there is a policy imperative to increase graduate, especially research, student numbers. Departments are encouraged to expand, rather than constrained from admitting to graduate programmes.

Diversity of admissions practices also exists across subjects in Warwick. To give just one example, 80 per cent of the programmes specifically designed for non-traditional adult students have non-typical entry qualification requirements (only one A level), whereas this proportion falls down to 20 to 38 per cent in all the other undergraduate programmes. More markedly, two faculties (science and the former education) did not allow admission without any qualifications, mainly for compelling reasons of professional accreditation in education or curriculum demands in sciences and mathematics, while arts and social studies allowed it for 31 per cent and 27 per cent of programmes. For part-time and 2 + 2 programmes, the proportion is again 80 per cent. However, it should be emphasized that many departments which are restrictive in respect of departmentally managed degrees are quite open to non-traditional students who come to them via part-time and 2 + 2 routes.

Admission policies: a comparison

On the whole, admissions appear more routine and automatic at Louvain compared with Warwick. For qualified young persons at UCL entry is exercised as a right, using the course catalogue rather than relying on interview persuasion and special qualities. This is especially true for first-cycle level programmes. For second- and third-cycle admissions, conditions and procedures may vary more across programmes and are therefore less routine. At Warwick – as at other popular universities attracting as many as ten qualified young candidates per undergraduate place – requirements, procedures and conventions vary between departments and the position is much more confusing, not to say idiosyncratic. Entry to Warwick undergraduate degrees is relatively difficult and restrictive, but for those who win a place, with completion rates well above 90 per cent an honours degree is all but guaranteed. At UCL by contrast, it is easier to enter but a significant proportion, often approaching half of all students on a programme, fail to proceed to the second level.

For non-traditional mature-age students, Warwick is perhaps surprisingly open in particular subjects and programme areas. Well-motivated and determined local adults can be almost certain of entry to the specially designed part-time and full-time 2 + 2 programmes in those subjects where they exist. In some departments, access to the conventional departmental single honours degree is quite easy.

At UCL non-traditional entry at first level is all but impossible. On the other hand, it is much easier at Louvain for a non-traditional student to enter university, for instance via non-university HE, at the second level, in particular through open faculties programmes. These in some ways resemble and correspond in function to Warwick's part-time degree and 2 + 2 systems. It is also much easier at Louvain for a 'non-traditional' student to enter university via non-university HE at the second level, or year three of study. At this point many conventional, young students have fallen away or been 'cooled out'.

There is no analogous inflow at Warwick within the three-year honours degree. Only a very small number of students enter with 'advanced standing' or credit exemption, despite the University's long-standing membership of the national credit accumulation and transfer system. On the other hand, entry at Master's level at Warwick (normally the fourth year) may be seen to resemble the somewhat more open possibilities found at Louvain at second level (year three). Alternatively, entry to second-year engineering with a non-university higher vocational qualification might be a more accurate analogue to UCL's second cycle.

Flexibility by place and time

The accessibility of an HE programme is related not only to the admissions policy but also to programme provision. In particular it appears from our study that flexibilities in terms of course scheduling and location are among the most significant factors of accessibility (that is, the most correlated with adult participation, see Chapter 4). Flexibility in terms of time arrangements is reflected in evening courses, weekend courses and any other scheduling which deliberately bunches courses together in ways that might be calculated to make them more accessible to adults with other, especially working, commitments. Flexibility in terms of space is gained by off-campus teaching. Decentralization or 'relocation' is seen as an important principle for enhancing access. Outside all these modes of flexibility and lying beyond the normal range of provision in most of the work of both universities lies the field of distance provision, now commonly IT-supported and often referred to as 'virtual'.

Flexibility by place and time at Louvain

Overall we found quite a low proportion, only 11 per cent, of UCL programmes offering flexible time arrangements, with restriction of flexible locational arrangements to four programmes specially designed for adults. We also found unevenness of distribution between the Louvain faculties. Special adult programmes (open faculties), psychology and education, and economics, social and political sciences have the highest proportions of programmes showing time flexibility (63 per cent, 53 per cent and 13 per cent respectively), whereas four faculties offer no flexibility whatsoever. Looking at all time-flexible programmes at UCL and comparing faculties against the institutional average, we find psychology and education to be 20 per cent above the norm, open faculties 13 per cent above, and economics, social and political sciences 3 per cent above, with humanities lowest (−15 per cent), and then engineering (−8 per cent) and science (6.5 per cent). In some cases, a given programme (for example the licence in law) may be delivered in parallel both in evening and weekend format as well as daytime format. The latter is accessible only to in-service professionals in the field, while the former cater for the traditional 18–22 student clientele. However, some evening and weekend programmes have no daytime equivalent. In those cases, the programmes are designed for adults specifically – either non-traditional in the case of open faculties, or professionals with the standard entry qualifications in many other cases. Sometimes, however, although they are designed primarily for adults, they also admit young students under

certain specified conditions. This has become the case with the licence programme in education subsequent to the survey being carried out.

The quasi-absence of off-campus teaching in Louvain (except for the two
open faculties) can easily be explained by the national legal framework
which denies the right for a university to develop teaching activities outside
its local area. In fact, what is more remarkable is the availability of such
arrangements in two programmes. It is, however, less surprising that those
two programmes are the open faculties which are specifically designed to
cater for non-traditional adults. It should also be noted that Louvain is
involved together with other French-speaking universities in the management
of decentralized licence programmes outside their respective local areas.
Finally, distance-learning arrangements remain quite marginal, probably
because of the small size of the country.

Flexibility by place and time at Warwick

Warwick offers the Master of Business Administration (MBA) degree taught
as a distance-learning programme. Although there are explorations and some
investment in curriculum development for distance programmes in other
subject areas, nothing else was on offer at the time of this research. Warwick
also validates a number of academic programmes mostly in colleges local
to its region. There are, for example, two validated Master's degrees in
community education provided by the Community Education Development
Centre (CEDC) in nearby Coventry, and taught at different sites around the
country. A Master's degree in counselling, as well as lower levels of qualification, is validated at a nearby FE college, and other programmes are validated
to diploma- and B Phil- (honours first degree) level at colleges as far away as
Oxford. All of these arrangements lead to formal degree and other awards of
the University of Warwick, like the University's Certificate of Further Education programmes which are franchised to three colleges in the Midlands.
Thus the University makes it possible for students registered or otherwise
recognized through its central administrative systems to work for degrees and
diplomas at times and places more convenient to them than the university
campus or its own programmes. Our picture of admissions and flexibility of
time and place for accredited Warwick programmes and awards would be
incomplete, and distorted, if these arrangements were omitted.

Similarly, the local Open Studies (OS) Programme, administered on behalf
of the University by the Department of Continuing Education (DCE), was by
the early 1990s enrolling some 7000 students, mostly in evening courses of
one term's duration, some on weekend day-schools, a few at daytimes during
the week, and a very few for study tours. Some of these courses are currently
available on campus at night. Many are offered at different locations in the
University's local region – the three local government areas of Coventry,
Solihull and Warwickshire with which the university has multiple links, including representation on Council, its supreme governing body.

This large programme, which in terms of head-count roughly matches the total undergraduate population of the University, thus displays strong characteristics of flexibility in respect of both timing and location. It is also almost entirely open in terms of admission, which is handled through DCE under the policy supervision of the centrally administered University Board of Flexible and Continuing Studies. The majority of OS courses in the early 1990s were non-accredited; hence in part their omission from our survey of programmes. A number, however, led over two years of linked study to an Open Studies Certificate (OSC), valued at that time at 30 credit points or one quarter of a full-time year of degree work, and subsequently revalued upwards to 60 credit points. OS courses provide a bridge into degree programmes, with a measure of advanced standing, for students interested in moving on to more systematic, accredited study. Aspiring students applying for a part-time degree place are on occasion referred instead to an OSC programme if this seems better matched to their circumstances and interests. Thereafter they may move on, subsequently or concurrently in their second year, to 'regular' part-time degree study.

Subsequent to our survey, procedures were set in train to accredit virtually the whole OS programme. It has thus come rapidly to represent a substantial element of the University's degree-level accredited provision, but a part which is characterized by continuing very high levels of flexibility and accessibility as measured by the three criteria of admission, time and place. In practice only a small minority of OS students, who are classically self-motivated 'lifelong learners', are interested in registering for a degree. There may be, therefore, a difference between formal access arrangements and the actual participation of adults in university programmes.

Comparative flexibility

Although the two institutions have different faculty and department configurations, the academic fields at UCL and Warwick display themselves similarly on a spectrum of traditionality, or high scientific/professional status. At both universities this correlates negatively with accessibility, as shown by both admissions conditions and time/place arrangements.

Each university has a special focus and form of access and provision for non-traditional adult students – the open faculty and 'bridging' programmes at Louvain and non-departmental part-time degree and 2 + 2 programmes at Warwick. In a country where young people still typically 'go away to university' the latter are emphatically local. In Belgium, with its ease of travel and different university traditions, the stress is less evident. These special programmes sit somewhat outside regular mainstream academic management in each case, and students may share problems about perceptions of status and institutional centrality in consequence. They tend to be available in areas of the social sciences which also display relative openness through regular faculty- (UCL) and department- (Warwick) administered programmes; but to be remote from and offer no access towards the more esoteric, high-status areas such as mathematics and medicine. Within these commonalities we may discern differences which are explicable in terms of local cultural diversities, but also some surprising analogies. Thus law at Warwick is unusual in its orientation towards the community cultural context rather than to black-letter legal training. It appears more accessible than stereotypes of law might suggest. Analogously, special efforts have been in law at UCL. There is a licences evening degree course connected with a candidature course offered at another university (*Facultés Universitaires Saint Louis*). With these two programmes it is possible to get the complete curriculum in law from first candidature to third licence through evening courses.

Other flexible forms of adaptation

Although flexibility by time and space appears to be the most significant factor of accessibility, other programme characteristics clearly play an important role. We are thinking here of pedagogical arrangements which are designed to accommodate the characteristics of adult learners and enhance their academic achievement: emphasis on formative evaluation, small group co-operative learning, experiential learning, peer learning, student supervision and services, student participation in the course design and evaluation, independent study, and, more generally, emphasis on faculty development.

As could be expected, at the time when we carried out this survey such arrangements appeared to be concentrated mainly in the programmes that are specifically designed for an adult student clientele, in particular non-traditional adults. In this respect at Louvain there has long been a division between two main categories of programme. The first category includes the large majority of degree programmes, designed mainly to cater for the young traditional 18–22 clientele. They are quite conventional in terms of provision. They have virtually no time and space flexibility, offering daytime campus-teaching only, and appear quite conventional in terms of teaching methods and delivery systems. The other category includes those programmes that are designed for adults specifically. Most have at least some flexible time arrangement – evening and/or weekend courses. However, a further distinction should be made within this category between the programmes catering for adult advanced students, mainly in-service professionals with a university degree returning to the university to update their skills and knowledge in their field, and those very few programmes designed to accommodate non-traditional, second-chance adults. While the former have long remained quite traditional in terms of pedagogy, the latter have always been characterized by quite innovative pedagogical policies and practices and they have always been a kind of pedagogical laboratory for the university. Recently, though, the picture has become far less clear-cut. There has been growing, university-wide concern about teaching quality. In particular, under the impulsion of a newly created university pedagogy development centre, many of the innovative pedagogical practices which had long been confined within marginal adult programmes now tend to disseminate university-wide. However, on the whole, most conventional programmes still remain little suited to adult learners.

Understanding the conditions for access

The second part of this chapter illustrates the wide diversity of adult access provision in HE across countries, institutions and subjects, departments and faculties. The first part of the chapter provides keys for interpreting such diversity. It points to the diversity of possible factors and levels of analysis to be considered in approaching the diversity of national and institutional access policies and practices. What we now wish to underline is the danger in over-emphasizing one level of analysis or one set of factors and ignoring the others. Let us take just a few examples.

A naive observer could be impressed by the differences between Warwick and Louvain in terms of space flexibility. We saw that in Louvain there is virtually no off-campus teaching. Does this mean that the adult access lobby is less powerful, or at least less strategically efficient than at Warwick (strategic interpretation)? Not so. The reason is more trivial. In Belgium universities are forbidden by law to organize teaching activities outside their local area. This factor can only be considered if enough attention is being paid to the (macro in this case) structure and context in which the actors operate (structural interpretation). Now, the next interesting question is, how does it come about that within the same national and institutional structure, two departments (namely, the two open faculties) have managed to develop an off-campus teaching policy, as opposed to all the others? Only a combination of structural and strategic interpretation can answer this question. For example, the *structuralist approach* would focus the analyst's attention on organizational factors, that could explain why the open faculty leaders and staff were so committed to the idea and goal of facilitating access of non-traditional adults through space flexibility. This would take account of the type of discipline (epistemological approach), the sub-unit culture (culturalist approach), the type of functional relationship between the sub-units and their environment (contingency approach), the legitimation principles prevailing in the sub-units (structuro-functionalist approach) or the type of biography of the actors involved (personalist approach). However, none of those structuralist approaches can show how those actors actually managed to achieve their goal in such a 'hostile' context of legal constraints. This question can be addressed only by a *strategic interpretation*. This would draw the observer's attention to the actors behaviours in the decision processes which led to the actual implementation of off-campus teaching policies in the open faculties. In particular, it would focus on the nature of the power-relationship patterns between all the actors involved, the power resources and strategies that have been used, and the interplay of actors' strategies and behaviours throughout the process.

The same reasoning could be applied to the differences observed between the two institutions, for example, in terms of admissions policies and practices. At Warwick the significant differences observed between the 2 + 2 or part-time programmes and the department-run conventional programmes in terms of flexibility of admissions criteria could indeed be explained in the light of a strategic approach. This would point to the factors which explain why the actors in some sub-units could achieve their goals quite effectively in terms of enhancing or restricting access to non-traditional students. However, such an analysis would probably distort the reality if it does not also account for structural factors, at both institutional (meso) and national (macro) level – a structural approach. For example, it can be hypothesized that the difference in accessibility is related to the organizational sub-cultures prevailing in those sub-units, the segment of the environment they cater for, the type of relationship they entertain with those segments, and so on. Likewise, the interpretation should not discard the fact that as a matter of national policy and practice, departments enjoy considerable discretionary power in admissions matters, which deeply conditions the actors' behaviour in this context. In this respect, the picture appears totally different in Belgium, as we saw above. Here, goverment regulations related to degree accreditation are far more specific and prescriptive than in UK about the conditions for admission to higher education.

4

Adult Students: Getting in and Keeping out

Introduction

In the preceding chapter we looked, generally in terms of theoretical perspectives, at the nature and behaviour of universities and at what particular universities actually do and do not do to facilitate adult participation. This chapter examines in more detail the adults who are found in universities. The basic questions are 'Who gets in and who does not?' and 'What are the characteristics of the adult students?' The chapter title refers to getting in and *keeping out*; we also need to ask if it is not rather a case of being kept out.

To answer these questions we have first to consider problems related to the definition of the *adult student* at university. This requires both a conceptual and a methodological approach. Secondly, we identify adult groups represented in the university student population. This includes looking at which degree programmes are chosen by adults, and identifying adult students' sociological profiles. In so doing we take into account the motivations and the personal and sociological backgrounds that lead them to enter the university.

Such an approach will also show which adults are being excluded from universities, and will enable us to see if the university is helping to reproduce and reinforce social inequalities or to counter social exclusion. Do we have a situation of 'wider access', with universities allowing entry and giving chances and support to new kinds of student, or 'more access', with universities merely making it easier for a larger proportion of their 'traditional' middle- and upper-class clientele to gain access, albeit somewhat later than their younger counterparts from the same social milieu? On the basis of this analysis, the chapter concludes by addressing the university's behaviour with respect to social exclusion and integration, the situation regarding which social segments the university does (or does not) reach, and the selection factors at play. To understand the issues fully, factors related to the university itself and also others relating to the societal context and the population under study have to be considered.

The definition of the adult at university

The first but by no means least knotty problem in conducting an international analysis of adult access to HE is the conceptual and methodological one of defining the concept of *adult student* and organizing the concept to describe the different situations encountered. When researchers, administrators or policy-makers speak about adult students they refer to a particular segment of the academic clientele that is not always clearly defined. Adult education literature talks about both adult students and non-traditional adult students, who can be seen as a sub-group of the larger group of students.

Peering through the mist

The conceptual mist which surrounds researchers and administrators looking at adults at university is made more dense by the myriad of terms used and the lack of explicit, well-stated definitions of adult education. Adult HE is usually characterized by a large set of terms rooted in a local or national context. Any reader of adult education literature has met the following terms at least once in their lifetime: recurrent education, university adult education, continuing higher education, further education, non-traditional higher education, extramural education, distance higher education, open university, extension university education, lifelong learning, in the English-speaking world; and *éducation continue, éducation continuée, formation continue, formation continuée* in the French-speaking world, and so forth. The same confusion arises from the diversity of terms used to designate the adult studying in HE: older student, second-chance student, adult student, returner student, re-entry student, extension student, part-time student, open university student, mature student, continuing education student, and school-leaver are some of the terms used widely in the specialized literature.

This conceptual diversity has implications for comparative studies, as it creates more ambiguity than clarity. As Kasworm (1993: 414) writes 'Because of the diversity of terms, it is difficult to define comparative activities in relation to particular adult student groupings, delivery systems, programs or forms of higher education. In addition, some terms refer to very specific experiences but gradually acquire broader meanings that eventually lose all pertinence. This is the case for the term *part-time student*.'

Some terms refer without distinction to adult learning in a formal or informal framework or in a credit-bearing or non-credit-bearing training. This can distort perception of what is going on. Other biases can be induced by the fact that some terms used in the field of adult HE refer to non-traditional curricula, programmes and experiences that are not limited by the student's age or life- or work-experience. In such a case, 'young' students participating in these non-traditional formations could be seen as adult learners, even if they are enrolled in traditional programmes, too.

Many authors, for instance, OECD/CERI (1987), Kasworm (1993), Davies (1995b) and Blaxter, Dodd and Tight (1996), have already underlined the polysemy of the concept of adult student. They have shown that it can relate to different meanings and populations, even in a single national context, and is defined by different criteria according to the country. The attempts to propose a 'universal' rigid definition seem to be irrelevant if we want to adopt a comparative perspective and to take into account the particularities of each educational system under study.

For example, the definition used by OECD/CERI in a comparative work published in 1987 did not take these particularities into account. It fixed a common criterion based only on age, whereby all students aged 25 and older were considered adult students. As a result, the survey had some difficulties dealing with some national contexts where, as we will see later, the legal definition did not match the one proposed by the researchers (OECD/CERI: 13).

Adult students in Belgium and in the UK

In Belgium there is no legal or official definition of an adult student. This lack of a standardized definition makes it difficult for researchers and academic managers to have a clear idea of trends in adult access to HE. Indeed, we were confronted with this problem in our own study. The adult student is clearly older than the young student; but how much older must he or she be? The answer will clearly vary with the level of study being considered. In our study, we set the following age criteria to define the adult student in each level of study.

• First year of the first-level degree programmes: 23 years old and over.
• First year of the second level Licence degree: 26 years old and over, increased to 27 and over for medical studies as the first level is one year longer than in other fields.
• First year of the second-level 'complementary degrees' and first year of the third-level degrees (except for the PhD): 29 years old, increased to 35 and over for medical studies.

Another approach to defining adult students in Belgium would be to consider the time elapsed between the student leaving the formal education system and re-entering it, regardless of age. This is the notion of adult students as 'returning' students which has been widely adopted in the literature (see, for example, OECD, 1992; Marchand, 1983). This criterion deserves to be considered independently of the age criterion, although they partly overlap. A 23-year-old who has been out of the system for several years and is entering the HE system for the first time has specific needs, expectations and perspectives which may differ significantly from those of another student of the same age who has never left the educational system.

A third possible approach to the concept of adult student is to look at the student's occupational status, whereby a student may be viewed as an adult to the extent that they work alongside their studies. In other words, studying is not the main activity in the person's life. This is the adult as a 'part-time' student. Again, this variable overlaps with the previous two, but not completely, so that it also deserves independent consideration. (Note that these last two approaches can also be useful in other national contexts.)

Ideally, all three approaches should be combined in order to identify the adult student, because each of them highlights a specific set of student characteristics that should be taken into consideration when conducting research into or making policies regarding access and participation of adults in HE. We come back to these points later. Unfortunately, the last two criteria are virtually impossible to take into consideration in the Belgian context, given the current state of the statistical system at both national and institutional levels.

In England, Wales and Northern Ireland the situation regarding the definition of an adult student is clear-cut, the official definition being 21 years and over for the first level and 25 years and over for higher degrees. The existence of this official setting allows the education system of these countries to present clear figures on adult participation in HE, unlike many other countries. As far as Scotland is concerned, the age of 21 delineates the 'adult' from other entrants to HE (Osborne and Gallacher, 1995: 229).

Towards a political or an operational concept?

Two types of definition of adult student can be identified. The first is more policy- and practice-oriented, while the other is more observation- and research-related.

We will begin with the operational approach. The concern is to design a definition that allows one to identify a particular population of students in the HE system. Analysis of the literature on adult HE shows that researchers have developed a large number of definitions and classifications in order to describe the different situations they analyse. Some core elements can be identified in these definitions and classifications, such as age and break in scholastic career. On the basis of these elements, the concept of adult student refers to different groups. Kasworm (1993: 412–13) identifies the following groups:

- students who enter or re-enter HE with a prior major break in their formal involvement in learning; these individuals seek focused academic study, an assessment of advanced knowledge, and subsequent award of a degree, certificate or credential of advanced specialized expertise;
- students enrolled in academic studies who represent specific chronological age categories, most of the time defined by a lower age limit of 21 years, 25 years or 30 years of age or older; this age categorization for university adult students is somewhat arbitrary, as in the research conducted

by Bourgeois *et al.* (1995), but is often used to identify groups of adult students who have interrupted their schooling and occupied adult roles;

- students who enter HE with mature life-experience reflecting past major full-time responsibilities in work roles, in family provider/breadwinner roles, in apprenticeship training, or in military service;
- adult students who have completed an HE programme or level of study, left the HE environment, and now re-enter to gain a second line of academic knowledge or expertise as a 'second degree seeker', certificate seeker, or professional development course student.

Other authors propose other categories. Schutze (1988) distinguishes four, as follows:

- adults who enter or re-enter HE to prepare for a first university degree;
- adults who already have an HE degree but re-enter to update their professional knowledge or to gain new qualifications in order to change jobs, to get a job or to advance in their careers;
- adults without any previous HE degree but who enter, often for a short period, for professional reasons;
- adults with or without previous HE degrees who enrol in courses to develop their general culture.

These different categories have different intentions regarding programmes, curriculum, course content, financial support and certification. The four categories do not have the same weight according to Schutze, as the first is still not very common in a lot of countries compared with the other categories which include adults in non-credit-bearing programmes. The second and third categories are increasing with the quickening pace of technological and economic change. The fourth category is more common in English-speaking countries.

The typology presented by West and Hore (1989) and West *et al.* (1986) is quite simple but very effective. It is based on scholastic career and likewise identifies four types of adult student (West *et al.*, 1986: 190):

- early school-leavers;
- recyclers (those who have already earned a higher education degree);
- returners (those who started higher education but discontinued);
- deferrers (those who left school with higher education entry qualifications).

Guyot (1996) puts forward a more complex typology of adult students that combines age and scholastic career criteria. This typology is presented in very general terms so as to be applicable to many different national contexts. The adult student population is far from being homogeneous regarding scholastic career, previous access to HE and degree completion in this educational system. Some have a continuous scholastic career, some have already had access to university, with or without completion, and some have already earned a university degree. On the basis of this, and taking into account age[1] and scholastic career criteria, a tree-shaped typology can be designed, as shown by Figure 4.1.

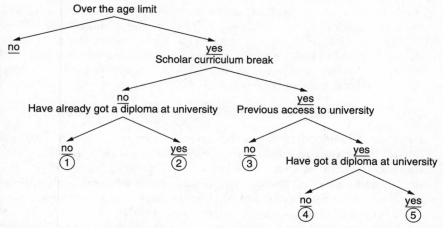

Figure 4.1   Typology of adult student according to Guyot (1996)

Five types of adult are identified:

- type 1: students with continuous careers but no university degree; these students' ages can be explained by frequent, repeated years of study or by the fact that the area of study was not taken into account in setting the age limit;
- type 2: students with no break in their scholastic careers and who already have a university degree; these students are enrolled in complementary or specialization programmes directly after getting their previous diploma;
- type 3: students with breaks in their scholastic careers who enrol at university for the first time;
- type 4: students with breaks in their scholastic careers and who enrolled in university study in the past but did not complete their training or earn a degree;
- type 5: students with breaks in their scholastic careers and who already possess a diploma at university; the break in the career may correspond to their entry into the working world.

This typology shows that the concept of adult student refers to a heterogeneous population. Taking the age criterion solely into account can lead to prejudicial amalgams to the development of research. So if possible it is better to take the scholastic career into account in order to be able to identify 'non-traditional adult students' (type 3 and 4). Note that there may also be 'non-traditional young students', who could be identified as being under the age limit but who are entering university after a scholastic career break. Unfortunately, information for taking the scholastic career into account is not always available, in which case it is not easy to distinguish the 'non-traditional adult students'.

Thinking of adult students in terms of traditional and non-traditional leads us to consider the second type of definition, the 'political' one. While the operational definition aims at helping the researcher in their empirical work, the political definition is practice- and policy-oriented.

In terms of policy and practice, as Davies (1995b: 287) explains, three types of student at university are identified.

1. 'deferrers'. These students have a similar profile to traditional students, who go on directly from secondary school (or equivalent), except that they took a longer time to get the traditional entry qualification or did not get into university (or HE) directly for various reasons (family, child-bearing, work, military or civil service, health problems, and so on);
2. the 'second chancers', who did not obtain the usual entry qualifications at school, often for reasons linked to some disadvantage (gender, social background, disabilities, ethnic origin, and so on);
3. the 'returners', who get back into the system to update or diversify their qualifications or to upgrade their level.

Davies notes that governments rarely set clear objectives in terms of equity, but focus in particular on the second category. Generally, policy is not concerned with equal opportunities in terms of class, gender or ethnicity. The most commonly pursued objectives relate to economic needs and focus on the third category: '. . . the concept of adult has moved away from a consideration of the whole person with cultural and social needs to one of an economic being with work related needs; the 'second chancer' has moved to the wings and the centre stage is now occupied by current and future workers capable of sustaining or regenerating economic competitiveness' (1995b: 287).

According to Goedegebuure *et al.* (1994: 346 – quoted by ibid.), besides striving for social equity and cultural enrichment, the more fundamental factors of expansion in HE are the need for skilled people, especially in applied science, technology and administrative sciences, and for more efficient management required for economic growth. The political focus on the 'returners' category has to be put into this context. Nevertheless, as mentioned by Davies, the development of adult training at university is characterized by an underlying tension: the economically most profitable fields, such as science and technology, are the most expensive to teach and, as we will see later, much of the expansion, in terms of adult participation, does not seem to occur in these fields.

Adult access to and participation at university

To get a more precise idea of the importance of university adult education and its characteristics, it is useful to apply the operational definition of adult student, and to observe this audience in different national contexts (macro-perspective) and within individual institutions (meso-perspective).

Table 4.1 Young and adult first-year entrants to higher education (excluding the Open University) in Great Britain by level of study (Thousands: percentage in brackets)[2]

	1981	1985	1991
Postgraduate			
Young	22.9	22.7	31.1
Adult	24.6 (52%)	33.0 (59%)	58.8 (65%)
Total	*47.5*	*55.7*	*89.9*
First degree			
Young	109.5	111.0	162.0
Adult	25.8 (19%)	28.7 (20%)	71.6 (31%)
Total	*135.3*	*139.7*	*233.6*
Sub-degree			
Young	57.5	58.2	66.4
Adult	89.2 (61%)	124.6 (68%)	147.6 (69%)
Total	*146.7*	*182.8*	*214.0*
All students			
Young	189.9	191.9	259.5
Adult	139.6 (42%)	186.3 (49%)	278.0 (52%)
Total	*329.6*	*378.2*	*537.5*

Adult access to and participation at university from a macro perspective

This section gives a general overview of the situation regarding adult access to university, first in the UK and then in Belgium.

Higher education in Britain has expanded rapidly over the last twenty years. The age participation rate (for 18–19-year-olds) in full-time HE increased from 13.7 per cent in 1984 to 29.0 per cent in 1993,[3] more than compensating for the demographic changes that reduced the size of age cohorts for entry to HE.

More adult students are now entering HE, particularly through the part-time route. Between 1981 and 1989, the number of adult students increased by 55 per cent.[4] A large number of adults also participate in other forms of post-compulsory education. If such training is taken into account, around 7 per cent of the adult population participated in some form of adult, further and higher education in 1991–92. Table 4.1 gives a breakdown of the numbers of young and adult students in HE by level of study.

As Parry (1995: 110) points out, the number of adult first-year students in undergraduate courses almost tripled between 1981 and 1991, from 26,000 to over 70,000. At the end of this period, nearly one in three entrants was a mature student. The growth was nearly as large at postgraduate level, while the numbers who entered sub-degree courses, the location of the majority

Table 4.2   Enrolments in Belgian higher education since 1961[5]

	1961–62	*1989–90*	*Variation (n)*	*Variation (%)*
NUHE	24,734	126,327	101,593	+ 411
University	31,312	109,297	77,985	+ 249
Total	*56,046*	*235,624*	*179,578*	*+ 320*

of adult students, increased by nearly two-thirds. According to Parry, this represented a faster rate of growth for undergraduate than for sub-degree education, despite the fact that the development of vocational education has been a particular concern of government policy. Just over half of the adult students who entered in 1991 were in sub-degree education, just over a quarter in first degree and one in five in postgraduate studies. Eight out of ten adult students enrolled in polytechnics and colleges. Parry also shows that six out of ten engaged in part-time study, and that expansion also occurred in the Open University for both associate students and first degree. Over 18,000 new undergraduate students enrolled in the Open University in 1991, joining a total continuing undergraduate population of 80,000 (compared to 14,000 and 60,000 respectively in 1981).

In the *French-speaking Community of Belgium* in spite of the smaller cohorts of younger students eligible for HE, the student population has increased, especially in non-university higher education (NUHE). This movement is related to several factors, especially the feminization[6] of the HE student population, the demand from the labour market for highly qualified workers, and unemployment trends. Table 4.2 shows how important the development of HE has been for the last 30 years. The number of enrolments in NUHE in 1989–90 is five times that of 1961–62.

The 'take-off' of HE is paradoxical. Given demographic changes and the shrinking younger age-groups of the population, we should have expected negative consequences for the level of enrolments but, instead, an increase has taken place. Therefore, we can say that more and more people access HE. However, from the way that statistics are presented[7] we cannot say *who* has access to degree education.

Adult entrants are fairly marginal, especially in universities (only 8.20 per cent of the Belgian students enrolled in Belgian universities for the 1990–91 academic year were 30 or older;[8] the comparable figure was 7.96 per cent for 1989–90). We do not have any recent figures for NUHE and there is no information about adult entrants in HE.

The information available for the universities in the French-speaking community is summarized in three graphs. The graph in Figure 4.2 shows the quasi-steady growth of the number of adult students[9] in the first year of the first-level degree and in the first year of the second-level degree from 1974 to 1988. After this academic year, the tendency is stabilized and there is no further increase.

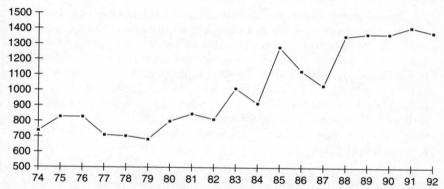

Figure 4.2 Adult students in Belgian French-speaking universities (first year of first- and second-level degree)[10]

The increase in the number of adult students does not parallel the trend for young students (Figure 4.3), and is actually more chaotic. The stabilization observed in the last five years for the adult students is not present for younger students, the increase in numbers of whom seems to be more constant.

The different tables and figures we have presented hint at a general increase in the number of adult students in universities. This trend has been discussed by some authors at an international level, such as Kasworm (1993), Schutze (1988) and Woodrow (1996). Their conclusions are similar. As Kasworm (1993: 414) writes:

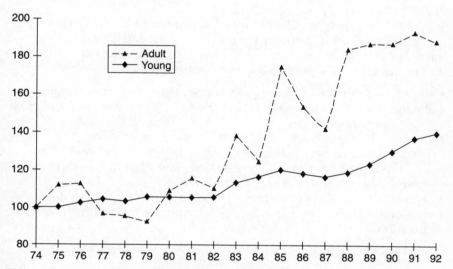

Figure 4.3 Numbers of students (adult and young) in Belgian French-speaking universities (first year of first- and second-level degree), indexed form: 1974 = 100[11]

Adult higher education is dramatically increasing. However, because of the recent development and the diversity of structures and forms of adult higher education, current statistics often lack comparative specificity . . . It is evident by the level of adult student participation that many industrialised countries have developed alternative structures, policies and programmes which serve access to higher education. Many of these industrialised countries reflect both modification of higher education institutions to provide access for students and also the development of innovative and non-traditional programmes and delivery systems directed to adult populations.

Nevertheless, the question arises: if adult access to HE is increasing, is there a qualitative change as well? Does this increased access benefit those who are traditionally not integrated into the HE system, or does it give opportunities only to those whose backgrounds are similar to those of traditional young entrants?

Adult access to and participation in university from a meso perspective

In this section we focus on what happens in terms of access in the two universities of Warwick and Louvain. We consider the levels of study and discipline in order to detect different patterns of access and participation and to state a hypothesis which will be developed in the following chapters.

Catholic University of Louvain (UCL)

We analysed the Belgian adults enrolled in principal studies or majors at the Catholic University of Louvain for the 1992–3 academic year. As we were interested in programmes that may be considered gateways to university study we did not take every programme into account, but only the following:

- the first year of the first-level programmes (*'premières candidatures'*);
- the first year of the second-level programmes (*'premières licences'* and assimilated programmes);
- the level I programmes that consist of one year of study (*'candidatures uniques'*, *'baccalauréat'*, *'épreuve préparatoire de premier cycle'*, and so on);
- the level II programmes that consist of one year of study (*'licences uniques'*, *'épreuve préparatoire de second cycle'*, and so on);
- the level II complementary programmes or specializations; and
- the level III (that is, graduate level) complementary programmes or specializations.

We considered the following criteria in relation to adult students:

- students enrolled in the first year of the first level and students enrolled in one-year candidatures and their equivalents who are 23 years old and older;

- students enrolled in the first year of the second level (*première licence* or its equivalent) or one-year licence (or its equivalent) who are 26 years old and older (this cut-off was raised to 27 and above for students in the first year of level II in medical studies); and
- students 29 years old and older who are enrolled in level II or III complementary programmes and specializations, the exception being specializations in medicine: the age limit was raised to 35 and above for this (it was not possible to break down the curriculum of level III medical specializations into separate years).

We thus considered 8491 students out of a total UCL student population of approximately 20,000. The analysis revealed that the proportion of adults in the total student population considered at UCL was 9.4 per cent or 796 out of a total of 8491 students.

Two indicators were used to find and understand where adults were located within the University as a whole. First, we considered the proportion of adults in the total student body by programme, faculty and degree level. Such ratios must be viewed with caution in view of the very different numbers involved. Thus Medicine's 9 per cent represents 166 adults out of the 1851 medical students considered, while Theology's 56 per cent refers to a total student population of only 27 for this faculty. The second indicator was the distribution of the total adult student population across programmes, faculties and degree levels. Psychology and Education contributed 5 per cent (36/796) of all UCL adult students. This indicator enables us, in turn, to rank the different faculties' relative contributions to adult 'participation' at university. Law for example, with 12.8 per cent of the student population, had only 4.5 per cent of the total adult population. We thus corrected for faculty size and examined to what extent the various faculties actually recruit adult students.

The breakdown of adult enrolment in the various faculties is presented in Table 4.3. The proportions of adults in the faculties' student bodies are displayed in Figure 4.4. The great majority (82 per cent) of the students enrolled in programmes from units that do not belong to any faculty (EUEN in abbreviated form) are adults, as one would expect from the intended function of catering to adults. Second comes the tiny Theology faculty with 56 per cent of its 27 students. Here many of the students are priests who are not young students. Other main contributors in declining order are Philosophy (37 per cent of the 87 students), Psychology and Education (19 per cent of the 681 students), then Economics, Sociology, and Political Science with 11 per cent of its large population of 2383. Proportions scale down through Medicine 9 per cent and Humanities 5 per cent to Law with 3.3 per cent, Engineering with 2.9 per cent, Agriculture with 2.5 per cent and Pure Science with 1.6 per cent.

If we look at the distribution of adult students compared with that of the total student population across faculties, we find that adults are particularly over-represented in EUEN and Psychology and Education, followed by the

Table 4.3   Distribution of adult students by faculty at UCL
(academic year 1992–3)

Faculty	Enrolments	Distribution (in %)	Adults	Distribution of adults (in %)
Theology	27	0.3	15	1.9
Philosophy	87	1.0	32	4.0
Law	1090	12.8	36	4.5
Economics, Sociology and politics	2383	28.1	259	32.5
Humanities	761	9.0	38	4.8
Psychology and education	681	8.0	131	16.5
Medicine	1851	21.8	166	20.9
Science	568	6.7	9	1.1
Engineering	658	7.7	19	2.4
Agriculture	282	3.3	7	0.9
Units that do not belong to any faculty (EUEN)	103	1.2	84	10.6
Total	*8491*	*100.0*	*796*	*100.0*

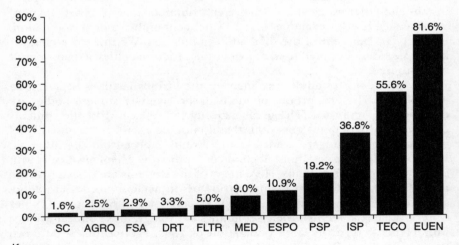

Key
SC: Faculty of Sciences; AGRO: Faculty of Crop Sciences (Agriculture); FSA: Faculty of
Applied Sciences; DRT: Faculty of Law; FLTR: Faculty of Humanities: MED: Faculty of
Medicine; ESPO: Faculty of Economics and Social and Political Sciences; PSP: Faculty
of Psychology and Educational Sciences; ISP: Institute of Philosophy; TECO: Faculty of
Theology; EUEN: units that do not belong to any faculty.

Figure 4.4   Proportion of adults in the programmes by faculty at UCL (1992–3)

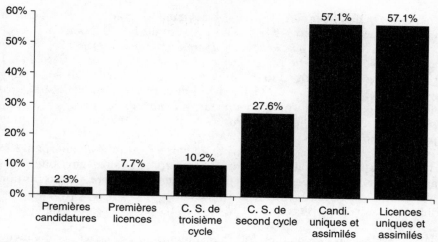

Figure 4.5 Proportion of adults by level of study at UCL (1992–3)

Social Sciences and Humanities, albeit to a lesser extent. By contrast they are very scarce in the traditional academic and vocational fields of Humanities and Pure Sciences, Law, Engineering and Agriculture.

Looking across degree levels we find a strong inequality of adult participation (Figure 4.5), with adult representation generally rising from a very low level of only 2.3 per cent in the *premières candidatures* (the first-level degree, normally taken in two years). This is essentially a direct school-leaver route rarely used by adults. Adults without the qualification for higher education will seek either direct entry to a licence degree where admission is possible, or entry via a *candidature unique*, depending on the subject. These possibilities are more attractive by virtue of speed alone (one year compared with the two-year *première candidature*). They are not, however, 'user-friendly' to adults in terms of scheduling, instructional design and so forth, as they offer no special arrangements and are composed of 'traditional' candidature courses. On the other hand, some of the licence programmes, for example in EUEN, offer direct access to non-traditional students and are generally more user-friendly to adults.

The proportion of adults in the *première licence* (second-level degree normally taking two to three years) is 7.7 per cent. This figure is low, partly because adults who already have licence degrees will prefer the *licence complémentaire* which is available in most fields. Consequently, only adults lacking a previous licence degree are likely to be found in these programmes. There is also the alternative candidature route. We may hypothesize that dropout and failure rates are very high in the *candidature unique*, so that very few adults reach the licence level. The course load in the candidature unique is extremely heavy and the scheduling, format and teaching methods ill-suited to adult returners. The other alternative is direct access to a licence programme in the 45 per cent of such programmes that have flexible admissions policies.

Licence complémentaire degrees are designed for graduates from another field, and normally take 1–2 years. Adults account for 10.2 per cent of the students in the third-cycle *licence complémentaire et specialisation* programmes and 27.6 per cent in the second-cycle *licence complémentaire et specialisation* programmes. Such programmes address two constituencies: those seeking a complementary licence immediately on completion of their first licence degree; and those returning to university from employment for a complementary licence. The latter appears to be the larger and mostly adult population.

The one-year candidature unique already referred to is an alternative to the candidature, generally for candidature degree-holders from other fields and for non-university degree-holders in the same field. Here, the proportion of adults (57.1 per cent) is predictably much higher, given these programmes' aims. Similarly, adults account for 57.1 per cent of the *licence unique et assimilé* students.

We find 'over-representation' of adult students in the licence complémentaire and the candidature unique. At the other extreme, adults are under-represented in candidature degrees, which illustrates the fact that adults seek to reach the second degree-level by routes other than the normal two-year candidature.

Licence degrees score low compared with the licence complémentaire. The concentration of adults in the licence complémentaire suggests that adults enrolled in second-level degree (both licence and licence complémentaire) consist mainly of adults with previous licence degrees. In other words, UCL is far more successful in providing opportunities for educational and professional updating and diversification (in the same or a different field) than in providing opportunities to adults seeking entry for a first licence degree. Its strength appears to reside more in accredited professional updating and upgrading than in second-chance access work.

The University of Warwick
The same type of analysis was conducted at the University of Warwick for the same (1992–3) academic year intake. The adult student populations in all first year undergraduate and taught master's programmes at Warwick were analysed, using the official definition of adult students. Adult participation was analysed by faculty and degree-level. The results are presented in Table 4.4.

Regarding the undergraduate programmes, science thus emerges as the largest faculty with the smallest proportion of adult students, principally because of its science and mathematical prerequisites for entry to its different programmes. Arts, however, also had quite a low adult proportion, reflecting restrictiveness at admission. Social Studies had the highest proportion of adults of the four faculties.

These faculty aggregations hide significant differences between programmes in different departments. In the Arts faculty the proportions ranged from 27 per cent in film studies and 20 per cent in English to 17 per cent

Table 4.4 Adults at University of Warwick (1992–3 academic year)

Faculty	Adults	Proportion (%)	Young	Total (adult and young)
Undergraduate				
Arts	49	12.4	345	394
Education	47	18.3	209	256
Science	75	9.6	700	775
Social Studies	158	21.0	294	452
Part-time degree	102	100.0	0	102
Total	*431*	*21.8*	*1548*	*1979*
Postgraduate				
Arts	204	51.6	191	395
Education	497	95.2	25	522
Science	1239	63.0	729	1968
Social Studies	1403	72.3	538	1941
Total	*3343*	*69.3*	*1483*	*4826*

in the history of art, 10 per cent in classics, 7 per cent in history, and from 0–3 per cent in the remaining areas. Education differed internally between arts and science education at 21 per cent and 12 per cent. In the Science faculty, adults accounted for 18 per cent of psychology majors compared with 10–11 per cent of computing, engineering, and mathematics and statistics majors, 6 per cent of the students in biology, 5 per cent in electronics, 3 per cent in chemistry and 1 per cent in physics.

The faculty of Social Studies, with the highest proportion of adults overall, also displayed striking internal diversity, from sociology with 42 per cent adults, followed by philosophy, also high at 21 per cent, and law with a surprisingly high 17 per cent. Politics and international studies had 14 per cent adults, with the business school at only 3 per cent and economics at 2 per cent. The business school's undergraduate section evidently conforms very much to the British 'old university' tradition of recruiting bright young school-leavers, despite its strongly professional adult flavour and orientation in other aspects of its work.

Eighty postgraduate programmes (MA, MPhil and PhD programmes) were analysed. Adult participation in full-time programmes was much higher at graduate level than at undergraduate level – 44 per cent compared with 18 per cent – and this holds true across all faculties. When part-time graduate students are added the picture changes even more dramatically. The proportions of adult students then rise from 23–63 per cent in the Science faculty and from 42–52 per cent in the Arts faculty, whilst the proportion in Education rises from 72–95 per cent; showing how heavily Education relies on part-timers at this level.

Comparing the two universities, there is great variety in adult participation by level of study and by subject area as identified by faculty or department.

At UCL hardly any adults enter the normal first level (première candidature) route used by successful upper secondary school-leavers, whereas this route is used by mature students at Warwick who are able to present access course credits or other alternative qualifications, or win entry through a department admissions process that recognizes their potential on the basis of work- and life-experiences.

UCL is clearly better geared to meeting the needs of second-chance adults at second level (open faculties and bridging programmes) and of successful graduates seeking further qualifications, than to providing first-level 'second-chance' access opportunities. Such graduates are either diversifying into a new field or specialization, or upgrading to a more advanced (second- or third-) level within their previous disciplinary track. Warwick provides much more open opportunities for adults to return to university for graduate study after a break from full-time education. When part-time as well as full-time students are taken into account the numbers and proportions are very substantial indeed in all faculties. As at UCL, most of the older people are continuing professional education students in the sense that they are improving (updating or diversifying) their existing HE qualifications. A small minority of such programmes admit formally unqualified non-traditional students, a few without even a first degree. At both universities, on the whole, admission procedures and arrangements appear more flexible at the higher levels.

Despite the première candidature restriction, there are channels for applicants to enter second-level programmes at UCL, either through a shortened candidature or by direct entry, and some effort is made to facilitate transition to this level from non-university HE institutions. In addition to allowing mature students into some 'normal' (single and joint honours) degree programmes mostly outside the sciences, Warwick has devised two special modes to draw adults into undergraduate programmes. They are partly differentiated from the core programmes, although with more or less common teaching. These are the part-time and 2 + 2 degree programmes. Here adults may work in mixed groups with students taking courses towards the more traditional honours degrees, or separately as evening part-time students at the university and as college-based 2 + 2 students in years 1 and 2 of the programme.

A familiar ranking of disciplinary 'academic tribes', as Becher (1989) puts it, may be discerned, although there are interesting differences in some subject areas between the two universities. Law and philosophy prove to be much more flexible and open at Warwick than at UCL, or than popular stereotypes might suggest. Medicine, absent from Warwick, is fairly restrictive at UCL in terms of genuine 'second-chance access', although significant numbers of students classified as adults do enter some of the programmes. Science is restrictive at both universities. With some exceptions, the humanities (arts) are also quite traditionally restrictive despite the absence of the compelling mathematics and science prerequisites that affect admission to science faculties. Leaving aside the special (largely social studies) provision of EUEN, part-time and 2 + 2 degrees for adults, the social sciences or studies (mainly sociology, psychology, education and politics) admit the highest proportions of adults at both universities. We return to these disciplinary differences and the factors underlying them later on.

The research conducted at Warwick and UCL also examined the connections between adult participation and admissions policies, course scheduling and location arrangements. At UCL, the proportions of adults are much higher (71 per cent compared with 5 per cent) in programmes where special course scheduling arrangements are made. The difference is more marked still when it comes to off-campus teaching (95 per cent in off-campus classes compared with 9 per cent in on-campus classes). This is natural enough, as the off-campus courses are arranged specifically for non-traditional mature students.

Adults then are greatly over-represented in programmes with special scheduling arrangements and off-campus provision. This effect is amplified by the fact that a third of these programmes are open to adults only. More surprisingly, almost 29 per cent of young students find their way into these time-flexible courses even though young people are generally thought not to be amenable to evening and weekend courses. The high level may be explained in part by the inclusion in 'flexible time arrangements' of 'block release' crash weekend packaging of courses, which young people may find attractive.

Turning to the relationship between adult participation and time and place arrangements at Warwick, it is helpful also to consider the type of programme and the social group of the students. Special scheduling is offered to accommodate part-time students who are working. These special arrangements facilitate entry for some students but exclude others. Thus an undergraduate part-time degree programme is offered in the evenings, but some adults take an undergraduate programme part-time in the day. Some graduate teaching is scheduled for evenings or weekends. The full-time 2 + 2 programmes attract different 'non-traditional' categories of students. In particular, those taking social studies are mostly working-class women with family commitments. Their tuition takes place in the daytime, preferably when their children are at school. As in the part-time degree programmes, students are without exception adults. However, some full-time undergraduate programmes not designed specifically for adults and taught in the day do have high numbers of adults (58 per cent in engineering design and appropriate technology, 50 per cent in sociology).

Whereas the adult participation rate is much higher at graduate than undergraduate level, and more programmes offer special scheduling arrangements at graduate level, there is no clear and simple relationship between scheduling and adult participation. Some graduate programmes with special scheduling have large numbers of adults or are attended exclusively by adults; others without special arrangements also have high numbers of adults. Thus, continuing education, educational studies and comparative labour studies all offer special scheduling arrangements and adults account for 96, 100 and 88 per cent, respectively, of their students. The proportions of adult students in engineering, applied social studies and quantitative development economics, which do not offer special scheduling, are 92, 100 and 88 per cent, respectively.

Teaching off-campus is not significant in relation to non-overseas adult participation in undergraduate degree programmes. Only the 2 + 2 programme is taught off-campus. This is on the campuses of the nine local colleges in the University's community partnership. The first two years of the four-year open access degree are thus made more accessible via more local and probably less daunting, more 'user-friendly', environments, before students move to the university campus for their two honours-level years. We should not overlook, however, the fact that the University teaches overseas and by distance mode in various Master's programmes, as well as off-campus at many sites around its region for non-degree 'open studies' students, some of whom follow a certificate trail into degree programmes. Open studies, then, is a form of off-campus outreach excluded from this analysis.

We found no significant relationship between open admissions policies and actual adult entries at UCL. The situation is quite similar at Warwick. So, one striking common finding of the comparative analysis conducted on the two institutions is how little formal conditions for admission correspond to or can predict actual adult participation. At UCL the special scheduling and location arrangements are what make it possible for adults to take part. At Warwick some apparently very open courses fail to recruit significant numbers of adults, whereas some rather restrictive programmes actually enrol large proportions.

A major difficulty in comparing the two universities lies in the structure of the degrees. Broadly speaking, England has a 3 + 1 + 3 structure for undergraduate honours, masters and doctoral levels. In Belgium a 2 + 2 (or 3) + 2 (or 3 or more) structure prevails. We can thus compare non-traditional access in one country at the beginning with access two years on in the other. Or we can compare levels 2 and 3 (second and third cycle) at UCL with the English fourth year or Master's level, in which case we find much greater openness in both systems – and quite remarkably high numbers of adults at Warwick. Overall, UCL shows an adult participation rate of 9.4 per cent. At Warwick the proportion among undergraduates is 21.8 per cent, but at the graduate level it is 69.3 per cent, allowing for the different modes of identifying 'adult' in the two situations.

The analysis also revealed the great variety that can be found within each institution and the 'counter-intuitive' discoveries that probing reveals – for instance, the behaviour of the law schools in both places. One of the most problematic tasks is teasing out which 'adult' participation involves non-traditional second-chance students and which is more simply the return, for career purposes, of the already well-qualified who are keen to upgrade or diversify their expertise (more of the initial study or moving into management, for example).

The critical reader interested in equity and participation will also have noticed how little we address gender – and the absence of ethnic and social class analyses. Here the differences in the data sets partly explain our silence. Social class is an old and abiding preoccupation in the UK but it does not feature very freely in institutions' admission and participation records. Whereas ethnicity is an increasing preoccupation in UK HE statistics, it is absent from Belgian records. More generally speaking, Belgian institutions do not seem to be interested in collecting data about the social characteristics of students at any level of the education system. This lack of interest could be related to the fact that the political authorities consider the educational system, and HE in particular, to be quite open to everyone. It could also be connected to a desire to hide social inequity in education. Nevertheless, the question of the backgrounds and characteristics of adult students cannot be overlooked if we are seriously to consider the relationship between the 'adult university' and social exclusion.

Adult students at university: who are they?

In many countries it is difficult to give an accurate description of the components of the intake of HE systems because of the poor quality of the statistics. In the experience of other researchers (Webb *et al.*, 1993), nothing accurate can be said about the origins (social or economic) and characteristics (gender, ethnic group) of students in HE, at least on a large scale. In these contexts it is even harder to have a clear understanding of the characteristics of the adult population (re-)entering university. The difficulty is considerable at both macro- and meso-levels of analysis.

Yet a question which frequently arises in discussions about adult HE concerns the meaning of the increase in the number of adult students. Does the development of university adult education correspond to a qualitative change, with an opening up to new audiences, or only to a quantitative change, without reaching non-traditional targets? This debate is often referred to as 'more access versus wider access'. It has important political implications. As Woodrow (1996: 1) writes:

> . . . different interpretations [of what is access] contribute to the construction of different political realities and outcomes. 'Access' used merely as a synonym for 'participation' highlights the positive, reporting on those who are participating, thus representing the status quo in a favourable light and justifying the continued allocation of resources to those groups already well-established within the system. On the other hand 'access', interpreted as wider participation, encompasses exclusion and non-completion, exposing immediately the limitations of current systems and the marginalisation of mature students, many of whom are late starters in the life-long learning process.

From the last perspective, access is related to equal opportunities, which means encompassing under-represented groups and embracing not only entry but also successful completion.

So, the crucial question is, who gets access to higher education and who does not? Adopting Woodrow's argument (1996), it is reasonable to answer the question by splitting students into two groups. A first group are those who actually get access. This is composed of students from middle- to high-income families of a dominant ethnic group whose parents have had experience of HE, who did not repeat any courses, got high marks on school-leaving examinations, and who have no disabilities. A second group are people who usually have no access to HE. In this group we find people from low-income families and/or minority ethnic groups, without parents having experience of HE, and who have experienced earlier education problems and/or who have disabilities. In terms of higher education, the people from this second group are disadvantaged as, even if they do enter HE, they will be more likely to drop out for financial reasons than those from the first group. Their academic performance is more likely to be disrupted by the need to earn income while studying. These people will also be more likely to study in less prestigious universities or choose a professional or vocational rather than an academic orientation.

In the light of these elements, any analysis of adult university education will be inadequate which does not examine the particularities of the mature audience at university. Despite the scant data, we will try to shed some light on this point. Before presenting the information, we should reiterate that the adult audience at university is far from homogeneous. The concept of adult student covers different types of student such as early school-leavers, recyclers, returners and deferrers. We can assume that the sociological profile and motivations vary from one type to the next. Recyclers will probably have particular educational and social backgrounds quite different from those of school leavers, returners and deferrers. Unfortunately we found few publications presenting the social and educational background of each group of adult students and, therefore, we will stick to a general level of description of adult students as a group. However, it should be kept in mind that the distinction between the different types of adult student is relevant for the debate about wider versus more access, as policies developed in a widening perspective will be less concerned with recyclers and probably focus more on school-leavers or second-chance students. Nevertheless, analysis of educational background alone is interesting as it gives an idea of the importance of second-chance students in the university systems.

Educational background and initial qualification

Although no national figures specifically on adult students are available except in the United States and the UK (Higher Education Statistical Agency (HESA) statistics), it seems that the level of qualification is quite high (OECD/CERI, 1987). Consequently it appears that (re-)entering adults turn to the university not because they have been deprived of previous training but because of a strong pre-existing scholastic foundation. Therefore,

Table 4.5 Adult students and school-leaving qualification: situation at University of Warwick – academic year 1992–3 (second-year undergraduates)

Qualification	% with qualification		
	Part-time students	2 + 2 students	Full-time students
CSEs	6.3	5.0	9.5
O Levels	62.5	40.0	57.1
CSE/O Levels	18.8	50.0	23.8
GCSEs	0.0	5.0	11.9
Vocational	50.0	50.0	33.3
A Levels	50.0	30.0	61.9
Access	6.3	10.0	30.9
Degree	6.3	0.0	0.0
Other	43.8	20.0	33.3

second-chance students can be said to be in the minority. For instance, as the OECD/CERI report shows, the qualifications of adults enrolled in HE are higher than the level for the total population. Even in Sweden, where adult students are the most common students in HE, the proportion of adults with low-level qualifications is small.

Case studies of particular institutions lead to the same conclusions. For example, Guyot (1997) showed that 95 per cent of the adult students at UCL already had a previous higher education diploma. There are similar findings from the University of Warwick (1992–3 academic year; Bourgeois *et al.*, 1995).

Table 4.5 reveals the small proportion of students without school-leaving certificates. The data also show that 30 per cent of the 2 + 2 students have A levels, while 50 per cent of the part-time students and 61.9 per cent of the full-time students have A levels. However, many obtained A levels at FE colleges as adults, not as 18-year-olds. The same type of situation was observed by Carp *et al.* (1976) in the USA. In their sample of 1207 adult post-secondary education learners, 42 per cent had at least some previous post-secondary education (versus 24 per cent for the whole sample of 3910 adults). Only 17 per cent of the learners did not graduate from high school compared with 33 per cent of the total sample. It thus appears that if the present trend persists, adult access to university will increase rather than decrease educational differences between social groups and reinforce social exclusion mechanisms.

Age

In the statistics, the adult student population is defined simply by age, so everyone identified as an adult student will be above a specified age limit. Nevertheless, it is interesting to have a more precise picture of the situation

Table 4.6   Adult students and age variation in student groups: situation at
University of Warwick – 1992–3 academic year (second-year undergraduates)

	21–30	31–40	41–50	51–60	Over 60	Total
Part-time students	31.25	25.00	25.00	12.50	6.25	100.00
2 + 2 students	40.00	40.00	20.00	0.00	0.00	100.00
Full-time adult students	50.00	45.25	4.75	0.00	0.00	100.00

regarding age. According to the OECD/CERI report (1987), the various countries' statistics reveal that the adult student is on average quite young. Many adult students appear to be people who either defer entering HE for just a few years or merely continue their training. If this is the case it means that many adult students are not second-chance students.

This assumption is backed up by some research findings. At UCL, Guyot (1997) showed that the average age in the sample of adult students analysed for 1993–4 was 33.4 and the age distribution was uneven (many 23–9-year-olds but few of 45+). In earlier work Carp et al. (1976) found that both interest and participation in learning activities began to decline in both men and women in their early thirties and dropped dramatically after the age of 55. The Warwick–UCL project found a relation between age and type of programme (Table 4.6).

In the OECD/CERI study the rather low age of the adult population is quite understandable: adults who (re-)enter are in the age corresponding to the most dynamic periods in their careers. Widening access for older adults, however, is an issue which needs to be considered more clearly by adult educators.

Location of the adult students in the university system

We have already considered location in analysing adult participation across disciplines and level of study. The University of Warwick and UCL case studies show that the level of entry varies from one national context to the next in line with national admission policies. While institutional particularities may be found within a country, the national context seems to be decisive in determining the most common entry paths. In contrast, the field of study seems to present characteristics that cross national borders. The small proportion of adult students in the natural sciences and in engineering, at least in the basic levels (undergraduate study in the UK and candidatures in Belgium), is a good example of this.

Relating adult students' positions within university programmes to their educational background reinforces the feeling that the development of adult education at university corresponds to a quantitative rather than a qualitative change, benefiting second-chance students. For instance, the survey of adult students at UCL showed not only that the majority of these students already have high levels of qualification, but also that most of them were not in the basic level of study. This survey identified these seven most important groups:

1. non-university (short cycle) HE graduates enrolled in one-year level I programmes (14.07 per cent of the adult students);
2. non-university (short cycle) HE graduates enrolled in the first year of the second level (18.15 per cent);
3. non-university (long cycle) HE graduates enrolled in level II complementary programmes or specializations (4.4 per cent);
4. university first-level degree-holders enrolled in first year of the second-level programmes (4.81 per cent);
5. university second- or third-level degree-holders enrolled in the first year of second-level programmes (7.41 per cent);
6. university second- or third-level degree-holders enrolled in level II complementary programmes or specializations (22.59 per cent);
7. university second- or third-level degree-holders enrolled in level III complementary programmes or specializations (7.04 per cent).

A high proportion of adult students at UCL cannot, therefore, be considered 'non-traditional' students. They already have university degrees (at least second-level) and want to get a complementary or higher qualification. Other mature students have a non-university rather than university degree and take advantage of level II bridging programmes to enter the university. Very few adult students have no previous HE qualification, and most of them enter by the first year of the first-level degree. This situation, which probably occurs in many other universities, even in different national contexts, is a good example of what the notion of adult HE actually often covers.

Gender

The number of women in HE, especially in universities, has risen in the last decade. However, the trend is not spread evenly over the total population or between different disciplines (thus women rarely enter engineering). Does this trend carry over to adult students? We might have expected an increase in the number of mature women entering HE, especially as women have become increasingly involved in economic activity and had fewer opportunities than their male counterparts to pursue their studies when they were younger. The rate of access of female adults to HE and the female employment rate are positively correlated: the higher the economic activity rate, the higher the proportion of women among adult learners in higher education (OECD/CERI, 1987). Yet the national figures show that the situation varies from one country to another (OECD/CERI, 1987).

Table 4.7   Mature home first-year entrants to higher education (excluding the
Open University) in Great Britain by sex, mode of attendance and level of study
(per thousand; percentage women in brackets)[12]

	1980		1985		1990	
	M	W	M	W	M	W
Postgraduate	15.3	7.6 (33%)	18.8	10.8 (36%)	26.5	22.8 (46%)
First degree	14.0	10.3 (42%)	14.8	12.9 (47%)	24.3	25.0 (51%)
Sub-degree	60.2	26.7 (31%)	66.8	44.1 (40%)	74.1	62.6 (46%)
Total	*89.5*	*44.7 (33%)*	*100.4*	*67.8 (40%)*	*124.9*	*110.3 (47%)*

In Sweden, Finland and the United States, women outnumber men in HE
(both in young and mature students) and study more frequently in part-
time programmes. In Germany and Austria, women are the minority in the
young student population. The situation for adult students in Germany and
Austria is even worse. In the UK the number of women has risen steadily,
as shown in Table 4.7, so that by the mid-1990s women consisted of half
of the undergraduate student population. Overall, the number of female
students has risen, with women making up the majority of mature incomers
to both full-time and part-time level I courses by the late 1980s, and attending postgraduate and sub-degree programmes in greater numbers than at
the beginning of the decade.

In France, women make up the majority of the younger student population
and are nearly equal with men in the adult student body (OECD/CERI, 1987).
In Belgium, the proportions of young men and women entering HE are fairly
equal, at least for the French-speaking part of the country (Dal *et al.*, 1994,
Dal and Dupierreux, 1996). Due to the lack of statistics nothing can be said
about the adult student population. Nevertheless, in the UCL survey women
made up 41 per cent of the sample of adult students (Guyot, 1997). Carp
et al.'s 1976 survey of American adult post-secondary learners indicates that
neither sex is more oriented toward continued learning than the other.

Social background and ethnicity

Many sociologists, such as Bourdieu and Passeron, have shown the strong
relationship between level of qualification and social position. They have
also stressed the role played by the education systems in social reproduction. So in light of what we have seen about the qualification level of adult
students, we may assume that the majority of these students do not come from
economically disadvantaged groups. Carp *et al.*'s survey (1976) underlined
inequalities between ethnic groups (under-representation of blacks among
adult post-secondary learners) and social classes (over-representation of
professionals and corporate executives).

Table 4.8 Adult students and social class (perceived): situation at University of Warwick – 1992–3 academic year (second-year undergraduates)

	% with qualification		
	Part-time students	*2 + 2 students*	*Full-time students*
Middle class	75.0	25.0	52.3
Working class	6.2	55.0	35.7
Classless	0.0	5.0	4.8
Unanswered	18.8	15.0	4.8
Do not know	0.0	0.0	2.4

Despite the democratization movement observed in the last three decades, available statistics on the social origins of students in HE, whatever their ages, indicate that low-income and minority ethnic groups enter HE far less often than medium- to high-income groups and dominant ethnic groups. The percentages may vary from one country to the next but are always low compared with the number of upper- and middle-class students from the dominant ethnic groups. The lack of specific data on adult students' social profiles prevents confirmation of this statement for mature students. Nevertheless, due to the low proportion of second-chance incomers in this audience, we can confidently assume that non-traditional students are under-represented in the adult student body. This is probably true for the Belgian HE system, especially in universities, apart from some limited exceptional experiences.

In addition to the lack of statistics, it is more difficult to analyse the social backgrounds of adults than young students because the usual indicators (parents' level of instruction, income bracket, profession, and so on) do not suffice. Most of the time, adult students are already working and the researcher has to take this engagement and their motivations for enrolling in HE into account. The 1987 OECD/CERI report underlines the fact that few adults enter HE with a view to social advancement, that is to say, to climb out of their social class. The proportion of adult university students with blue-collar jobs is close to the proportion of young students from working-class families. Interestingly, Slowey (1987) showed that for the UK around 70 per cent of adult students belonged to the two highest job categories (professionals and upper employees) while only a scant 20 per cent of these students were in the intermediary category of non-manual workers, and around 10 per cent in the manual worker category.

However, some empirical findings from our research show that the picture is not so clear-cut. Indeed, the social background of students in the University of Warwick survey appears to vary with the type of training. The large proportion of students registered on 2 + 2 programmes who identify themselves as belonging to the working class bears mentioning. In contrast, three-quarters of part-time students stated that they belonged to the middle class. The breakdown of these findings is given in Table 4.8.

Table 4.9   Adult students and family status: situation at University of Warwick – academic year 1992–3

	% Married/Partnered	% With no dependants
Part-time student	87	16
2 + 2 students	53	49
Full-time mature students	47	57
Ordinary students	0	100

To conclude, it is difficult to discuss issues concerning the social and ethnic backgrounds of adult students given the lack of data. We may wonder if this deficiency of information corresponds to a political will to hide the education system's failure to reduce social inequalities or its role in reproducing such inequalities. We may also consider these elements to be evidence of the relative failure of current second-chance HE policies.

Family status

Due to their age, adult students are more likely to be married and have children. This is not a minor issue as many studies have shown the importance of the 'family' factor in adult enrolment and completion of HE. The economic cost of studying can have negative repercussions on family life which is not easy to combine with student activities and can be a real barrier to success. For instance, Slowey (1987) identifies time management as adult students' main problem in the UK. About half of students questioned stated that the major difficulty was the lack of time because of familial obligations, rather than inconvenience linked to reduction in their professional activities.

According to the OECD/CERI (1987) report, there are no significant differences between the family status of the whole population and the adult student population. This is confirmed by Carp *et al.* (1976). Some empirical research gives quite detailed pictures of the situation of adult students regarding family status in particular institutions. Blaxter *et al.* (1996), for instance, give interesting information about the relationship between family status and part-time studying (see Table 4.9).

These figures show a clear split between the groups. In 1992–3, ordinary students are never married and have no dependants, while the majority of part-time students are in the completely opposite situation. The two other categories split fairly equally along both lines. The research conducted by the Warwick–UCL team revealed that 20 per cent of the 2 + 2 students who filled in the questionnaire were single parents. The difficulty of striking a balance between the demands of family life and study probably explains a great deal of these findings. What is more, this appears to be even more difficult for women (Pascall and Cox, 1993; Edwards, 1993; Merrill, 1999). At UCL, a large proportion of the adult respondents in 1993–4 (46.9 per cent) were not married (Guyot, 1997). However, this figure may include people who cohabited without being married. Nevertheless, many adults were married (46.6 per cent), while 6.5 per cent were divorced.

Economic activity and earnings

Is there a link between the increase in unemployment and the development of adult HE? On the one hand, students completing their HE degrees are likely to go on further in their training, for instance by enrolling for complementary degree or specialization programmes. In so doing, these 'late-leavers' find a way to improve their academic resumés and to delay their entry into the labour market or possible unemployment. On the other hand, jobless adults without high levels of education sometimes consider it useful to get into HE in order to increase their chances of getting a job. This could be a good strategy but since many countries forbid people who are drawing unemployment benefits from engaging in studies, they may have to make a difficult choice between entering HE, which means losing their benefit, and continuing to draw benefit but not improving their level of education, which compromises their chances of finding employment.

Some adults combine a part-time or even a full-time job with study so as to have an income while working towards a degree. This leads to the development of part-time programmes, which seems to be very attractive for adult students. Nevertheless, combining the two types of activity is often difficult. It frequently reduces the chances of successful completion, especially when the adult student has family responsibilities. Such adults run higher risks of dropping out or failing than students who do not have to work.

The research conducted at UCL (Guyot, 1997) showed that 55.8 per cent of the adults were full-time workers, while 21.8 per cent were part-time workers and 22.4 per cent did not work at all. Analysing by gender, family status and economic activity, we found the following to be the most important categories:

- 26.2% were married men with full-time jobs;
- 9.5% were unmarried men with full-time jobs;
- 8.8% were unmarried men without jobs;
- 7.9% were unmarried women with full-time jobs;
- 6.9% were unmarried women without jobs;
- 6.9% were unmarried women with part-time jobs;
- 6.3% were married women with full-time jobs.

These figures indicate that a majority of adult students had at least a part-time job. The high proportion of full-time workers should be related to our earlier observations about education level: that a high proportion of these students are not new incomers and probably do not belong to disadvantaged social groups.

Table 4.10 Distribution of the adult students by gender, economic activity and most recent qualification: situation at UCL – 1993–4 academic year (%)

Type	Gender	Activity	Latest diploma	Distribution
1	Male	Without job	Secondary school	2.84%
2	Male	Without job	Non-university HE (short degree)	3.15%
3	Male	Without job	University (second- or third-level)	3.47%
4	Male	Full-time job	Non-university HE (short degree)	11.36%
5	Male	Full-time job	Non-university HE (long degree)	4.42%
6	Male	Full-time job	University (second or third degree-level)	31.45%
7	Male	Part-time job	Non-university HE (short degree)	2.84%
8	Male	Part-time job	University (second or third degree-level)	2.52%
9	Female	Without job	Non-university HE (short degree)	3.15%
10	Female	Without job	University (second or third-level)	4.73%
11	Female	Full-time job	Non-university HE (short degree)	7.57%
12	Female	Full-time job	University (second or third-level)	7.57%
13	Female	Part-time job	Non-university HE (short degree)	7.26%
14	Female	Part-time job	University (second- or third-level)	5.05%
Total 1–14				97.38%

Other interesting information emerges when we take into account both economic activity, gender and the most recent degree. Table 4.10 shows the breakdown of adult students according to the fourteen most important categories identified. The proportions of jobless women and men without a secondary-school qualification are less than 2 per cent and 2.84 per cent, respectively. In contrast, we find a very high proportion of full-time male workers with a second or third-level university degree (31.45 per cent). Types 4 and 5 (full-time male worker with a non-university HE degree) account for nearly 16 per cent of the sample. For female, full-time workers with a second or third-level university degree and full-time workers with a non-university HE degree (short degree) are the most common situations (both 7.57 per cent of the entire corpus).

Once more we see that the most needy non-traditional target groups are not really being reached by HE. On the contrary, it seems clear that adult HE is here benefiting the socio-economically and educationally already advantaged, and helping to reinforce and reproduce social inequalities. Further empirical research needs to be conducted to examine the situation in other institutional and national contexts. However, it is doubtful that the situation will prove to be any different.

The information presented by OECD/CERI (1987) tends to confirm our conclusion. Two features are underlined in that report. First, in each country analysed (Sweden, UK, USA and Canada) the majority of adult part-time students worked as well. Secondly, many students were both full-time

Table 4.11 Adult students and factors influencing decision to take a degree as %: situation at University of Warwick – 1992–3 academic year (second-year undergraduates)

Factors	PT students	2 + 2 students	FT students
Career	43.8	25.0	76.1
Money	0.0	5.0	11.9
Degree	0.0	10.0	2.4
Need for qualifications	6.3	25.0	14.3
Age of child	12.5	15.0	2.4
Challenge	6.3	15.0	0.0
Accessible/local	6.3	25.0	0.0
Timetable suitable	6.3	10.0	0.0
Personal development	18.8	15.0	7.1
Enjoy studying	43.8	15.0	16.6
Influenced by others	12.5	0.0	4.7

workers and full- or part-time students, yet managed to earn their university degrees. The percentage of unemployed in the adult student body was consistently lower than in the whole adult population. However, it appears that some unemployed people take advantage of their situation to undertake college-level studies.

Statistics about earnings are rare. According to OECD/CERI (1987), American and British data show that high proportions of full-time adult students belong to lower-income groups whereas a high proportion of part-time adult students belong to middle- or high-income groups. Nevertheless, more recent data are really needed to confirm or disconfirm this trend. From a policy perspective the financial support given to adult students in some countries may have a real impact in terms of enabling or discouraging the participation of non-traditional adults.

Study purposes and motivation

We have already identified the several different types of adult student, such as early school-leavers, recyclers, returners and deferrers. Each groups' reasons for (re-)entering the university will be different. As shown by West (1996), some adult students will insist on their career needs, some on their personal development, and others on the need to acquire new skills in order to get or improve their jobs. Adult students at Warwick were asked why they had decided to study for a degree (see Table 4.11). Disparities and differences between the groups are apparent, for instance, 'career' is clearly chosen less by the 2 + 2 students (25.0 per cent), whereas it is chosen by more than three out of four students (76.1 per cent) in the full-time student group.

In the Carp *et al.*, 1976 study, 1207 American adult learners in post-secondary education were asked to give their reasons for undertaking their studies (see Table 4.12). The most frequently mentioned reason was

Table 4.12   Reasons for learning in Carp *et al.* (1976) survey

Reasons	% of learners checking why they participated
Knowledge goals	
Become better informed	55
Satisfy curiosity	32
Personal goals	
Get new job	18
Advance in present job	25
Get certificate or licence	14
Attain degree	9
Community goals	
Understand community problems	9
Become better citizen	11
Work for solution to problems	9
Religious goals	
Serve church	10
Further spiritual well-being	13
Social goals	
Meet new people	18
Feel sense of belonging	9
Escape goals	
Get away from routine	19
Get away from personal problems	7
Obligation fulfilment	
Meet educational standards	4
Satisfy employer	27
Personal fulfilment	
Be better parent, spouse	19
Become happier person	26
Cultural knowledge	
Study own culture	8
Other reasons	2
No response or other response	3

explicitly continuing education and knowledge. The second most common item referred to vocational reasons ('get a new job', 'advance in present job', 'satisfy employer'). According to the results of this survey, men reported job advancement more often than women (especially housewives) while the latter chose personal fulfilment. Learners mentioning a new job are most frequently in the youngest age-group, while learning out of curiosity increases with age. The 55–60-year-old age-group is nearly twice as likely as the under-35-year-old to give curiosity as a reason for their studies. Black learners cited certification or licensing, a degree, new job, study of their own culture and community goals more often than whites, while white students were more concerned with career advancement, getting away from the routine of daily living, and knowledge for its own sake.

Regarding education level, individuals who had experienced high school most frequently mentioned social and community goals and were more likely to learn in order to gain knowledge than students with merely elementary education. Students with top occupations most frequently mentioned better information as the reason for studying, while learners with unskilled or semi-skilled jobs were most likely to learn for self-fulfilment. Students with full-time jobs learned in order to get promotion and to meet the requirements of employers or authorities, more often than those not fully employed who, in contrast, more frequently gave religious, escape and personal fulfilment reasons.

Adult students' motivations cannot be discussed without considering the barriers encountered by these students. Despite the increasing demand for adult education and training, adults still find it hard to get into universities. Researchers have long underlined the existence of barriers hindering adults from getting into college (OECD/CERI, 1987, Cross *et al.*, 1976). According to Cross, there are three types of barrier. The first type is the adult's own attitudes – the way they perceive the education system and the possibility of being a student. The second type is education provision, its content and characteristics, such as the absence of special scheduling arrangements which is sometimes a nearly insurmountable barrier. The third type is the adult student's 'objective' characteristics, including family situation, occupation and place of residence.

Research shows that the most common obstacles to entry identified and owned up to are the costs incurred and lack of time. These may be more commonly mentioned by adults because they are more socially acceptable than other motives and problems, such as lack of interest in studies and low self-confidence.

Barriers can also vary from case to case. For instance, women are more often concerned with child-care and family duties while workers are concerned with time management. Attitudinal barriers, which are hidden behind the would-be learners' discourses, cannot, however, be neglected. It seems that a major obstacle is the adult's opinion that HE is not for them but for young people only. This feeling is probably stronger for less qualified people with no prior experience of HE. This makes it all the more difficult for policy-makers and programme managers to reach non-traditional targets and to attract second-chance students. Nevertheless, objective barriers must not be minimized. They do have a negative impact on adult participation, even though reduced over recent years, in at least some national and institutional contexts. At this point, many more political efforts can still be made.

The limits of access

The development of adult education at university, then, relates to a 'more access' process rather than to a 'wider access' one. The changes that have occurred in recent decades are quantitative rather than qualitative. As a rule groups which are marginalized from the HE point of view are still not being reached by the university system. On the contrary, current access opportunities seem to reinforce social and educational inequalities: the adults most likely to (re-)enter are those who already have good educational backgrounds and come from middle or upper socio-economic classes.

The increase in the returner population and growth in the demand for continuing education to provide complementary or specialized training is far higher than the development of opportunities for second-chance students. This can be put in parallel with what is observed at the general level of HE, and especially at the level of the universities. The 'massification' of HE, which profits mainly the middle- and upper-social classes, has been marked for years by implicit demands from civic society and economic actors to think of HE and university programmes in more vocational terms. More and more universities are urged to train people as professionals rather than intellectually or as citizens. This trend is echoed in the adult education field, as individual demands for adult training more often correspond to career requirements or vocational needs, and the collective demand is linked to economic purposes, exacerbated by the present crisis. An indicator of this movement is the increasing number of non-credit-bearing programmes in universities that are now offered in many countries to enable people to update or upgrade their knowledge, mostly in scientific and technological disciplines and in medical sciences. In this context, 'humanistic' or egalitarian objectives are not on the agenda and non-traditional students' access to HE is not a priority.

To conclude, it is clear that the adult student population is far from homogeneous. Its heterogeneity relates to social and educational background, and to motivations and location in the system. Despite this heterogeneity, the population will probably go on increasing because, as globalization increases, the need for continuous training, if not lifelong learning, will rise. Nevertheless, adults who wish to (re-)enter HE still encounter barriers. Attitudinal barriers, that education is not for them, continue to exist. Changes in attitudes towards lifelong learning need to begin with initial schooling. 'Objective' structural barriers are still hard to overcome, even though some efforts have been made at national and institutional levels. Adults with previous HE experience and socio-economic advantages have more chances of clearing such hurdles, whereas adults who come from low-income groups with a low educational level are thereby disadvantaged, especially if they are older.

We turn now from this analysis of adult students according to their social and economic characteristics to hear what some quite diverse adult students who have entered the system think of it, and it of them.

Notes

1. The age limit can be defined by the researcher, as do Bourgeois *et al.* (1995) taking into account the discipline of study in which the student is enrolled, or by official administrative decisions as in England.

2. Source: Statistical Bulletin 18/92 and private Parry communication (Department for Education) – quoted in Parry, 1995: 111.
3. Source: Education Statistics for the United Kingdom – Department of Education and Science; quoted by Bourgeois *et al.*, 1995: 79.
4. Source: Education Statistics for the United Kingdom – Department of Education and Science, Statistical Bulletin 18/92; quoted by Bourgeois *et al.*, 1995: 83.
5. Sources:
   - Rapports Annuels du Bureau de Statistiques de la Fondation Universitaire (1962–1992)
   - Annuaires Statistiques de l'Enseignement (1961–1971), Ministère de l'Education Nationale
   - Etudes et Documents, Ministère de l'Education Francophone (1972–1988)
   - Statistische Jaarboeken van het Onderwijs, Ministry of Dutch-language Education (1972–1988).
6. In 1974, 40.91 per cent of the students enrolling for the first time at the first year of the first level of French-speaking universities were women. In 1989, this ratio was 48.53 per cent.
7. Due to the federalization of the country, national statistical agencies suffer from management problems and community agencies are not yet ready to supply satisfactory data, especially in the French-speaking community. On the other hand, there is strong competition in the HE market; therefore data on education are considered strategic and institutions are not ready to publish figures that could help to compute comparisons between them.
8. Source: Rapports Annuels du Bureau de Statistiques de la Fondation Universitaire (1991–1992). This figure includes people who began studying at the university several years ago and have not yet finished, so it is not a very good indicator for measuring adult access.
9. Adult students are defined on the base of the following age criteria:
   first year of the first-level degree programmes: 23 years old and over.
   first year of the second-level Licence degree: 26 years old and over, increased to 27 and over for medical studies as the first level is one year longer than in other fields.
10. Source: Base de données de la Fondation Universitaire (1974–1989), Base de données du Conseil de Recteurs de la Communauté Française de Belgique (1989–1992), Guyot (1995).
11. Source: ibid.
12. Source: Statistical Bulletin 18/92 and private Parry communication (Department for Education) – quoted in Parry, 1995: 113.

5

Staying in and Coming to Terms

Hearing student voices

What brings people into university after being away from education? Often it is because adults want actively to change their lives, and also to prove to themselves that they are capable of studying at this level. Many have been out of the education system for a long time. For some, initial schooling was a negative experience in the UK. They were failed by a system based on class inequalities (O'Shea and Corrigan, 1979; Willis, 1977). For others, school was an enjoyable experience but they were unable to reach their potential. Class and gender expectations denied them the opportunity to stay on and complete their education (Deem, 1978, Spender, 1982). Assuming the role of mature student is not easy; initially it can be daunting. Although access has widened the mix of the student population, it is uneven across the university sector. Students in the 'old' UK universities still overwhelmingly consist of 18-year-olds. Most adults are to be found in the 'new' universities (old referring to those institutions that were universities under the binary system, new referring to the former polytechnics). Adults mostly have to learn in a minority situation alongside younger students, although part-time degree students may be taught as an adult group. University structures and facilities thus remain largely oriented towards younger students and, for the latter, being a student is the dominant role in their lives. Adults, particularly women, are taking on another role which often has to compete, for example, with being a parent, partner, worker and carer. Drawing on Goffman's (1974) terminology, they are constantly moving from one frame to another.

This chapter looks at the 'adult university' from the perspectives first of adult students then of lecturers. Employing a life histories method, the voices of adult students are used to inform our understanding of the issues and problems of adult access. This enables us to examine key questions and issues in a rich and meaningful way. How do adults perceive themselves as students? Do they experience university life differently according to the mode of study (full- or part-time), and their age, class and gender? Do they feel included or excluded by the institution? Do they leave university as changed people? What policy recommendations would they suggest to improve the life of mature students in universities?

Mature students are not the only actors involved in the access of adults to universities. Lecturers and admissions tutors are also part of the picture. University staff both as individuals and as members of a department play an important role in either supporting or inhibiting the access and learning experiences of adults. For many adults, particularly part-time students in full-time employment, lecturers are their main and sometimes only point of contact with the university because of other commitments. To what extent do admissions tutors act as gatekeepers in relation to adult applications? Does teaching adults affect their teaching styles? Is their relationship with adult students different from that with younger students? To what extent does the departmental culture affect their attitude towards mature students?

The 'voices' heard in this chapter are mostly drawn from a four-year study undertaken at the University of Warwick during the early 1990s. A small sample of adult students from four departments, Arts Education (a degree with teacher training), Law, Sociology and Biological Sciences, were identified and interviewed via a questionnaire. The latter two departments were chosen because they have an average adult student participation rate. In contrast Biological Sciences has very few adult students while Sociology has a high proportion. A second interview took place towards the end of the final year of study (1995). Lecturers from the same four departments also received a questionnaire, and a smaller sample was interviewed later. Students quoted are referred to by their mode of study. Those interviewed have been given a pseudonym to ensure confidentiality.

Literature on access from the viewpoint of the actors is sparse but growing, particularly in relation to the experiences of mature women students (McLaren, 1985; Edwards, 1993; Pascall and Cox, 1993; Merrill, 1999). A recent study by West (1996) offers a comprehensive social psychoanalytical perspective on the experiences of mature students in HE by extensive use of the biographical approach. Other studies, however, such as Woodley *et al.* (1987) and Bourner *et al.* (1991), draw largely on quantitative and descriptive approaches. Such perspectives provide only a partial understanding of mature students in HE. Listening to the voices of adult students offers an insight into the problems and issues of being a mature student at university:

> Qualitative research helps to expose a new language – the language of genuine lived experience. It is a mode of research that does not predefine the nature of learning and adult learners' experiences . . . Research that is grounded in a concern with meaning and relevance rather than measurement and typology can shift the ground from which we seek to understand the experiences of adult learners. It has the capacity to enrich – and to re-define – theory and practice related to adults' learning (Weil, 1989: 18).

A biographical approach enabled us to penetrate the social identity of mature students by looking at both their understandings of themselves and lecturers' understanding of them. In this sense identity is 'no more essential than meaning; it too is the product of agreement and disagreement, it too is negotiable' (Jenkins, 1996: 5). How is the self-identity of participants defined and redefined, individually and collectively, as they embark and progress along the student career? The self is socially constructed through the process of socialization and interaction with others. It is, therefore, a 'synthesis of (internal) self-definition and the (external) definitions of one-self offered by others' (Jenkins, 1996: 20). Jenkins summarizes this process as the 'internal–external dialectic of identification' (ibid.). Our understanding of the self is influenced by symbolic interactionism, particularly the work of Cooley, Goffman and Becker. The mature students in this study were faced with presenting the self in a new social situation to which they had to adapt quickly in order to learn the student role:

> Fundamentally group action takes the form of a fitting together of individual lines of action. Each individual aligns his action to the actions of others by ascertaining what they are doing or what they intend to do, that is, by getting the meaning of the acts . . . In taking such roles the individual seeks to ascertain the intention or direction of the acts of others. He forms and aligns his own action on the basis of such interpretation of the acts of others (Blumer, 1964: 184).

Action theory can be combined with the structural theories of Marxist sociologists and feminists to provide a more comprehensive understanding of individual and group behaviour within an institutional setting. Sociologists in analysing the social world have constructed a macro/micro paradigm divide, dichotomizing human behaviour (Cicourel, 1982). However, people live their daily lives in an interconnected macro and micro world. The students in this study were actively changing their lives through education but were also constrained by employment, university policy and practices and, for some women, by family life. Berger and Luckmann's *The Social Construction of Reality* (1966) was an early attempt to integrate macro and micro theories, emphasizing the dialectical relationship between objective and subjective reality:

> It is important to emphasize that the relationship between man [*sic*], the producer and the social world, his product, is and remains a dialectical one. That is, man (not, of course, in isolation but in his collectivities) and his social world interact with each other. The product acts back upon the producer. Externalization and objectivation are moments in a continuing dialectical process (ibid.: 78).

The majority of participants at Warwick were women. With this in mind we could not ignore the impact that the inter-relationship of class and gender had had in shaping both their past and present lives. Drawing on feminist sociology we wanted to '. . . place women and their lives, and gender, in a central place in understanding social relations as a whole' (Acker, 1989: 67). How did the interaction of public and private lives shape their student career? Questions of gender, therefore, raised the issue of the extent to which women's experience of being a student differs from men's.

First contacts and impressions

Life transitions and critical incidents, such as children growing up, divorce or unemployment, led several participants to reflect upon their past and current life. For others the decision to return to learn was less dramatic. Instead it was a gradual culmination of life-experiences: failure to reach their educational potential at school and discontent with working and domestic lives. To varying degrees all were seeking a fresh start. For the women, domesticity and low-paid jobs highlighted the contradictions, lack of power and fulfilment in both past and present lives. Many of the working-class men realized that they were in unskilled, boring jobs and that without qualifications they were not going to escape from 'dead-end jobs':

> It was a factory setting. You go in from 9 until 5, do what you are told and leave. It was very monotonous work. Same thing day in day out. The only interest came when something went wrong with the job and you could enjoy yourself. There was not much appreciation and no chance of moving up. That was one reason why I left. It became very staid. Redundancies were also looming. I thought; I have had enough of this place, it is time to move on (Paul).

Similarly the women were aware of being in a rut either at work, in the family or both:

> I did not know exactly what I wanted to do. All I knew was that I did not want to go back into an office and be a secretary. There was always the idea that I could have achieved more from education but there was always the problem of how would I do it with the children being young (Hyacinth).

All shared the feeling that something was missing, and that education held the key.

On entering university they had high expectations of what learning and achieving a university degree could potentially do to their lives in relation to self-development and employment. However:

> At the same time a university education and the role of being a student were experiences that needed to be demystified. The working class background of the majority of participants precluded them from having such knowledge. Despite this they were convinced that a university education was now for them and wanted to prove to themselves that they were capable of studying at this level. Along with this were fears and anxieties about entering a new social world (Merrill, 1999: 138).

New social interactions called for a workable and meaningful definition of the situation if such students were to survive at an élite university like Warwick. The pace of 10-week terms meant that understanding and socialization into the student world had to be achieved quickly. These mature students had to make a presentation of the self and gain acceptance in a social situation dominated by younger students, a situation in which they stood out in terms of age, class and, for some, ethnicity. In relation to its undergraduate student population Warwick is not, and probably never will be, an 'adult university':

> Underlying all social interaction there seems to be a fundamental dialectic. When one individual enters the presence of others, he will want to discover the facts of the situation . . . To uncover fully the factual nature of the situation, it would be necessary for the individual to know all the relevant social data about the others . . . Full information of this order is rarely available; in its absence, the individual tends to employ substitutes – cues, tests, hints, expressive gestures, status symbols, etc. – as predictive devices. In short since the reality that the individual is concerned with is unperceivable at the moment, appearances must be relied upon in its stead (Goffman, 1959: 241, 1971 edition).

It tends to be assumed that those entering an institution adjust to the rules and norms of that particular organization to become an 'organization person'. The emphasis is on the individual changing rather than the organization. However, mature students enter university with more past history and cultural baggage than younger students:

> The adult, therefore, brings with him [*sic*] into the classroom his conceptions and experience, based on extra-institutional factors and influences. On the basis of these he interprets his role, not in terms of the normative expectations of his tutor and fellow students but in accordance with his pre-existing social norms. In turn, these provide the source of and continuing support for his interpretation of his role as a student (Harries-Jenkins, 1982: 28–9).

The student role is shaped by both past and present experiences. What influence does the presence of mature students have on the ethos and structure of a university? At the same time, what is the impact of the institution upon the self of the mature student? To what extent is their former self deconstructed and subsequently reconstructed by the student role? It is at these levels that the dialectics of structure and action occur.

The initial point of contact with a university is through the admissions procedure. For adult students who may have been out of the education system for a long time this can be a daunting step. Many were nervous about the interview. A positive and welcoming approach to adults is essential as they will react to the messages given out by the institution (McGivney, 1993). Mature students quickly perceive which HE institutions are 'adult universities' by their behaviour at admissions interviews. Sally, for example, had a negative experience at her first interview at another university in the region. She experienced the interviewers as sexist. She was asked how she was going to cope with studying and looking after children rather than about her academic ability. She responded to that institution by walking out of her interview. This contrasted with her experience at Warwick:

> He did not ask me irrelevant questions about my domestic responsibilities but asked me about my work with the Trade Union and Employment Service and my recent educational experiences with the Open University. I found the interview interesting unlike at X (Sally).

Being put through to the right person or department on a telephone enquiry about course opportunities was also cited frequently as a critical factor when initially contacting a university.

For several participants age was not a factor in their interview. Lecturers were judging them on their ability to study rather than by age. Most felt that admissions tutors were supportive of mature students. Some gained an insight into the attitudes of certain departments towards mature students:

> The interviewer explained that Warwick is keen to facilitate adult students. I was told that the Sociology Department attempts to fit lectures into school hours so that mothers attending are not disadvantaged (Sue).

Participants entered Warwick with a diverse range of entry qualifications. Some 2 + 2 and part-time students possessed no formal qualifications. Others had gained GCSEs, A levels, Access credits, vocational qualifications, diplomas or open studies certificates. These candidates had two main concerns in applying to universities. The first was choosing a suitable and interesting course. Secondly, was the institution sympathetic to and aware of the learning needs of adults? For women this included an understanding of the problems of studying and rearing children and, for part-time students, of the strain of working full-time. All participants began their mature student career with the perception that Warwick was a university for adults. To what extent did rhetoric match reality?

Interviewing mature students: the lecturer's perspective

University admissions tutors, acting as gatekeepers, can play a powerful personal role within the framework of institutional and national policy, in deciding whether or not to admit mature students. Frequently attitudes are shaped by the culture of particular disciplines and departments. 'Different academic disciplines develop different criteria for evaluating the capabilities or intelligence of the students who apply to them' (Ainley, 1994: 120). In the old universities in the UK the debate about admissions and mature students centres on the determination to preserve the 'gold standard' of A levels. Adults without good A-level qualifications are labelled non-traditional and viewed as undesirable by some institutions, this despite the fact that Access and BTEC are now recognized as formal qualifications for entry into HE. As A. Thompson points out, 'underpinning the practice of admission to higher education are assumptions about legitimacy and entitlement' (1997: 108).

Most 18-year-olds are offered a place at Warwick without an interview. In contrast, all prospective adult candidates are interviewed. The Law department designated one admissions tutor to deal solely with applications from adults. Departments do not have a policy or a fixed quota in relation to the numbers of mature students to admit. In Sociology, for example, 'we do not have a fixed quota. It would not be feasible to do that but in my mind out of 25 this year I was looking for 8–10 mature people. It is very much a rule of thumb' (Sociology admissions tutor). Law admits about one hundred students per year and out of this total they aim to enrol 10–15 mature students. The subject matter of Law at Warwick is different from most other law departments as the emphasis is on law in a social context:

> We do not have a formal policy but the Department is disappointed if we cannot take that many . . . We see the admission and contribution of mature students, especially with their backgrounds in industry and trade unions or whatever, as being an important contribution to the Warwick law in context (Law admissions tutor).

The Sociology admissions tutor used his role to address issues of inequality in society:

> I do not enjoy ploughing my way through the application forms but the one thing that I do enjoy is the feeling that I can just slant things a little way towards those who are relatively disadvantaged and slant things a little way towards those who are patently extremely advantaged. But it is only a little way. What I enjoy about it is the contact with people. Whether or not we can offer them a place here I can give them some encouragement or advice (Sociology admissions tutor).

Admissions tutors admitted to adopting a different interviewing stance with adults compared with 18-year-olds. Using a sociological explanation and endorsing the need for a second chance in education the Sociology admissions tutor declared: 'However, the interviewer stance has to be different – eighteen year olds are the ones who have been the 'successes' of the education system. Adults very often have been failed by that system' (Sociology admissions tutor).

The varied life-experiences which adults bring to a degree course were viewed positively in departments such as Sociology, Arts Education and Law. Alternative modes of entry such as Access were not regarded as being inferior to A levels. What was important was the commitment and the capacity to learn. On the other side of campus, metaphorically and literally in terms of geography, perspectives on mature students are different. The different tribes of academia (Becher, 1989) became apparent. Biological Sciences admit very few adult undergraduate students, typically between one and six a year.

The admissions tutor and lecturers generally were sceptical about the ability of mature students to succeed in biological sciences. The consensus was that the sciences are not suitable for adults as scientific knowledge moves at a rapid pace. What was learnt at school soon becomes out of date.

At Warwick, Biological Sciences focuses on a specialist aspect: molecular biology. As a result the department is scathing of local Access courses after the experiences of a small number of Access students joining the department. Gatekeeping now ensures that Access students do not get admitted:

> We have had a great deal of problems with these Access courses. To say that you can do a one year course and it gives you the biology and chemistry background to get into what students have done for two years at A level and if you have been out of it for a long period of time is absolutely ridiculous. It is scandalous (admissions tutor, Biological Sciences).

Lecturers in this department did not consider it to be a problem for adults studying other non-science disciplines:

> Science is not like Arts where you read a book and you know something about it . . . My feeling is really that anybody can go and do an English or social studies degree if you are prepared to read the books to get the knowledge. You cannot understand a science book without the basic knowledge (lecturer, Biological Sciences).

These attitudes betray an assumption that scientific knowledge has a higher status than other forms of knowledge. As Young asserts: 'academic curricula in this country involve assumptions that some kinds of and areas of knowledge are more "worthwhile" than others' (1971: 34). Biological Sciences at Warwick is, therefore, largely inaccessible to adults. Those that are admitted tend to be in their early twenties. Who has access to biological knowledge is carefully controlled: 'those in positions of power will attempt to define what is to be taken as knowledge, how accessible to different groups any knowledge is, and what are the accepted relationships between different knowledge areas and between those who have access to them and make them available' (Young, 1971: 32). Non-traditional adult students, in this instance, are not considered to be real students. The high academic reputation of the department rests on teaching high-flying young students with good A-level grades.

Coming to terms with the university

Adjusting to a student career

For a minority of participants the second hurdle was finding the courage to enter a large, and for some, alienating educational institution. On the first day of term some almost did not make it. An induction day helped others to survive the ordeal:

I really had to make myself come to the mature students' induction day. I can remember sitting in the car park wondering, and scared, why the hell have I done this? It would have been so easy to have driven off. By the end of that day I was so relieved that I had done it. I knew a few faces. It was chaos on the Monday (start of term) and if I had walked into that I would not have survived. The induction day was useful (Sue).

Jill was reassured by the presence of other mature students on campus and in her department. Interacting in an unfamiliar social situation raised questions of academic confidence and feelings of intimidation. Other studies here revealed similar experiences (McLaren, 1985).

To ease the entry of adults, an adult university needs to provide particular support both pre-course, such as induction days, and in the early stages of first term. The situation was less traumatic for those who had participated in an educational programme, such as an Access course, open studies or return to learn, in the year prior to commencing the degree course. The 2 + 2 students were confronted with adjusting to two different educational institutions; an FE college and the University. As discussed later in this chapter, settling in to life at Warwick was more traumatic than at an FE college.

Becker and Strauss's work (1970) on adult socialization provides a useful way of understanding how adults adapt to problems of change in institutional settings. Becker and Strauss describe it as a process of situational adjustment:

The person, as he moves in and out of a variety of social situations, learns the requirements of continuing in each situation and of success in it. If he has a strong desire to continue, the ability to assess accurately what is required, the individual turns himself into the kind of person the situation demands (Becker and Strauss, 1970: 279).

Goffman's 1961 study *Asylums* offers greater insight. He identifies two stages to the processes of dealing with institutional life: primary and secondary adjustment. Although Goffman is looking at inmates in a 'total institution', the conceptual framework is applicable to the mature students in this study. On entering Warwick adults had to learn the ropes and get familiar with a new institutional setting. This is primary adjustment. Once this had been learned the mature students, in a similar way to the inmates in *Asylums*, used their acquired knowledge to manipulate the system to their advantage, such as getting seminar times changed. Goffman describes this as:

. . . secondary adjustments, defining these as any habitual arrangement by which a member of an organization employs unauthorized means, or obtains unauthorized ends, or both, thus getting around the organization's assumptions as to what he [*sic*] should do and get and hence what he should be (1961: 172).

Mature students are not a homogeneous group although this is assumed in much of the literature. The mode of study was an important factor in determining how participants perceived themselves as students. Part-time students were less immersed in the student role than 2 + 2 and full-time students: many expressed feelings of marginalization within the institution. To cope with university life the mature students formed sub-cultural groups within the wider, dominant student culture according to mode of study. Within these sub-cultures women formed further female sub-cultures: a sub-culture within a sub-culture. Culture here is being used in the manner defined by Clarke *et al.*:

> We understand the word 'culture' to refer to that level at which social groups develop distinct patterns of life, and give expressive form to their social and material life-experience. Culture is the way, the forms, in which groups 'handle' the raw material of their social and material existence . . . A culture includes the 'maps of meaning' which make things intelligible to its members (1976: 10).

The mature student sub-cultures were rendered visible by the establishment on campus of territorial spaces which were symbolically owned by adults, such as particular coffee bars and the mature student common room. Equally there were territorial spaces dominated by younger students and only penetrated by a minority of adult students, particularly the students' union.

The learning experience: lectures, seminars and assessment

Participants who had not completed an access course arrived with preconceived ideas about teaching styles at university. For those whose educational experience was limited to initial schooling there was an assumption that teaching would resemble the didactic and formal approaches used in schools in the 1960s and 1970s. 'When I first came I thought it was going to be like school – teacher tells you what you do and you do it' (Helen). For some it was initially a shock to discover that they were not going to be spoon-fed, that they had to learn to become independent in their learning approaches.

Spending time attending lectures and seminars is a central part of student life, particularly for adults. Married women and part-time students attend campus for lectures and seminars and perhaps a visit to the library but there is rarely time, because of other commitments, to use more of the facilities which the campus has to offer. However, few studies discuss lectures and seminars as learning environments for mature students. Those that do mention this only briefly (Edwards, 1993; McPherson *et al.*, 1994). Participants were asked about their attitudes towards lectures and seminars, and to what extent these aided learning. Attitudes varied as to whether or not lectures or seminars were preferred. The critical factor pivoted on the teaching skills of the lecturer rather than the different teaching contexts of lectures and seminars. For 2 + 2 students the situation differed in that they compared varying lecture and seminar styles in the FE college and university.

Initially, concern about lectures was to demystify and decode the academic discourse used in disciplines: 'I wondered what on earth I was doing here because of the language used but I persevered and now I enjoy it' (Ben). A Biological Sciences student felt that lectures made abstract concepts, described in books, understandable. 'Sometimes it is hard to picture or imagine something in a book, but a lecturer will simplify this so as to make reading it a reminder of what has been said, plus they can give life to a subject' (Laura). Another part-time student declared that listening to lectures was like 'being on another planet at first'. Once this obstacle had been overcome, lectures were viewed as a useful tool and framework for guiding one's own learning. More importantly, many students adopted an instrumental approach to lectures: they clarified the issues and provided a coherent structure for essay-writing, and material for examinations. In particular, they provided a valuable introduction to new topics.

For part-time students obtaining concise information for essays and examinations was particularly important, as time is a critical factor for them. One explained that 'some lectures are dynamic and I come out of them feeling really good' (Jill). However, not all participants held favourable opinions about lectures and some were critical of the lecturers' ability to teach. In critiquing lecturers' teaching styles they were indirectly presenting their perspectives on what constitutes good pedagogy for adult students: 'Some lectures are not very well structured and delivered. It creates a sense of confusion and anxiety because you do not understand what the lecturer is trying to explain' (Lynne).

The quality of a lecture, therefore, 'varies tremendously depending on who the tutors are, quite horrifyingly so' (Sue). Some lecturers were deemed to be 'more competent' than others. Several students were amazed that lecturers do not receive training in teaching skills as they bluntly stated that some could not teach. (Since this study was completed a course has become available for lecturers.) During this research one of the younger mature students changed from part-time to full-time in order to complete her degree more quickly. She was surprised to discover that the teaching approaches differed between the two modes of degree:

> Lectures and seminars did not exist in part-time degrees. You would come in for a two hour class. I had never been to a real formal lecture before. In my first law lecture I was really gobsmacked, wondering what is going on here. I was completely lost and did not know how to take notes. I would try and write everything down, whereas now it comes as second nature. One sociology lecturer tries and crams a lot into a lecture and it can get a bit muddling but she is very good at giving out copies of her lecture notes. Otherwise we would be stuck if she did not. I prefer lectures this way than I did coming from a two hour mish-mash of trying to get everything in. This is a lot more formal and better. You have a whole hour of a good lecture and you can get all your notes down. Then you have an hour's seminar. It is a lot more clearer [sic]. You

know about the subject, whereas before I never felt that I had a grip on a module. Now I feel as if I have a good foundation of the subject (Dalvinder).

Other part-time students explained that attending a two-hour class after work was often exhausting. As with lectures, participants held a mixture of positive and negative attitudes towards seminars. Again the quality of seminars varied according to the skill of the lecturer:

If the tutor is sensitive and responsive to the educational needs of students, seminars are very fertile in intellectual stimulation. Sometimes tutors indulge themselves in seminars in their favoured ways, values and ideas and they clock watch if they have not prepared and it shows (Stephen).

Several preferred seminars to lectures as being interactive and not passive. However, common complaints included the fact that the topic discussed in a seminar did not always relate to the lecture and it was therefore interpreted as not being relevant. This was particularly the case when the tutor who led the seminar was different from the person who gave the lecture. Tutors were also criticized for 'going off at a tangent' or a being 'waste of time' in that discussions meandered rather than adhering to a clear structure: 'Sometimes you can come in and you need not have bothered. Sometimes you can come in and they can be really good and you can get a lot of notes. You need good notes for revision. Sometimes they are just waffle' (Dalvinder). However, a year later, after changing from part-time to full-time, Dalvinder was more positive about the functionality and instrumentality of seminars:

Seminars are all right as you get to do group work and you get to see where the other students are coming from. You get to talk to them about how they are doing and about their essays, whether they have any information they can give you, where to get books (Dalvinder).

Inconsistency in the delivery of lectures and seminars was a common theme echoed by most participants. Seminars, however, provided an important social space for mature students to interact with lecturers and younger students. Goffman's (1959) dramaturgical approach is relevant here. Seminars offer a stage for mature students to present the self to others. Participants discussed extensively their relationships with younger students, particularly in the social situation of a seminar. Within this setting two diverse student sub-cultures confronted each other. The intermingling of younger and older students was, on the whole, considered to be both positive and beneficial by most participants.

The minority who favoured an exclusively mature-age seminar group were largely part-time students who had no experience of learning with younger students, being taught as an adult group. In common with the findings of Edwards (1993) this group declared that the age gap meant that they found it hard to communicate with younger people, whose behaviour they felt was immature. Having other mature students in a seminar was viewed as vital for support and avoiding feelings of isolation. Several stated that they would not be able to cope if there were no other mature students in the group. Laura, as one of three mature students in Biological Sciences, had a qualitatively different experience of university life from that of other adults studying social sciences or humanities: 'I would like to learn in a mixed group as I would be able to relate to someone my own age.' A few felt intimidated at first by younger students, undermining their confidence in seminars: 'I used to feel that other students knew more than I did so I kept quiet. But then you realise that they do not know any more than you do. They are just more able to talk' (Helen).

Other participants stated that younger students were less conscientious about their work than adults. This occasionally caused friction. The norm, however, was to welcome the presence of younger students in seminars as it resulted in cross-fertilization of ideas, perspectives and learning processes. It also eradicated age and, to a lesser extent, class barriers. One woman describes younger students as being 'lovely' while another reflected:

> That was very strange actually. There is only one other mature. You wonder at first about the legitimacy of being there but it worked quite well. It is a bit daunting when you first go in and you feel like a mother. I do not think that that is a problem. It is just an initial problem of getting over the age gap. The shock of all these youngsters! If you are willing to go and meet them on their level and joke with them and help them in some way as I have access to photocopying [*sic*]. We share information. If you go in there and see yourself as different, if you are not willing to get on some rapport at some level then you are going to get isolated (Valerie).

Many recognized that younger students were more ideological than adults but that the mixing of the two approaches was beneficial.

The 2 + 2 students did not experience mixed seminar groups until year three of their degree course. For the first two years they were taught in the FE colleges as adult-only groups. Seminars and lectures are more informal in the colleges: 'at the college the group was small and the person who taught us went out of his way to be helpful' (Sarah). Karen lamented on this point:

> If I left here tomorrow (Warwick) they would not miss me. Lecturers have so many in the group that they do not know you. I do not feel like anybody would miss me. It is so different from college. You would not miss classes because the lecturers would know (Karen).

Several remarked that there were disjunctions concerning teaching approaches between colleges and university. A few felt that they had not been adequately prepared by the college for seminars: 'I was terrified of going to seminars at Warwick at the beginning as the word seminar is off-putting' (Mike).

Studying: writing essays and doing assessments

Note-taking in lectures was something to be learnt quickly by those who had been out of the education system for a long time. Others who had taken access courses or who were taking the 2 + 2 degree were better informed and equipped about study skills. Some attended study skills courses organized by the senior tutor's office at Warwick.

Writing the first essay was an anxious and nerve-racking time as it was a new skill to be learnt. Most admitted that the quality of their first essay was poor. Paul explained: 'it was knowing what they wanted and the way they wanted it written'. Anxiety centred around the uncertainty of not knowing what level of work was expected for a degree. Those who had recently studied A levels or an Access course or whose employment involved writing reports felt slightly more confident about writing essays. Initially some were nervous about going to see a lecturer for help with an essay. This was partly related to being unclear about the role of a lecturer. However, this problem was soon overcome:

> Lecturers always say that if you want to see them about essays or are concerned about the marking, they always say come in and see us. At Christmas I had a bit of a bad time as during the holiday I worked. I was getting low in funds. Law books are very expensive and we were advised to buy them. I worked during Christmas and I had three assessments to do. I had got out of the routine of working and studying so I was having difficulties. When I got back I had a law assignment to hand in and I had been rushing it all week. I went and told the lecturer that I had to work. He was really good because he gave me an extension. I had never had one before (Dalvinder).

The 2 + 2 participants from some colleges noticed a tremendous increase in the number of essays that had to be written at Warwick. In their second interviews participants reflected upon their acquisition of study skills:

> I feel like now that I can finally understand it all. It is all coming together and making sense. The way I write has grown, changed and evolved. I feel that I am writing sense and that every now and then I have a reasonably original thought. That is great watching it all (Avril).

Attitudes towards assessment evoked contradictory thoughts. Assessment at Warwick is a mixture of assessed assignments and examinations. Some expressed a strong dislike of examinations. They produced feelings of fear, anxiety, exhaustion and nervousness. Research by Bourner *et al.* (1991) also indicates an aversion to examinations by adult students. All felt that they under-performed in examinations. Sitting in an examination hall brought back memories of schooldays:

> I am scared stiff quite frankly sitting there at an exam because I have not done it for years. That is one area where I would have liked a

pre-run, a mock exam. That would be beneficial. I did not achieve what I thought was my potential because of my lack of skill in doing a written exam (Adam).

Yet at the same time a pragmatic approach was taken. Several wanted examinations to be included as part of the assessment procedure, as they were less time-consuming than assignments:

The snag with assessments is that you can go on for ever trying to make sure that they are perfect. You will only end up with a few more marks for three or four more hours work. It is very complicated really. I think on the whole I prefer assessments but there is a tendency to do just the work for assessments and not worry about the rest of your work (Jean).

These comments echo some of the dilemmas mature students experienced with their studies. On entering Warwick they had preconceived ideas of what studying would be like at university. The reality did not always match their ideals. Weil (1986) also found evidence of a mismatch between non-traditional adult students' expectations and their actual experiences. The adults were eager to learn, and to widen and expand their knowledge base. They wanted to read as widely as possible, study a topic in depth and spend time perfecting assignments. However, they were soon confronted with institutional constraints. Participants discovered that the pace of 10-week terms is hectic and does not allow time for all the books on a reading list to be read. Reading widely simply put pressure on the workload. At the beginning of their student career many found this difficult to come to terms with, as it contradicted their image of studying at university:

I am thorough with my essays and I like to read as widely as I can but I am struggling at Warwick because of the workload. I find it difficult to cut down on the reading. It has been a major problem for me. I got behind with my work and I do not like working like this. I like to be on top of my work. I realised that this is not possible at Warwick but I did not know this beforehand (Mike).

These dilemmas almost caused Mike to leave Warwick at the end of his third year of the 2 + 2 social studies degree. To survive, participants had to change their attitudes towards learning. For example, some chose not to write class essays:

Lectures and seminars are much easier this year as I am able to rationalise the workload more. You get brutal and say to lecturers 'I am sorry but I am not doing that class essay. It is my final year and I want to concentrate on my finals'. You take more responsibility (Joyce).

Over the period of their study the adult student culture was maturing. Collectively students learnt how to cope with the system: fewer topics were chosen for revision, fewer books were read. Passing examinations and being successful with assignments became the prime goal of studying, rather than pursuing knowledge for knowledge's sake. Realism replaced idealism. Using Goffman's conceptual framework, they were exhibiting signs of secondary adjustment to the institution. Reducing the workload was essential because of domestic and employment commitments. Studying, although important, was only one fragment of their lives:

> As a group they were constructing the boundaries of a mature student role and setting norms. Consciously cutting down on their workload also had an important latent function: it eased pressure on university, domestic and, in the case of part-time students, working life. Choosing not to complete all essays was a part of this strategy (Merrill, 1999: 157).

This pattern of behaviour was noted in an early study of the culture of medical students. 'Students reason from their definition of the situation: if there is more to do than can be done in the time available, we can solve the problem by taking short cuts' (Becker *et al.*, 1961: 117). In doing so the 'group reaches a consensus on how to deal with much of what is problematical in its environment' (Becker *et al.*: 135).

Bringing life-experiences to learning

What differentiates adult learners from other learners is the life-experience they bring to the learning situation (Knowles, 1984, Brookfield, 1996). Social science and humanities subjects are popular with adults because the discourse is conducive to inclusion of life-experiences. Essays and, particularly seminars, enable participants to give them expression. Among the Warwick part-time students three men, all trade union shop stewards, opted for a labour studies degree as the nature of the subject related closely to their working lives. They were quick to criticize any course which they felt was too academic and out of touch with 'the real world'. The areas of life from which experiences were discussed in the public arena of seminars differed according to gender. Women, for example, as noted by Edwards (1993) discussed family lives, bringing up children, and gender experiences in sociology and law seminars. In contrast, men refrained from discussing their private lives; the public world of work, however, was acceptable. Many women believed that their life-experiences made a valuable contribution to learning and to seminar discussions:

> The older people feel: I cannot do it. I have not written essays for years. I do not feel that they realise the knowledge they have. They bring knowledge to the lecture and bring it alive. I think that mature students as a whole have got so many different experiences of life in general. A student who has just gone from education to education does not know any more than an educational setting so you cannot bring any more to it (Jenny).

Mature students are far from homogeneous. Some younger adults in their early twenties criticized older students for drawing on their life-experiences too much in seminars. One common theme, however, was that academic study enabled both women and men to reflect upon past life-experiences more theoretically and critically:

> Studying sociology has made me look more critically. Your experiences are put into theory. Maybe that was the factor for me, being able to do that more than the younger students and also with being Asian and being a woman. I have got so much knowledge of my own personal life to think about – even issues which relate to my parents (Dalvinder).

Sociology lecturers also discussed the fit between adults choosing sociology as a subject to study and life-experiences. 'Sociology is a very popular subject for mature students. I guess at the end of the day that they think that it is about life. It is one which I think most do extremely well at' (Jane, lecturer). More succinctly, another lecturer explained: 'I think it is autobiographical for adults to do sociology' (Hilary).

Encounters with lecturers and attitudes to them

What did students expect lecturers to be like? Many expected them to be aloof and on a higher level, immersed in a world of intellectual knowledge. They were people of high status. Social interaction on an individual level would centre on help and advice concerning essays, or talking to a personal tutor largely in relation to personal problems.

On the whole, contact with lecturers revealed that they were 'human' and approachable, not elitist and arrogant. Only a minority of lecturers were categorized as being unhelpful. These were from departments where the culture was antithetical to mature students. Most admitted that lecturers had told them to come and see them if they had problems with their essays. For Valerie the level of help varied: 'With essays some lecturers are more helpful than others in providing feedback such as verbal and written comments.' In contrast Dalvinder remarked that 'lecturers have been very helpful, especially X. I think that he is very good. All of them go out of their way to help. They encourage you to go and see them and discuss essays.'

The mature students found lecturers easy to talk to because of the similarity in age. Married women students with children discovered that they shared issues and problems with female lecturers, establishing a bond between them. These findings contrast with the study by Edwards of mature women students, who

> . . . saw their lecturers as very different people from themselves. Lecturers could thus only be approached for help for purely academic reasons, which the women felt was, after all, what they were there for. They were not regarded as interested in other, more personal aspects of the

women's lives. This was mostly seen as acceptable because the women wanted to keep the private side of their lives separate and could feel uncomfortable discussing personal problems with their tutors even where they affected their studies (1993: 94).

All students at Warwick are allocated a personal tutor who undertakes a pastoral role with their tutees. Several contacted their personal tutor about academic or personal problems during the course of their student career. Lecturers' perceptions in this study were that mature students took up a larger proportion of their personal tutor's time than younger students. This evidence supports that of Edwards (1993) and Maynard and Pearsall (1994) in their studies of mature students. Responses from participants indicated that they had found personal tutors to be helpful and supportive in solving their problems. More serious cases were referred to Warwick's senior tutor's office. The following comment was typical: 'Marvellous. I have had some problems since I started the course at home and I just came in and told my personal tutor who informed other people. They were really helpful and considerate' (Jill). Some pointed out that there were inconsistencies in the tutorial system as they had not met their personal tutor.

Part-time students were less certain about the role of a personal tutor. Many chose to go and see the director of part-time degrees if they had any problems. A few of the older mature students remarked about the age gap between themselves and a younger lecturer: 'I always feel like his mother when I am speaking to him – that is not his fault' (Kate).

Moving from college to campus: the transition of 2 + 2 students

Warwick University's 2 + 2 students confronted two contrasting institutional experiences during their student careers. In Becker and Strauss's (1970) terms they underwent two periods of 'situational adjustment'. The transition from college was for the first few weeks a traumatic and alienating experience. Initially, as they learnt the culture of a new, large institution, Warwick did not feel 'adult friendly'. The definition of self had to be reconstructed to meet the culture, structure and constraints of a new institutional setting. At Warwick they were no longer taught in small distinctive groups but they had to slot in with second-year undergraduates already familiar with the system. A new student identity had to be quickly reasserted both individually and collectively, as they established their own social and territorial spaces:

It was horrendous, a nightmare. Probably one of the worst experiences I have ever had. Effectively first year students on second year courses. It traumatised two other female students because you feel isolated as everybody has made their friends. The first couple of weeks can be really intimidating, especially with all the volume of information and work. My head felt like it was going to explode with all the information and work. Everything is still going on at home, the kids etc. By the end of the second week I was prepared to quit but a friend persuaded me not to. After a while it calmed down and you got to know the routine (Joyce).

As college students they had all had some contact with Warwick, through both lecturers and facilities, such as the library. Yet less than half of the 2 + 2 students experienced no problems in relation to the transition, even though 'the University went overboard in making the transition easy as everything was done for us' (Kate).

One point of continual discontent was labelling by individual lecturers and certain departments. The 2 + 2 students wanted to integrate into the 'normal' undergraduate population at Warwick and did not want to be stigmatized as different. This labelling made them feel like outsiders. For some lecturers, however, 2 + 2 students do not conform to the model student in terms of social class and, they believe, in terms of academic ability. Harries-Jenkins (1982) documents that in relation to adults:

> ... the 'good student role' is defined solely by the tutor within a framework of educational criteria and assumptions which value cohesion rather than conflict, excellence rather than equality and achievement rather than participation ... In part the problem which arises here is the result of a persistent reluctance to examine critically the extent to which the traditional interpretation of the good student role is essentially subjective. Many tutors themselves are the product of an education system which emphasized the importance of academic achievement. Their appointment is, in effect, their reward for attainment as students (ibid.: 23).

In a top-rated, research-led university like Warwick the presence of the first cohort of 2 + 2 students, who were perceived as clearly different, raised issues of quality and standards in certain quarters and amongst certain academic tribes. Some lecturers were sceptical, believing that such students would not successfully complete the degree course. As Becker stresses:

> Professionals depend on their environing society to provide them with clients who meet the standards of their image of the ideal client. Social class cultures, among other factors, may operate to produce many clients who, in one way or another, fail to meet these specifications ... All institutions have embedded in them some set of assumptions, and their embodiment in actual social interaction, in order to fully understand these organizations (Becker, 1971: 113).

Others were more supportive and helped to 'champion' the cause of adult students across the University. The 2 + 2 students were conscious of being labelled, and of the possible effects this might have upon their academic career:

I would like to drop the 2 + 2 label. It sounds simplistic. Younger students never mention it but it is just in your own mind that you are different from the others. It would be nice just to be able to integrate with the others. You feel that some lecturers might treat you differently because you have not come the same route and have not got A levels. I am not saying that it does happen but you feel that it could (Judith).

Particular departments were identified where the labelling process was more overt. Many felt, for example, that politics lecturers separated them out as a group, making them feel that they were not 'proper students' taking a 'proper degree course':

I think occasionally that the 2 + 2 label in the Politics Department meant that you were not taken as seriously. They group you in seminars according to which course you are on so that 2 + 2 are grouped together which I do not think is particularly good. It does not get me angry like some people but it is a little bit demoralising. It knocks your confidence a bit. I think that we work as hard as anybody else (Jayne).

This was also identified as a department which participants believed did not welcome and support mature students. This led some to change from majoring in politics to another subject area, usually Sociology, as that department was perceived as acting positively towards adults.

As seen from the other side

Teaching mature students: lecturers' perspectives

Warwick is a department-centred university. Any whole-university initiative such as part-time or 2 + 2 degrees will only succeed if there is support at department level. Departments are not culturally homogeneous. This study revealed much diversity across the departmental system. For Becher the behaviour of departments is closely linked to the nature of the academic discipline: 'It would seem, then, that the attitudes, activities and cognitive styles of groups of academics are closely bound up with the characteristics and structures of knowledge domains with which groups are professionally concerned' (1989: 20).

Certain departments at Warwick were clearly more favourable and supportive towards the access and teaching of adults in universities than others. However, even within negative departments there are individuals whose attitudes conflict with the department culture. There were also signs of contradiction as the majority of lecturers in Biological Sciences, a department whose culture is antithetical to mature students, admitted that they did enjoy teaching adults because of their motivation and enthusiasm. Practices and attitudes towards mature students varied within the same faculty, for instance Social Studies where Politics contrasted sharply with Sociology. As learning is the focus of mature-student life, the characteristics of a department play an influential role in determining the quality of undergraduate student life for adults:

> The ideas and actions of the faculty, residents and interns affect the students, first of all, by seeing the conditions under which students' problems arise. The rules the faculty makes, the way the faculty organizes and defines the situations in which students must perform, the way the faculty interprets and applies their rules and definitions – all these constitute a major part of the environment in which students act. The faculty and others in this way create the problems to which the perspectives of the student culture comprise some kind of solution (Becker *et al.*, 1961: 48).

Lecturers were asked if they enjoyed teaching mature students. With very few exceptions all were positive. Reasons given shared a commonality across the four departments studied. Words such as highly motivated, enthusiastic and committed featured frequently:

> More interesting, rewarding, stimulating and challenging teaching mature students. There are a number of reasons. The strongest thing which comes through is that people are more interested. They are more receptive to thinking about ideas. I think people are also more likely to ask for assistance, be open about the difficulty and that in some ways is quite rewarding. A lot of undergraduate students who are younger tend to be much more defensive if they do not follow the work whereas older students just seem more open about that and at least you feel you can engage with the problems they are having (Sarah, Law lecturer).

Teaching methods in the old universities tend to be traditional and didactic, relying largely on formal lectures and seminars. Poor teaching skills among some lecturers was a source of criticism by many mature students. Good teaching is about using student-centred approaches to learning and taking into account the different learning needs of different groups of students in a class. Lecturers were asked if they had modified their teaching styles as a result of having adults in their groups. Most had not. A Biological Sciences lecturer declared: 'Teaching adults does not change my teaching style. I do not see why they should need different methods.' Those that reflected upon their teaching were predominantly in Sociology: 'I have moved towards group work and accessible seminar discussion teaching. My aim is to make these courses accessible and useful to adults who may not have been in an educational environment for many years' (Sociology lecturer). Another pointed out that adults are less passive in their student role than younger students: 'Mature students facilitate a more interactive approach. They are less inclined to take things on trust and, therefore, ask more questions which necessitates a teaching style that accommodates their queries' (Sociology lecturer).

A law lecturer observed that adults responded better to interactive styles of teaching than younger students, while another sociology lecturer elaborated that mature students bring to the attention of lecturers what constitutes good teaching practice. Another stressed that her teaching style took into account the life circumstances of adult students: 'I am conscious of the need to be organized well in advance and clear in my requirements because they often [the women in particular] have less time available to them and less experience of the requirements for academic study' (Law lecturer).

The presence of mature students is welcomed by many lecturers in seminars. Mature students help seminars to become interactive and dynamic. Several lecturers stated that they were always pleased to have mature students in seminars for this reason; 18-year-olds tend to be passive and quiet. An arts education lecturer complained about the difficulty of getting a response from younger students while 'mature students realize that talking is part of the learning process' (Kathryn). For her, teaching mixed groups of younger and older students has become problematical. It feels as if she is teaching two distinct groups:

> What struck me first on the undergraduate programme here was the difference in confidence between the mature students and the students who are straight from school. Even after three years I have never really properly resolved that because it is what one of our tutors calls 'the hegemony of the mature students' because they are more confident, they are more likely to be the ones who respond in seminars and who have more experience of the world, have their own children and so they can do different things with the information you give them because they have different places to put it in their head. I have never resolved the difficulty of having both sets of people in lectures and seminars. It is like two different audiences ... I do not enjoy the tension between them and feeling that I am perhaps doing a disservice to the younger students who are certainly more diffident and sit at the back whereas the confident mature student will sit at the front. I have not learnt a way of getting round that yet (Kathryn, Arts Education).

In contrast, a sociology lecturer enjoys the synergy of younger and adult students. The difficulty for him as a teacher is seminars containing *only* mature students:

> I think my own experience is that the best seminars, the most interesting and dynamic seminars tend to happen when there is a mix. This is the type of seminar I like. With this group of just adult students (part-time degrees) I find that I am not terribly skilled in it and so I have to find my way this year and it is a very different sort of seminar and different sorts of discussions (Rick, Sociology).

One reason why mature students are vocal is because they are able to relate life-experiences to the subject matter, particularly in the social sciences. Adults also inform lecturers if they do not understand what is being discussed in a seminar or, as an arts education lecturer explained, 'they give me feed-back about my teaching'.

One sociology lecturer had to adjust his teaching approach in seminars to take into account the vociferousness of the mature students:

> They are less inclined to just take what you say and not come back at you if they feel that they do not understand or there is a problem with what you are saying. It comes back to the issue of them being challen-ging and so on. I have adopted a teaching style which is more interactive. In the context of seminars having a certain number of matures in one sense makes life easier as they are willing to participate in discussions so that discussions can be student-centred rather than having to make a large input oneself. The difficulty arises when there is a mixture of matures and non-matures and the ones who are not mature are not as expressive so you have to bring them in so that the seminar does not become swamped by the matures (Stephen, Sociology).

Adults commonly dominate the verbal space in seminars, something which many mature students themselves recognized:

> Adults dominate seminars in a quantitative sense but domination in a very welcoming sense as they do talk. They do have something to con-tribute. They will draw on their own experiences. Somehow they have the confidence to admit when they are stuck which is a good. Also atti-tudinally confronted with a group with a collective task, perhaps because of their maturity, they see it as part of their responsibility to make the group a success (Hilary, Sociology).

Some felt that the domination by adults can be intimidating to younger students.

> Talking to younger students they informed me that they did feel drowned out by matures in seminars. There can be problems in balancing seminars between relatively vocal mature students and relatively passive school leavers. There are obviously exceptions on both sides (Stephen).

However, several thought that, on the whole, it is beneficial to have a mixture of ages in the teaching group for the students themselves:

> I think it is a mutual benefit to the mature and eighteen year old student. I do not think that it is just one way. The eighteen year old shows them the ropes in some ways and how to get away with things whilst mature students do bring younger ones on. You see it particularly if you have a relatively large proportion of mature students (Paul, Sociology).

Some lecturers recognized the importance of life-experiences in relation to the learning process of mature students and tried to incorporate the use of life-experiences in their teaching. For example, an arts education lecturer who teaches literacy and teaching skills for the school classroom to students explained:

The subject is very appropriate for their learning needs and most of the mature people are very interested, in that a lot of them have had their own children and can refer directly back to their own experience even if they have not been in the classroom very much. In the third year they write an extended piece on learning to read and a lot of them use their own children as a model. In fact it is a very interesting piece of work (Kathryn).

Law lecturers remarked that experience of family life and the legal system through divorce, for example, or at work or with housing, provided adults with first-hand experience which was useful in seminars. However, one young lecturer did not share his colleagues' experiences, perhaps reflecting more his own teaching approaches than mature students' behaviour.

Many people feel that mature people bring something to the course but again I have been disappointed. It would be great to have people talking about contract law but you do not get that. You do not get people who say well in practice it does not work like this or find someone who is articulate about the law. You would think that as people are older and had experience of insurance etc. they would bring this into discussions. It may be more difficult in biology to bring in experience but in law there are so many things which these people have done; marriage, divorce, children and all these things they could talk about (Ken).

While most lecturers valued the life-experiences which adults bring to the learning process, some stressed that it can also be problematical. Attitudes may become entrenched by life-experiences, often in a narrow way. A lecturer who teaches labour studies noted:

Part-time degree male factory workers are rough and ready Marxists when they arrive in the sense that they see manual workers as the core of the working class, male manual workers, and a nice simple division between us and them. It is nice to see them branching out or realise that 'them' are not just bosses and that this army of women workers have different things to offer. To see these sorts of things opening up I have found very enjoyable (Paul, Sociology).

He also believes that mature students come to study to escape from or transcend their life-experiences:

To some degree it is bringing a wider experience but my view is that people come to be students, not to dwell in their experience but to get away from it. I tend not to encourage people to draw too much on their experience . . . It is people moving on from their past experience (Paul, Sociology).

Another problem is that some adults find it difficult to acquire the skills to enable them to conceptualize and theorize about their life-experiences:

Quite a few find it hard to generalise beyond their experiences and tend to be rather anecdotal. Anecdotes can be quite interesting but my task is then to try and not to suppress the anecdotes but draw the anecdotes into a more generalising conceptual framework. Other adult students get fed up with those who keep using anecdotes and are very keen to develop their conceptual vocabulary. I think that they really like it when they leave a seminar with a new concept (Rick, Sociology).

On a relational level several lecturers found it easier to talk to older students than 18-year-olds, as the ages are more close. Gender could also be important:

I have had some domestic problems this week and a student had similar problems and you can have a conversation. You can relate to that person which I like to do. I like to do it with the younger ones but I have not got as much in common. By the fourth year I feel that the mature students are friends. You can go out for a drink with them. It is very easy to forget that the relationship is anything but a colleague (Elizabeth, Arts Education).

From a different angle one young female lecturer talked about her relationship with adults from the point of view of being younger than they were:

One thing which does surprise me is that I am pretty young and younger than mature students and that is not a problem. They treat you more on an equal level but there is more mutual respect than with some younger students who can be quite arrogant such as young men who are incredibly arrogant. The way they sit. It is like who are you and what are you doing teaching us. Just the whole message they give off is really revolting. The older students are much more courteous. It is nicer (Sarah, Law).

Academic perceptions of mature students

The overwhelming majority of lecturers enjoy teaching adults, but differences between departmental cultures emerge in discussions of academic abilities. Within the sciences it is the norm to continue with academic studies in a linear fashion without breaks from study. Work or family experiences are less valued. 'Once they get beyond 25 you begin to think what they have been doing with their time and why they want to come back' (Rob). Rob was critical of local Access courses which he felt were not an adequate preparation for a degree course at Warwick. As an admissions tutor he questions mature students carefully:

We look for a reason for doing the degree . . . We try and probe to what their background is. Is it going to put pressure on any relationship? Have they got a stable background? I still think a mature would be better off going through the less difficult background of new universities where there is more emphasis and they have been used to teaching people who have got other problems . . . I must admit I do advise quite a few of the people I interview to do that to go to a less hectic environment (Rob, Biological Sciences).

Several emphasized the unsuitability of biology for Access students who were regarded as needing more help and support with essay writing. A lot of time has to be spent in the laboratory each week. One lecturer feels that this is difficult to manage if you have a family. Another expressed his thoughts more bluntly:

I think that we probably feel that we ought to make it a little tougher for mature students because we have the feeling that they do not do as well so we feel that they have to be that little bit better. When they have stuck the course they have tended to get poorer degrees. We would provide study skills if we were a charitable organisation but is it cost-effective? We would say we would rather not have them. I feel rather that if mature students were to come to this University, and they are very welcome, they have to be very much on their own and they have to appreciate that. They will get informal help from individual members of staff but no major formal assistance . . . I do not see why we should make any particular arrangements for mature students. Why single out mature students? . . . I do not think the sorts of degrees we teach are really the sorts of things mature students want to take . . . It is not like a sociology degree where anybody feels they can take it at any age (William).

He was, however, in favour of widening access in other parts of the University. Asked about the 2 + 2 degree programme he replied: 'Sounds like a super idea. I would be all in favour of it.' Mature students are clearly perceived to be a problem in science. The assumption is that the student has to adjust to meet the needs of the department, rather than the department changing to meet the needs of adults.

In contrast, both Law and Sociology found that some of their best students, past and present, were adults:

Mature students do just as well if not better statistically than non-mature students and some of our best results, our outstanding students, have been mature students. I think that the general view of the Department is that mature students do just as well and that mature students make the life of the Department healthier in some sense. In that latter way it has made the whole experience of teaching more rewarding (Rick, Sociology lecturer).

Another observed that 'most students who get first-class degrees in this Department are mature students' (Paul, Sociology). In terms of academic performance the learning curve is steeper initially than for school leavers.

Some lecturers consciously gave more support and constructive feedback to adults when marking essays. One commented:

I try to give constructive feedback, particularly in the early stages of the year. I work on the assumption that any sort themselves out during the first year. Some adults can write essays straight away, some cannot. The learning needs of adults may be more than eighteen year olds in terms of writing essays but it is a problem which can be overcome as long as they are reasonably capable (Stephen, Sociology).

Another compared the academic abilities of part-time students to those of full-time students:

> . . . the part timers struggle more. The part-time degree is getting pretty near to open access, not quite as there is some selection procedure. People can start the part-time degree who would not stand a chance in the competition for the full-time degree. So you get people coming in whose skills are less well developed. You take greater chances. In part-time degrees there is a greater ability and skill range. There are also some part-time degree students who are in the very top flight. They sometimes take you by surprise when you get a first essay and it is marvellous because you think why are they not doing it full-time. Life circumstances is the reason (Paul, Sociology).

It is commonly held that adults are more demanding of lecturers' time than younger students (Bourner *et al.*, 1991). At Warwick most lecturers did indeed feel that adults took up more of their time than younger students, but on the whole this was not viewed in a negative sense.

> Adults are more likely to come and ask advice about writing essays and they often act as spokespeople for the groups. They articulate every-one's grievances which is good. The habit of studying and examination techniques are the main issues. As a personal tutor matures are more demanding on time but it is different. With younger ones there is never much of an exchange, you feel that you never get to know them as well as older students possibly because they are nearer in age to you. If you have got mature students as personal tutees it is much more rewarding. I would rather have mature students as personal students. Whatever prob-lems they have they always make an effort to overcome them. They do get things sorted out just because they are older (Chris, Arts Education).

Lecturers were aware that mature students face a different set of problems from those of younger students. They have to juggle several roles, they have family and financial problems, and these can impact upon their studies. Most were sympathetic, Biological Sciences being the exception:

> One of my tutees has been a pain but it is because of her background. Her husband left her and she was left with two young children. She is fighting a custody battle through the courts. It colours my view of what Access students are like. They are more demanding on our time because they have holes in their knowledge which they want filling in (Rob, Biological Sciences).

Private and public lives

Traditionally geared towards meeting the needs of 18-year-olds, institutional structures, regulations and procedures may make life harder for adults on campus. Mature students, particularly women, are constructing and pursuing a student career while juggling with often conflicting roles such as worker, parent, carer, or partner. As Joyce illustrates: 'I am a single parent and although my ex-husband is supportive he works in London four days out of seven. All my family live in London, therefore, I have to do a juggling act with my daughter/childminder/ex-husband to ensure that she is cared for' (Joyce).

Some students are committed and attached to multiple institutions (see Goffman, 1961). For married women private lives often interact with public life as a student in a constraining way. Time for studying is scarce. Many have to study late at night, and ensure that domestic life is undertaken without interference from their studies:

> I have found it very difficult to organize time for studying. It is very difficult to get them [her family] to understand how much time you need for your studies. They seem to want you to do well but at the same time they do not leave you alone or help with practical things that need to be done in the home to give you that time to get on with it (Hyacinth).

Some women received little or no support from partners. A minority of husbands and partners perceived the studying by their wife or partner as a threat to their dominant position in the family (Leonard, 1994). In extreme cases divorce or domestic violence ensued. The men in this study, however, were not affected in their studies by having also to undertake domestic work. They had more freedom to remain and work on campus after lectures and seminars, particularly as, with one exception, they did not have to collect children from school. However, relationships with partners were not completely unproblematical for men. Two admitted that studying had caused friction at home. For example: 'Predominantly I think that it is because I have got locked into myself. I think the economics course did that. My wife thought that I was ignoring her. It did create some problems and I think that I am less supportive than she was last year' (Bob).

The problems mature women students experience are now familiar (Edwards, 1993, McLaren, 1985, Pascall and Cox, 1993). Jane Thompson summarizes the issues succinctly:

> In almost every other respect women who embark on courses without men fare better than those who have to square what they're doing with husbands, partners or lovers. Men who re-enter education as mature students probably need to make some adjustments too, but it is unlikely that their initiative is seen as anything other than important by their wives and children. Working class women's return to education – if it is

tolerated at all – is only usually condoned if nothing noticeable changes at home. Women still retain the major responsibility for child care and domestic work and often feel they have to 'do it even better' so that their absence at college doesn't become a major source of grievance (1997: 65).

Using Becker and Geer's terminology, adult students were confronted with 'problematic situations', both in the family and at Warwick. To cope with the problematic situations and act upon them they developed 'group perspectives' (Becker *et al.*, 1961). For married women, problematic situations arose at department level. Many were critical of departments which were inflexible in relation to the timing of lectures and seminars. For them it was imperative that classes took place within the hours of the school day. Course choice was therefore limited and many had to take courses which they were not particularly interested in. In this sense the women felt the University's policy to be hypocritical. On the one hand, access and participation of adults is promoted. On the other hand, practical policies mitigate against it:

> The only thing for me is the lack of child-care facility which feels like a lack of support for students with children. It does not actually feel like they want children here and if you are a mature student with children it is very important. I do have to come in and bring him even if it is to run into the library. Quite often I have to bring him in when I have a meeting with a lecturer so I hurry. There needs to be somewhere where he can go and he would enjoy it (Avril).

The Sociology department was considered to be the most favourable in terms of access policies and support for adults. Yet one woman felt that even this was largely rhetoric spoken at interviews. She understood that it would be possible to accommodate all her classes within the school day:

> For the first year this seemed to be the case but the second year seemed like a free-for-all. I am not saying that there should be concessions but I think that certain things could be done that would make it somewhat easier for women with children. It is not that I do not want to be in by nine o'clock, it is just that I cannot be in very easily by nine o'clock. If you are going to say yes we welcome mature students then I think that you have to accept the fact that there are extra difficulties and do something about that. It seems idealistic if you say yes we welcome you but we are not actually going to do an awful lot to make it a bit easier for you (Sue).

As the institution showed no signs of changing, some women took positive action to try to change it in a small way. Individually and collectively they negotiated a new reality with the lecturers and departments concerned. Cicourel's (1968) work is useful here in illuminating how the women, acting from the group perspective of a sub-culture, negotiated justice to alter department rules and norms in a way which they judged to be fair within the confines of organizational regulations. To draw also on the discourse of Goffman (1961), 'the various strategies for making out are part of the "underlife" of any institution' (Manning, 1992: 112). For example, Helen, a single parent, and others visited campus two weeks before the start of a new academic year to enquire about seminar times. On realizing that none of the times fitted in with the school day, the women successfully negotiated with Sociology staff to alter them. Joyce discovered that the culture of the Politics department was rather different. In making a similar request to change the time of her seminar she was told by a lecturer: 'we do not want to hear anything about child-care arrangements. If you cannot fit in, just do not come.' Another 2 + 2 student remarked that 'Sociology are accommodating but with Politics you would think that you were in a different university'. School half-term holidays were another major problem for women students with children. Sociology staff and some lecturers in other departments did not object to the children being brought into lectures and seminars. As A. Thompson points out, most HE institutions are not flexible:

> Institutions of higher education make few concessions to mature students and even less to mothers. Creche and nursery provisions are limited and expensive and do nothing to solve the problem of school age children after school, children who are off school sick, or in half-terms and holidays. Lectures, tutorials and seminars are arranged to suit the logic of the timetable and the convenience of the institution, rather than the domestic responsibilities of the students (1997: 64).

Interestingly, some women did not think that the University should change to suit their needs:

> I know that there has been a lot of conversations about the University should do this and should do that but I do not agree with that. As we are Warwick University students I think that we should behave as every other student. I do not see why they should make the exception because we knew the ground rules before we started . . . I have been very impressed with Warwick (Kate).

Part-time degree students faced a different set of institutional problems. Their criticisms centred on access to and availability of books from the library. Borrowing core books from the short-term borrowing section of the library (student reserve collection) was problematical because of employment hours and living off campus. Complaints by students led the director of part-time degrees to negotiate with the library to establish a special section for part-time degree students, whereby they could take out books on more convenient terms to suit their dual role as student and worker.

Evening courses are essential for students in full-time employment. Several part-time participants declared that the number of evening courses on offer seemed to be narrowing each year, limiting their choice of courses and subject areas. Getting departments to offer evening courses is not easy, although some like History and Sociology have always offered a wide range of courses for part-time students. A questionnaire to lecturers revealed that many would be willing to teach in the evening provided they were given remuneration for time. Others spoke about the problems it would cause for their own family lives: 'It is an issue that I am very torn about as I can see the need for flexible teaching hours for some adults. However, if you are a member of staff and have a young family it is important to go home at 5.30 pm because if not it is an imposition on your partner' (Derek, Law). Others stressed the necessity of using evenings and weekends for research at a university like Warwick: 'To have a teaching commitment at weekends would interfere with my research which the University holds me under a contractual obligation to perform' (Arts Education).

Access policies: departmental views

Departments at Warwick do not have formal policies for the recruitment and teaching of adults. However, lecturers in Law and Sociology feel that they have a strong informal policy advocating the further access of adults to their department. One indicated how attitudes had shifted within the department:

> When I first came to Warwick the department had a student handbook which was badly written as it said to mature students, 'do not think you know everything about the world because you do not'. We rewrote that saying that mature students have something very positive to give to the degree and we welcome them. We also try and recognize that mature students can have special problems (Brian, Law).

In Sociology, mature student open days were thought to have improved: 'they were diabolical in the beginning. The process of widening access has taken place (in the Department). I would not like to see it stopped' (Rick, Sociology).

Some lecturers, were unaware that the University's mission statement advocated widening access for local adults and knew nothing about the 2 + 2 and part-time degree programmes. For some the debate about access was discussed within the framework of Warwick being a top research-led university, and whether or not the two identities can easily coexist within the same institution. 'We have to keep going with part-time degrees and 2 + 2. I think people feel that in a research driven University it solves their consciences to see these things happening and being dealt with' (John, Biological Sciences). From the same department came a stronger note:

> As far as the University is concerned it is of course important to give equality of opportunity but because it may not be able to be top at everything it should accept that in some areas of study some of the adults might be better served at another institution which is able to put on more the kind of course in which they can succeed (Fiona, Biological Sciences).

Others were uncertain whether or not access should be widened further, others again more positive, and some critical of the University's progress:

> There is a lot of adhocing and perhaps the University is sometimes too self-congratulatory about what it has achieved. Perhaps there is still plenty of room for improvement within resources constraints. There is a lot to sort out . . . I feel there is a positive constituency within the University to address these issues (Ben, Sociology).

A few noted the failure to attract local black adults despite being in a region with a high multicultural population.

Final reflections from mature students

Many UK universities have taken steps to widen access, but non-traditional adults remain a minority. As an unusually small minority the pressure is overwhelmingly on adults, particularly in the old universities, to change to meet the needs of the institution: 'Although further and higher education now have large numbers of mature students, there is evidence that staff attitudes and institutional practices have not entirely caught up with the needs of this clientele' (McGivney, 1996: 131). Some perceive Warwick as a middle-class institution:

> It is full of people with professional qualifications, middle class people. The part-time degree brochure is off-putting for people like me. It needs some case studies of people like me who left school at fifteen and are working class. It must be even more off-putting for black women (Valerie).

For the participants, completing their student career was a significant achievement. It was often a struggle juggling other roles, dealing with the constraints of the institution and relationships in the family. Struggles were alleviated by support through the mature student sub-culture. Reflectively, all the mature students in this study valued the opportunity of a second chance, enabling them to realize their educational potential. They all felt that they had changed as a result of being students. They could not return to being the person they were before entering university. As noted by Pascall and Cox 'there had been a heightened awareness of the self, a search for a new identity, or for the "real" self that the contingencies of life had suppressed' (1993: 120). Learning had brought about self-development and individual empowerment: 'Knowledge is wonderful. I am questioning things. Why did I get to forty before I went to university? I have learnt so much. Whatever happens no one can take the three years away. It has been like gold. I have really enjoyed it' (Pamela). Studying made students feel 'more educated', 'more critical about the world' and more confident about themselves:

Studying has widened my horizons. It has helped me to develop my personality as there are things that you are totally ignorant of and it is amazing the things you learn and you go through life and do not know anything about. It is interesting how it develops and your craving for learning continues. I think that without any continued education you get blinkered in life – just do your job and anything else you do you do not need to know a thing about. Part of your brain just dies. There are a lot of people who say what on earth do you want to put yourself through doing that and I find that a strange attitude. Learning gives you confidence as a person. I think it is very good (Jenny).

More collectively, the women's gender consciousness was raised. By the end of their studies they had also become in Goffman's (1961) term 'institutionalised'. Campus life had become integral to their lives. It offered an alternative to domesticity and inequality in the home. As Avril remarked; 'I do not want to go back to the real world'. For another:

You start day one, year one and suddenly it is the last day, year three. I cannot believe that I am nearly at the end of it now. I have gone from that naive person not knowing anyone to swanning in as if I own the place. When I do stop there is going to be an awful lot of sadness. I am not looking forward to going back to being a housewife (Sue).

The mature students' careers were thus shaped by the interactions of structure and agency. Class, gender and age influenced their perceptions and experiences. Yet at the same time they were, albeit in a small way, able to impact upon the culture at Warwick, particularly at department level. Their student experience was also determined by key factors such as age, marital status and mode of study. Compared to full-time students, part-time students frequently felt marginalized. Many did not consider themselves to be students: 'I do not really feel part of the University. I am an outsider looking in. Being part-time can be a lonely experience' (Dalvinder). The younger mature students in their early twenties were closer in age to the young students. They were looking for the full student experience, and felt that they did not have anything in common with the older married women. The latter had to resolve the competing and conflicting demands of study and domesticity. This often meant that they were unable to be as involved in university life as they would have liked.

Adult students are perceptive about what an institution should or should not be doing to accommodate them. They are informative voices for policy-makers to listen to. At Warwick some departments are more 'adult' than others. Over the past few years, with the growth of part-time and 2 + 2 degrees, the number of mature undergraduates has steadily grown. While change on a small scale has occurred in some parts of the campus there is still a long way to go before Warwick becomes an 'adult university'. Looking at the UK university system as a whole, West outlines different possible scenarios for the future:

The arrival of larger numbers of adults into higher education might tilt the pedagogic and epistemological balance towards a dialogical and more integrated learning culture. There is, at present, a powerful struggle between different conceptions of knowledge and about what higher education is for, which widening access has intensified . . . Higher education, like many learners, is in transition. As the doors are pushed open, as the student population alters and becomes more articulate; as adult learners feel that they represent the majority; as the sense of wider cultural unease and social dislocation increases and the need for dialogue becomes paramount; and as continuing education becomes a mainstream rather than marginal activity, conversations in higher education might shift towards adult learners, their needs and stories . . . On the other hand, if the democratization of higher education means managing on decreasing resources, relationships will suffer and the space for renegotiating selves, relationships and for creating new social formations will be severely constrained (1996: 204, 205).

It is only at the microscopic level of the individual student's experience of the secret life of the university in the coffee bar, the tutor's office and the lecture room that accessibility in the end acquires meaning. These are students who are, at least from their own self-reflections, 'different'. Many of them represent wider and not just more access, although the change is modest: gradual rather than transformational. Bureaucratic and interpersonal behaviours as students encounter them vary with different departmental cultures and according to individual idiosyncrasies. Not all conform to departmental cultures, which themselves vary remarkably.

Our close-up interrogation of mature age students and their various tutors at Warwick illuminates the distance between national policy prescription (although funding mechanisms clearly can influence local departmental behaviour depending, as we saw in an earlier chapter, on the market strength of the department or unit). Each university is distinct. Yet in its very uniqueness as well as its internal diversity, Warwick is entirely normal and typical.

We turn now, more generally, to the subject of the 'struggle for adultification'. This chapter has made eloquently clear that for those who do overcome the various barriers, of an individual as well as an institutional kind, take a deep breath and enter their first lecture or seminar, the struggle is by no means over. Our Warwick student narrators told tales of quiet frustration, heroism and usually significant personal transformation. They also indicated the limited extent to which their university is really combating social exclusion on any large scale, and they remind us that it is as much a series of local hand-to-hand combats as of grand vision and institutional leadership.

6

Innovation and the University: the Struggle for Adultification

Adultification as an organizational change process

Making the university more accessible to adults always implies some form of organizational change. It challenges not only the institutional practices of teaching, curriculum structure, course location and timing, admissions, and so on, but also the organizational structure, the transformation of current departments, or programmes, or creation of new ones. Most importantly, it challenges the social construction of what the university's missions and priorities should be, which is shared by its members. This is especially true when it comes to widening access to excluded social groups and categories. In the university as a particular type of organization described in Chapter 3, and in the particular context of resource restrictions, implementing adult access policies most often competes directly with other goals which are equally if not more valued within the academic community. At institutional level, the picture looks more and more like a zero-sum game as the resources needed to develop and implement adult-oriented policies are necessarily diverted from elsewhere. The same prevails at individual level. The time and energy invested by faculty members in the development and management of access policies, or in adult teaching, cannot be devoted to other activities that are also expected from them by the institution.

In such conditions, 'adultification' of the university most often looks like an on-going struggle or bargaining process. This raises the question what factors can make such a process successful. In the light of the theoretical distinction introduced in Chapter 3 between strategic and structural approaches, our basic working hypothesis is that the success of adultification results from a combination of successful actor strategies in decision- and policy-making, and conducive conditions related to the organizational structure and context. The object of this chapter is to provide some theoretical perspectives for a better understanding of those conditions of success. The following propositions are based on a review of the literature, and two empirical studies conducted at the University of Louvain. One is a case study focusing on the development of a non-traditional adult education programme in economic and social policy studies (called FOPES[1]) at UCL in the 1970s. The aim of this study was to analyse the decision-making process which led to the creation of that programme, and more specifically the interplay of the actors' power strategies in the process (Bourgeois, 1990; 1991; 1993; Bourgeois and Liénard, 1992; Bourgeois and Nizet, 1993; 1995). The other study was part of the previously mentioned Warwick–Louvain comparative study. Its goal was to understand the differences observed across departments in terms of adult access policies and practices (Guyot, 1998).

Actors' strategies underlying adultification

To review and discuss all the possible types of strategy for implementing change in academic organizations would be an impossible task. Likewise, there would be no point in generalizing observations collected in single case studies in relation to the effectiveness of change strategies. Our intention in this section is not to present an additional account of innovation management strategy in an academic institution. Such accounts abound in the literature (see, for example, the excellent book edited by Slowey, 1995). Rather, we present a broad conceptual and theoretical framework for analysing such strategies. This framework has been developed on the basis of an interaction between empirical observations collected in the above-mentioned FOPES case study and theories on academic decision-making provided by the relevant literature.

The creation of FOPES is a remarkable and unique event in the history of the University, not only because of the particular innovativeness of the programme itself, in terms of student clientele, admissions policy, teaching practices and so on, but also because of the originality of the programme management structure. The programme is run outside any established faculty, by a board composed of representatives of UCL and representatives of an external organization called MOC,[2] on a parity basis.

A conducive context and interest group configuration

Any major organizational change such as the development of a non-traditional programme for adults in an élite university is possible only if there is an interest group which: for whatever reasons is committed enough to the change intended and therefore ready to struggle energetically for it, has at least some capacity to influence the decision process leading to the change, and encounters a favourable organizational context. The existence of such a group and context was evidenced in the FOPES case. More importantly, the study showed that the successful implementation of change ultimately results from a combination of both a conducive context at the outset and the effective use of influence strategies by key actors within that context.

A relatively conducive context. At the origin of the creation of FOPES there was the will of a few individuals to commit a large, élite, research-oriented university – the Catholic University of Louvain (UCL) – and a large labour organization (MOC) to the development of joint co-operative projects in the area of teaching and research. The emergence of the idea of co-operation between such different organizations is to be understood in the light of a favourable context, in at least three respects:

1. The two institutions were closer than it may look at first glance. Although they were operating in quite different segments of society – higher education and labour – they were part of the same institutional network as both French-speaking and Catholic institutions.[3] They were entertaining various types of tie. They had both formal and informal links, for example, through representatives on each other's boards, or through individuals belonging to both organizations (for example, UCL faculty members who were also activists or leaders in MOC).
2. The ideological context of that time (post 1968) was rather conducive to the perspective of widening access to HE for workers. More and more voices, both inside and outside the university, were claiming for more commitment and responsiveness from the university to social concerns such as the democratization of HE.
3. In the context of that time, both institutions could expect objective benefits from increased co-operation. In short, UCL could expect the political and financial support which it definitely needed and which it could draw from MOC, given the latter's close and multiple links with the social democrat party.[4] The appointment of the MOC president at the head of UCL board of trustees could be viewed as part of that support-building strategy. Moreover, by demonstrating its willingness to strengthen co-operation with the largest labour organization, UCL could expect to improve its public image with respect to the circle, in particular political, from which support was sought. On the other hand, MOC also had an interest in co-operating with UCL as it was likely to facilitate the access of its activists and leaders to HE and training opportunities.

Now it should be stressed that potential for opposition to such a project did exist, at least within the University, to the extent that the resources invested in the project were necessarily to be diverted from others and the prospect of co-operation of the University with an external, labour-oriented institution, was not compatible with an elitist view of the University that was shared by a large part of the academic community. In fact, it appeared that the potential for opposition was not so much directed against the general idea of co-operation between the two institutions as against the concrete form which this co-operation was to take, that is, the creation of a non-traditional credit-bearing programme for workers.

A conducive interest group configuration. Even in a favourable context, the FOPES project would never have come to fruition if there had not been an active interest group, committed to the idea of strengthened UCL–MOC co-operation, and therefore ready to strive energetically together to achieve such a project. This group (henceforth called the 'active co-operation supporter group', abbreviated ACS) consisted mainly of individual faculty members, most of whom were also MOC activists or leaders. These people were particularly sensitive to the May 1968 ideals, and especially to the idea of widening university access to working-class adults. They were eager to see their university undertake reforms in that direction. However, most of them were not in a particularly high-status position in the academic hierarchy, and hence could not expect to be able to bring about the desired changes in their institution by themselves. MOC was therefore regarded as a powerful institutional ally and the prospect of UCL–MOC co-operation was regarded as strategically a very important opportunity to be seized. The ACS group within UCL had its counterpart within MOC. It consisted mainly of some MOC local and national leaders who had a strong interest in the development of UCL–MOC co-operation for both ideological and organizational reasons.

On the other hand, the ACS found leading figures of both MOC and UCL, who were sufficiently willing to respond to their claims because they were quite sensitive to the benefits their institutions could draw from strengthened co-operation, and sufficiently influential to translate these demands into appropriate decisions because of their key positions in the organizational structures. In this respect, both the UCL rector and the president of MOC, who also happened to be the president of the UCL board of trustees, played a critical role.

On the whole, the context appeared to be quite conducive to the prospect of co-operation between these institutions. However, even though the MOC and UCL partners were somehow bound to do 'something' together, none of them had a clear idea at the outset what this something should be. On the other hand, the heterogeneity of the interest groups involved was a source of conflict. As indicated above, they showed significant divergences in their preferences as to what the something ought to be.

As predicted by the political model of academic decision-making (see Chapter 3), this combination of co-operation (interdependence) and conflict (divergence in goals, values and preferences) did in fact result in the use of politics (that is, influence strategies) throughout the decision-making process underlying the determination of what form of co-operation to choose. The decision outcome, that is, the programme as designed, approved and, eventually, implemented, gradually took shape through the interplay of influence strategies used by the actors involved at all stages of the decision process. It is to this that we now turn.

Bringing about change through the use of influence strategies in decision-making

In an organizational context of high conflict potential, how can an active interest group manage to influence the organizational decision-making process so as to achieve its goals and overcome resistance? Presenting the details of the actors' strategic behaviour in the decision-making process under study would be beyond the scope of this section.[5] Rather we present the conceptual framework which stemmed from the case study to identify and analyse those strategies, along with a few illustrations taken from the case study.[6]

Macro strategies across the whole decision-making process
One possible approach to analysing the actors' strategies is to look at their behaviour throughout the decision-making process as a whole and try to identify the theme underlining the actors' course of action throughout the process, which we call macro strategies. From this perspective, each stage of the decision-making process can be viewed as a strategic step used by the actors to achieve their final goal, that is, the implementation of the desired change. As a first step, such an analysis requires a theoretical framework for identifying the different stages of the observed decision-making process. In our case, we have already referred to the political model of academic decision-making (see Chapter 3[7]) which identifies four typical stages: the activation, design, final approval and implementation stages. These stages were clearly identified in our case study.

Activation stage. This stage starts with the formal request addressed by an MOC leader to the UCL rector (May 1969) to set up an MOC–UCL *ad hoc* committee whose mission was to work out recommendations for possible forms of co-operation between the two institutions. This committee, which was called CTU,[8] was officially established by the rector several months later. It consisted of MOC and UCL representatives on a fifty-fifty basis. Its mission ended one-and-a-half years later with the submission of its final report to the UCL authorities. Amongst its recommendations was the creation of a UCL degree programme in economic and social policy studies which would eventually become the FOPES programme, and the establishment of another committee to further the examination and development of the CTU's various proposals.

Design stage. The UCL authorities formally approved the CTU's final report and established the new committee proposed by the CTU. This committee, called STU,[9] was established as a UCL committee. Like the former CTU, it was composed half of representatives from MOC and half from UCL. For the seven months following its creation, STU focused almost exclusively on one of the CTU's recommendations, namely, the FOPES project. It worked intensively on the development of all the programme components (curriculum, teaching methods, admissions policy, course format – scheduling and location, governance structure, and so on). The final draft of the FOPES proposal was then submitted to both MOC and UCL authorities for final approval.

Final approval stage. During that stage, the project was thoroughly examined, discussed and amended by the competent bodies of both institutions. Direct and personal negotiation took place between the top leaders of both institutions. The FOPES project was finally approved by the UCL faculty senate 10 months later and a decision made to start the programme in the next academic year.

Implementation stage. The status of the FOPES programme as formally approved by UCL and MOC stipulated that it would be governed by a board composed of both UCL and MOC representatives on a fifty-fifty basis. Once established, the FOPES board worked intensively for four months to make the programme operational. FOPES finally opened its door in January 1974.

The ACS's strategic behaviour in the whole decision-making process appears remarkably consistent. In the first stage, we see this group raising the co-operation issue and bringing it to the forefront of the University's competent bodies' decision agenda. The political model pays a great deal of attention to that critical stage of decision-making. As indicated in Chapter 3, politics in decision-making starts with the activation or de-activation of a decision issue. According to their interests, organizational actors may choose to raise an issue (a problem, a concern or an objective) and increase its visibility as a decision issue to be dealt with by appropriate decision-making bodies or, on the contrary, to avoid it. In our case, ACS not only activated MOC–UCL co-operation as a decision issue but also managed to have the appropriate decision-making structure (that is, the STU committee) installed to deal with it effectively.

The way an issue is activated at the outset determines to a large extent further participation in the decision-making process. It was noted in Chapter 3 that the political model does not imply that all the actors potentially concerned with the decision issue will actually get involved in the decision-making process. They will do so only if certain conditions are met, including perceived interdependence, divergence in goals and preferences, importance of the issue and power distribution. Now, the way the issue is activated at the outset may affect those conditions and therefore the decision of both potential opponents and supporters whether to get involved or not. The issue may be activated so as to enhance the actors' perception of whether it is vital or not for their interests to mobilize actively in the decision process. For example, supporters may minimize the importance of the issue in the eyes of potential opponents to keep them away from the decision process, or they can enhance their perception that the decision outcomes will not affect their goals anyway.

In the next step (*design stage*), they managed to have another decision-making body created in order to deal with the recommendations emerging from the previous stage, and to ensure that those recommendations be transformed into a concrete proposal that would best fit their interests, that is, a proposal which would both meet their goals and demands and be the most likely to be accepted with the least delay by the competent decision-making bodies. The political model points to the design stage of the decision process as critical from a strategic point of view. The argument is that this stage (search and elaboration of decision alternatives) determines the final decision outcomes to a large extent. It is therefore essential for the actors seeking to influence the final decision outcome to have access to and control of the design stage of the decision-making process.

ACS then appeared to be very active in the *approval process* in order to secure that the most essential characteristics with respect to their interests of the emerging project be eventually preserved in the final agreement. Finally, they also managed to exert enough control over the *implementation process* to ensure the preservation and development of the essential characteristics of the programme as actually implemented.

In summary, the innovation promotors' behaviour throughout the decision-making process can be viewed as a four-step 'macro' strategy towards the achievement of their goal:

1. activation stage, consisting of activating the relevant decision issue on the institutional agenda and transforming it into 'satisfying' proposals;
2. the transformation of the initial proposals into a single project that appears to be both feasible and desirable to the actors;
3. approval stage, the attempt by the supporters to influence the final decision so as to secure their interests in the resulting decision outcome;
4. implementation, to control the decision implementation process in order to ensure that the project as actually implemented best fits their interests.

Each step therefore appears as a link in a global strategy that leads the actors or innovation supporters gradually towards the achievement of their goals. In a way, each step can be seen both as a means to the next step and as a goal that is aimed at in the previous step. In the next section we focus more specifically on the actors' strategic behaviour within each stage of the decision-making process.

Meso strategies within each stage of the decision-making process
Each stage of the decision-making process can be viewed as a step in a more global strategy. It can also be viewed as a combination of more specific strategies contributing to the achievement of a common goal. From this perspective we observed a quite consistent pattern in the actors' strategic behaviours in the case under study. In each stage we identified a similar combination of strategies. This combination can also be described as a four-step sequence. As an illustration, we shall describe this sequence in the activation stage.

1. *Securing an appropriate decision-making structure for dealing with the issue.* In the initial contacts between the MOC top leader, Mr B (who was one of the ACS key figures), and the UCL rector, the former raised the issue of MOC–UCL co-operation, along with arguments to highlight the import-ance of the issue for both institutions and initial suggestions as to possible forms this co-operation might take. He also suggested the immediate cre-ation of an *ad hoc* committee (which would become the CTU) to explore the issue further and work out recommendations. Furthermore, it was

requested and agreed that this committee would be composed of both MOC and UCL representatives on a fifty-fifty basis.

The ACS thus secured not only a guarantee that the issue would be actually dealt with institutionally, but also the possibility of influencing the process in the subsequent stage of the decision process. The same step could be observed at the beginning of all subsequent stages, although in the final approval stage there was no creation of a new *ad hoc* structure, only the activation of an existing one – the competent bodies of both institutions had been captured.

2. *Occupying the newly created (or activated) decision-making structure.* The composition of the STU committee revealed that all the UCL and MOC members, including its chairman (Mr B), were in fact ACS. This suggests that the ACS managed to 'occupy' the newly created decision-making structure and thereby were in a strategic position to influence the decision process directly at that stage. The same 'occupation' strategy was observed in subsequent stages.

However, in reference to Pfeffer (1981), we distinguished two types of occupation strategy: 'homogeneity' and 'heterogeneity'. The homogeneity strategy, which was observed in the first two stages, consists of including as many supporters as possible in the decision-making body. By doing this, the supporters increase their chances to control and influence the decision process directly and thereby to obtain the desired decision outcome. The heterogeneity strategy, which was observed in the final approval stage, consists of including potential opponents in the decision-making body. This strategy has two advantages. It exposes potential opponents' members to social influence processes which, if effective, may change their minds and turn them into allies – a co-optation effect. Moreover, it legitimates the decision process and outcomes in the eyes of the potential opponents outside the committee. The implementation stage revealed a sort of mixture of both strategies: heterogeneity at the top level of the programme's management structure in the programme board, and homogeneity on the bottom level – choice of the programme director and staff.

3. *Influencing the decision-making process from inside.* Once within the newly created structure, the ACS managed to influence the decision process at that stage in order to obtain the outcomes that would best fit their interests. In the activation stage, they managed to work out a list of recommendations which would both meet their goals and preferences and be the most likely to be accepted by the decision-making bodies to which they were to be submitted for approval. They also managed to propose the creation of an *ad hoc* committee (CTU) which would secure the follow-up of their recommendations. The type of influence strategies they used to obtain those outcomes are discussed below.

4. *Legitimating the decision outcomes.* Various strategies were used by the supporters to legitimate the decision outcomes vis-à-vis the decision-makers who were to approve them and decide to carry on the decision-making process.

Micro strategies within each stage of the decision-making process

The four-step pattern described above can be viewed as a meso-strategy in itself to achieve the intermediate goals that are aimed at in each stage of the decision-making process. However, each of these four steps can in turn be looked at as a set of micro-strategies which jointly contribute to the achievement of the strategic objectives that are aimed at in each of these steps. The question is how, through which influence strategies, do the supporters manage to obtain the desired decision-making structure to deal with the issue. How do they actually occupy this structure, to influence the production of decision outcomes within the structure, and ultimately to legitimate those outcomes?

Let us come back to the design stage. The CTU committee was officially charged with working out concrete co-operation proposals from the set of recommendations previously made by STU. Those recommendations were quite varied, and the idea of creating a degree programme especially geared to the MOC activists' and leaders' constituencies was only one of those recommendations. What happened then is that instead of working out different, competing proposals for eventual submission to the top authorities of the University, the committee (where supporters were in a majority) chose from the outset to focus its attention and energy only on the degree programme (FOPES) project. Only that proposal was eventually submitted to the university authorities. This choice can be explained by the fact that the project was perceived by the ACS: as one of the most suited to their preferences and goals (widening university access to working-class groups) and; in the current context as the most feasible and likely to be implemented in the short run. By doing this, they were restricting drastically the margin of freedom of those who were to make the final decision. The only choice that was left to them was to approve, to reject or to amend the single proposal submitted to them. In other words, by not presenting alternative proposals they were forcing their preferred proposal onto the decision-makers' agenda.

However, this strategy of the 'one best choice' raised two strategic problems for the ACS. On the one hand, by avoiding presenting 'second-choice' alongside their 'first-choice' proposal, they were taking the chance of having the latter rejected by the university authorities, which would, of course, have seriously jeopardized their ultimate goal to have some acceptable form of co-operation between MOC and UCL implemented in the short term. Therefore, they had to minimize the risk of rejection of the proposal by making it appear as acceptable as possible to the final decision-makers, including potential opponents. In other words, they were obliged to legitimate the proposal towards the decision-makers to whom it was submitted.

On the other hand, the ACS in the committee stage were also careful to make the proposal acceptable, not only to the potential opponents but also to the other supporters outside the committee to whom they were accountable. In their attempt to make the proposal as acceptable as possible to potential opponents they also had to reduce the risk of coming up with a proposal that would not please supporters outside the committee.

Such a 'two-direction' legitimation process involved a combination of legitimation strategies. One was concerned with the use of language in the final draft of the proposal. For example, the previous drafts discussed within the committee stated that FOPES was to cater for 'people who belong to certain organizations, who are activists and committed to the building of a more democratic society'. It further specified the social groups to be addressed and stipulated explicitly activism and social commitment as formal admission requirements to the programme. Now, interestingly enough, those sentences disappeared in the final draft. There was no longer any explicit reference either to any particular group to be catered to by the programme, or to activism as a formal entry requirement. Instead, it was simply stated that '*all other things being equal, priority will be given to those candidates who . . . seek to develop their ability to develop projects for socio-economic change*'. Such a sentence, as opposed to the previous versions, was more likely to reassure those who were concerned about the ideological neutrality of the University and the preservation of its emphasis on academic excellence, or feared to see UCL publicly committed to any particular ideology, social group or institution. At the same time it did not close the door to the idea of having activism actually taken into account in the admissions policy. It could therefore reassure supporters who were particularly sensitive to the programme openness to the MOC clientele in particular.

The final draft also included a reference to a market study previously conducted by some STU members, which highlighted the existence of a significant potential student clientele for the programme. Such a reference was likely to reassure those who were concerned about the economic viability of the programme.

These actions were aimed at mobilizing support and soothing opposition to the proposal by enhancing a positive perception of it by the final decision-makers to whom it was addressed. Such legitimation strategies affect the way the proposal itself is expressed and presented. Another type of legitimation strategy was identified. It was fulfilling the same function as the former (enhancing a positive perception of the proposal by the decision-makers), but more indirectly, by raising a positive perception of the decision-making process from which it resulted. For example, STU set up a consultation meeting which addressed a large part of the UCL and MOC memberships to collect feed-back on the project in preparation. It emphasized in the final report that only authorized expert sources that had been thoroughly examined were used in the design process. The working drafts and minutes of meetings were regularly sent to the UCL and MOC authorities to keep them posted on such aspects as the development of the committee.

By doing this they were enhancing a social construction of the decision-making process which emphasized its transparent, democratic, rational and expert character. This in turn was likely to legitimate the decision outcomes.

Nature of the influence strategies: towards a typology

The examples above indicate the wide variety of possible forms of influence that can be exerted in a decision-making process underlying organizational change and innovation. We now review various types of influence strategy more systematically. This review is conducted in reference to a typology that was worked out on the basis of the FOPES case study and by reference to the literature.[10]

Two basic forms of influence: pressure and legitimation

On the basis of a review of the literature on power in organizational decision-making, we distinguish between two basic forms of influence: *pressure* and *legitimation*. Pressure is a form of influence that is based on a dependence relationship between two actors. It was summarized by Bourgeois and Nizet (1993) as follows.

> Pressure (or 'dependence-based' influence) has probably been the most studied mode of influence in academic organizations (see, for example, Salancik and Pfeffer, 1974a; 1974b; Moore, 1979). In this paradigm, originally developed by Emerson (1962), the power of an actor A over B is directly proportional to B's dependence on A, with B's dependence on A defined as a function of
>
> A's ability to control resources that are crucial for B (i.e., resources that are necessary for the achievement of goals perceived as crucial by B),
>
> and the non-availility of these resources to B outside of A (see Emerson, 1962; Blau, 1964; Crozier, 1963; Crozier and Friedberg, 1977; Hickson *et al.*, 1971; Pfeffer, 1981; Reitter and Ramanantsoa, 1985).
>
> In this mechanism, influence is used in the form of *pressure*. B's dependence on A means that A has the ability to threaten B with withdrawing (or not providing) those resources, regardless of the concrete form under which the threat is communicated to B (it might be implicit). As for B, he will comply with A's demands because he is somehow forced or pressured to do so. In other words, A exerts influence over B through pressure. To be complete, we should mention that A's power may derive not only from his ability to control those resources that are indispensable for achieving B's goals but also from his ability to control constraints that can compromise the achievement of B's goals. This distinction is close to that introduced by Etzioni (1961), French and Raven (1968) and Gergen and Gergen (1984) between the 'power of reward' and the 'power of coercion'. Various authors have emphasized that aspect of power (Biersted, 1950; Baechler, 1978). (Bourgeois and Nizet, 1993: 389–90.)

Influence through legitimation operates quite differently from pressure as it does not require any dependence relationship between the two actors. As Bourgeois and Nizet put it:

In this paradigm [Legitimation] A's ability to influence B lies in A's ability to make his demands (or decisions, or propositions) perceived by B as legitimate, that is, as complying with norms and objectives valued by B (e.g. Boudon and Bourricaud, 1986; French and Raven, 1968; Maroy, 1988). In this case, B complies with A's demands (or decisions, or propositions) not because he is forced to do so, but rather because he has come to perceive them as legitimate. This mode of influence can therefore be exerted regardless of the actual degree of B's dependence on A. The common characteristic of legitimation strategies is that, in one way or another, they all aim at modifying actors' perceptions (or representations). Pfeffer (1981) also suggested that legitimation may be used both to quiet potential or actual opposition or to mobilize support. (1993: 390).

In the FOPES case study we found very few instances of exercise of influence through pressure. One of them was evidenced in the following event which happened in the final approval stage. When it examined the FOPES project, the faculty senate, which was the competent body to make the final decision, decided not to approve it immediately. Rather, it set up an *ad hoc* committee to examine particular aspects of the project. Two months later, it heard the conclusion of that committee but no formal decision was made at that time. At that point in the decision-making process, time was playing against the supporters' interests. The more time passed, the more opposition could build up. A few days after that meeting, the MOC president himself wrote a letter to the UCL rector to urge the University to make a quick decision. The main argument he used was that if the University did not hurry, MOC might turn to another university partner to implement the FOPES project.

In this example, the pressure exerted by the MOC president is obvious, pressure in the threat to turn to a competing partner or, to put it in Pfeffer's terms 'to play groups off against one another'. In other words, the threat was to deprive UCL of a partnership with MOC from which it could draw benefits in terms of resources much needed by the University at that time to achieve some of its goals (in particular, a successful move to Wallonia). Moreover, this letter was sent to the rector personally, as he had proved to be particularly sympathetic to the argument.

Besides these few instances of pressure, most influence strategies that could be evidenced in the case study were predominantly legitimation strategies, illustrated in the events presented above. We suggested earlier that different dimensions can be considered for distinguishing legitimation strategies specifically. An example is one concerning the target of the legitimation process.

Targets of legitimation strategy. While the ultimate function of legitimation is to enhance B's positive perception of the decision outcome (or alternative) supported by A, it can be achieved in three different ways. One is to legitimate the decision outcome (or alternative) directly. The others both legitimate it indirectly, by legitimating either the decision-making process or the decision-maker.[11] These three types of legitimation are summarized by Bourgeois and Nizet as follows.

A can try to legitimate the decision outcome (or alternative) directly. For example, A will systematically highlight the advantages of the decision for B while keeping its disadvantages in the shadow. The target in this case is the *decision* itself. A can legitimate a decision outcome (or alternative) by legitimating the process through which it has been (or will be) reached. In this case, the target of the legitimation strategy is the *decision-making process* itself. For example, A can try to have B accept a decision outcome by highlighting the fact that the decision has been reached through a democratic procedure or by emphasizing that B's interests were duly represented in the decision procedure.

A can legitimate a decision outcome (or alternative) by legitimating himself as a decision-maker. For example, A can refer to his formal status or his expertise to have B perceive his decision as legitimate. The target here is the *decision maker* himself (1993: 390).

The first two types of legitimation were clearly illustrated above. The strategic use of language, or rhetoric, in drafting the final proposal is an example of direct legitimation of the decision outcome, first type. The strategy which consisted of emphasizing the transparent, democratic, collegial and rational character of the procedure through which the FOPES proposal was worked out by CTU is an example of the second type of legitimation.

Legitimation for conservation, succession, and subversion. Another dimension for distinguishing legitimation strategies stems from Bourdieu's 'theory of fields' (*théorie des champs*).[12] Bourdieu's central assumption is that a social field (for instance, a university), is characterized by competing systems of norms and values (called legitimation principles). Those legitimation principles are hierarchized within the field. For example, in a given university, such as UCL or Warwick, scientific excellence may be the dominant system of values and norms, as opposed to excellence in teaching or accessibility to socially excluded groups. The actors belonging to the field have certain characteristics in terms of competence, resources, image, and so on which are unevenly distributed among them. For example, a department or a faculty member can be excellent in terms of scientific achievement and rather poor in terms of teaching excellence or accessibility to non-traditional students, or the other way around. Bourdieu's central argument is that the power of an actor in the field is a function of the degree to which he or she possesses those characteristics that conform with the dominant legitimation principle. For example, in an institution where scientific excellence is the dominant legitimation principle, the department which can prove to be excellent in terms of scientific achievement will be in a better power position than one that may be excellent in terms of accessibility to non-traditional adults but poorer in terms of scientific excellence.

Under those conditions, legitimation plays a central role in the struggle for power within the field. It may take three forms. Those who are in the better power position because they possess the characteristics that are valued by the dominant legitimation principle will strive to maintain their power by *both* maintaining the domination of this principle in the field *and* enhancing others' perception that they indeed possess those characteristics to the highest degree. In the above example, the department with a reputation for scientific excellence will struggle to maintain both its image of scientific excellence (for instance, by emphasizing the quantity and quality of publications produced in the department) and the dominance of scientific excellence as the dominant legitimation principle (for instance, by securing the predominance of this criterion in the institution's internal resource allocation policy). This is the use of legitimation as a *conservation* strategy.

Those actors who are in the weaker power position, to the extent that their characteristics are less valued in relation to the institution's dominant legitimation principle, may struggle to increase their institutional power in two ways. One is to modify their characteristics, or to modify the others' perception of their characteristics, so as to appear to conform with the dominant legitimation principle in use. For example, a department with remarkable and efficient adult access policies but with a poor reputation in terms of scientific achievement may attempt to co-opt some faculty members with high scholarly credentials, or it may take action to have its staff improve its scholarly achievements. It may also make an effort to advertise its scholarly achievement and promote a better image, in terms of scientific excellence, within the institution. This is the use of legitimation as a *succession* strategy. A quite different strategy may be adopted by those who struggle to modify the current legitimation principle hierarchy prevailing in the institution in order to promote the principle in reference to which its current characteristics can be valued. In the example above, the department which can prove excellence in terms of accessibility to non-traditional students may struggle to promote widening access as a top-priority mission for the institution, or at least to increase the perceived importance of that mission within the university, as occurred at Warwick. In this case, legitimation is used as a *subversion* strategy.

Influence and organizational resources

The exercise of influence in decision-making through either legitimation or pressure involves some use of specific organizational resources. This point has long been discussed in the literature on power in organizations. In fact, most typologies of power or influence strategies distinguish them on the basis of the type of resource involved. The well-known Crozier and Friedberg's (1977) typology distinguishes between four basic forms of power in organizations according to the resources used, namely, expertise, relationships, information and rules. On the basis of a meta-analysis of those typologies, Bourgeois and Nizet (1993) distinguished seven types of organizational resource that could be involved in influence strategies, that is, expertise, monetary resources, information, time, rules, coalitions, and language and symbolic actions. They further argued that each of them could be used *either* in pressure *or* in legitimation strategies. Therefore, on that basis their typology distinguishes 14 (2 × 7) possible strategies, most of which were evidenced in the FOPES case study. Here we present only a few example of possible strategic uses of an organizational resource, namely, information.[13]

Pressure can be exerted by A over B to the extent that A controls information affecting the achievement of B's goals. A can, therefore, threaten B not to provide them with the information needed or to disclose information that could compromise B's goals. Information can also be used for legitimation. For example, A could provide specific information that is likely to change B's perception of the decision outcome.

In our case study, during the design, the ACS had a market analysis conducted to provide evidence of the existence of a student market for the proposed programme. The communication of those results was likely to legitimate the proposal to those who were sensitive to the economic viability of the programme. Information can also be involved in indirect legitimation of the decision outcome, through legitimation of the decision-making process.

It was noted above that during the design stage, the STU members kept the university top administrators posted on the development of their work by sending them minutes of the meetings alongside working drafts. In this example such a procedure fulfils two functions. It reassures the administrators that they *can* exert some control over the decision-making process, while there is little chance that such control would actually be exerted. It also somehow binds the top administrators to the proposal arising from the committee.

Another instance of the use of information is found is the STU committee's initiative to set up an open consultation meeting about the project during the design stage. This can be viewed as a symbolic action to legitimate the decision-making process by making it appear democratic and transparent to the academic community. It also provided the supporters with useful information about potential objections to the project that could be raised. Therefore it enabled the supporters to adjust during the design process, and hence increased the chances of ultimate approval.

Conclusion

Given the specific nature of both the organizational context and the issue at stake, the dynamics of adultification of the university can be viewed as essentially a struggle, or more precisely, a *political* process. That is, it is a process in which decisions and policies result from the interplay of influence strategies used by the actors. Politics is involved at the outset in the activation of the decision; in the fact that some actors decide to step in or keep out of the decision-making process; in the selection and elaboration of the decision alternatives; in the making of the final choice about the proposed decision alternatives; and in the actual implementation of the resulting decision outcomes.

The differences that are observed in adult access policies and practices across institutions and in sub-units within institutions can, therefore, be explained to a large extent in the light of the interplay of power relationships and strategies displayed by the various interest groups in the decision-making processes that underpin those policies and practices. However, as argued in Chapter 3, this is only one part of the story. The structural characteristics of the organization and its environment may also contribute to the differences by serving as a framework in which actors operate and which conditions the actors' positions, behaviours and strategies to a large extent. The question can therefore be raised whether there are particular structural characteristics of the organization and its environment which are more conducive than others to adultification. This question is addressed in the next section.

The organization's structure and context

Introduction

Among the structural factors likely to affect adult access policy-making in universities, we can first make a distinction between *external* factors, characteristics of the organization's environment, and *internal* factors which are the characteristics of the organization itself. External factors can be identified at the macro- and the meso-level.

The role of external structural factors

Macro-level external factors originate in the characteristics of the national context to which the organization belongs. As shown in Chapter 3, international comparisons reveal the extent to which national contexts closely shape access policies developed by HE institutions in different countries. As illustrated by the Warwick–Louvain comparison, cross-national differences in the structure of the HE system, mode of university funding and management, legal framework, ideological, cultural and historical context may account to a large extent for the differences observed in the adult access policies and practices developed by the two institutions.

The external factors at the meso level arise from the relationship between the organization under study and its local environment. They can explain differences in policies observed across institutions. HE institutions may cater for different environment segments and characteristics; for example, they may cater for different student markets, use different sources of funding, or in some cases be exposed to different governmental regulations. Moreover, academic institutions may differ in terms of what Baldridge *et al.* (1977) called environment vulnerability. In other words, HE institutions may be responsive to their environment to a varying extent. They can be differentially sensitive to governmental regulations, student-market demands, requirements imposed by private and public sources of funding and/or professional associations, or more generally, to the demands of civil society at large. To that extent their access policies may be more or less affected by the characteristics of the segments of the environment they cater for. For example, in Belgium universities clearly have more autonomy from governmental regulations than non-university institutions with respect to admissions, curriculum and instruction, and internal resource allocation. On the other hand, they are far more exposed than the latter to demands from the national bodies for research funding. Likewise, small universities (*centre universitaires*) are significantly more sensitive to the local student market and local sources of funding, in particular from industry, than are large, comprehensive, research-oriented universities such as Louvain. The same also applies in the UK especially as between the old and new universities, and indeed in most HE systems.

The role of internal structural factors

Internal factors may also play a crucial role in shaping access policies within academic institutions and therefore may also explain the differences observed in access policies and practices across sub-units. Academic departments have some specific structural characteristics which may explain the differences in their behaviours, for example, with respect to adult access and participation. This is what Guyot's doctoral study (1998) was intended to demonstrate. The Louvain–Warwick comparative study had previously shown significant differences across departments in terms of adult-access provision (admissions, curriculum, course schedule, and so forth) and actual adult-participation patterns. In response to this observation Guyot's study addresses the possible origins of those differences. He was primarily concerned with those characteristics of the departments themselves that could explain their differences in terms of adult participation and access provision. He suggested different sets of hypotheses, which refer to three distinct theoretical models. These were originally intended to account for differences in academic departments' *research* practices and policies. The goal was, therefore, to test the relevance of those hypotheses in explaining differences in departments' behaviours with respect to adult access and participation. An additional questionnaire survey was conducted at Louvain to address all 472 full-time faculty members, of whom 284 (60.2 per cent) responded.

The cultural approach

Hypotheses   This approach (for example, Becher, 1981; 1993; Gaff and Wilson, 1971; Kolb, 1981; Harman, 1989; Sporn, 1996[14]) is one of the most prolific in the sociology of academic organizations. Anthropological qualitative analyses mingle with quantitative research based on large surveys. The fundamental hypothesis is that there is a strong relationship between the sociological characteristics of the academic community working in a given discipline (*knowledge community*) and the epistemological characteristics of the discipline (*knowledge form*). Each academic community, therefore, has its own sub-culture (traditions, values, attitudes, norms, codes of conduct, means of communication, style of language, and so on) to which the members have been socialized not only in their initial education in the discipline but also throughout their career. Of course, the academic sub-culture prevailing in a given university department is partly influenced by local and national cultures. It also has features that are inherent in the specific culture of the academic profession as such, which it shares with the other academic sub-cultures. Nevertheless, there remain distinctive features peculiar to the discipline which transcend institutional and national peculiarities.

It can be hypothesized, then, that the specific academic sub-culture prevailing in a given department may at least partly explain its behaviour with respect to adult access and participation in two ways. First, academic sub-cultures differ typically as to the value awarded to the different activities performed by academics. In particular, teaching and research are not equally valued across disciplines, whether in attitudes and judgements expressed by faculty members about these activities, the relative amount of time actually devoted to them, or criteria for academic reward. The hypothesis is, therefore, that *adult participation is lower in those faculties where teaching appears to be less valued relative to research.*

Secondly, academic sub-cultures may also differ in terms of attitude and perceptions toward specific issues such as equal opportunity via access to HE, openness of the university to adults and non-traditional students, the role of the academy in society, the social mission of the university, and so on. The second hypothesis is, therefore, that *adult participation is lower in those disciplines where an 'elitist' view of the university prevails.*

Findings The results regarding the first hypothesis are not clear-cut. On the one hand, it was found that research is believed to be significantly more valued both by the departments and the university at large in the science division[15] than in the social science division. Teaching is believed to be significantly more valued by both the departments and the university at large in the social science division than in science. The medical school's position is intermediate on both scales. Moreover, a strong positive correlation was found between the perceived value of teaching in the department and the proposition of adult students attending the department. The first hypothesis, therefore, is confirmed by those observations, but other findings are not consistent with the hypothesis. Neither individual attitudes and preferences about research and teaching nor the proportion of time devoted to reseach and teaching vary significantly across faculties. Moreover, no significant correlations were found between either item and adult participation.

With respect to the second hypothesis, the survey investigated faculty members' attitudes toward various aspects of the university's mission and its relation to society. The only significant differences across faculties were found with respect to items dealing with the university's openness to adults. Except for philosophy and theology, social science faculties appear to be significantly more positive towards widening university access to adults than all the others. However, no significant correlations were found between these attitude indicators and adult participation in the faculties.

In conclusion, the situation is not clear-cut. The findings only partly confirm the hypothesis of a relationship between the discipline-related sub-culture and institutional behaviours about adult access and participation. This may be due to limitations of the study with regard to the choice of indicators. Further research is obviously needed. Qualitative approaches would allow for a finer identification of the features that characterize academic sub-cultures in the different subject areas. The study focused only on the correlations between sub-culture indicators and adult participation without looking at indicators of the actual faculty adult-access provision. Evidently, confident explanations of faculty attitude and behaviour in respect of access are elusive, and not to be won lightly.

The contingency approach

Hypotheses This approach (Barnett, 1988; Rothblatt, 1985; Becher and Kogan, 1980; Blume, 1985)[16] focuses on differences across academic disciplines concerning the type of relationship they entertain with their respective environment. In a way, it applies the environmental vulnerability argument to differences observed *within* academic institutions. The central hypothesis is that faculties and departments not only cater for different segments of the environment – such as student markets, sources of funding, regulations and demands from professional associations – but are also sensitive to the external environment to varying degrees. Originally this argument was used to explain cross-disciplinary differences in research practices and policies in academic institutions. Guyot suggested that the argument could be extended to account for cross-discipline differences with regard to adult access and participation. The central hypothesis is twofold. On the one hand, the more a discipline is socialized – responsive to the influence of the civil society – the more it is likely to be exposed, or sensitive to, the needs and demands of adults. It is, therefore, expected to find higher levels of adult participation in the most socialized disciplines. On the other hand, the segments of the environment with which the department or faculty interact will determine the nature of the adult needs and demands, hence the profile of the adult clientele, that will be catered for as a priority.

Findings In summary,[17] the study showed significant disparities across disciplines (divisions, faculties and departments) with respect to most socialization indicators. However, the observed differences are not consistent across the different indicators. For example, the science division appears to be the most socialized with respect to the research-funding indicators, whereas the medical division is the most socialized in terms of involvement of faculty members in community service activities. It is in the social science faculties that those activities are the most valued by faculty members and perceived by them as the most valued in their respective faculties and the institution at large. Faculties and departments also appear highly differentiated with respect to the nature of the external sources of funding which they rely upon, and the nature of the service activities performed by faculty members.

Despite such disparities, the UCL academic community on the whole appears quite homogeneous in terms of individual attitudes and preferences about the role and mission of the University vis-à-vis society at large. By and large, a positive attitude towards the idea of opening the University to the needs and demands from civic society prevails across disciplines.

Results concerning a possible correlation between adult participation and socialization indicators are rather disappointing. Most of the data available provided information mainly on socialization in the areas of research and community service, which can hardly account for cross-discipline variations in the amount and nature of external demands regarding adult access and participation to which faculties are exposed. With regard to the second hypothesis, a relationship between the segments of the environment with which the department or faculty interact and the profile of its adult student clientele was indeed found. Most of the adults studying in applied science, agronomics or medicine are typically highly qualified professionals seeking continuing education and training in their professions, whereas the adult students in education are to a large extent second-chance students, that is, mostly teachers or educators who do not have high levels of prior qualification (typically, they have a non-university degree) and who are entering the university for the first time in their life. Those differences can easily be related to the segment of the environment with which they interact.

The structural–functionalist approach

Hypotheses This approach is represented mainly by Bourdieu, 1984.[18] The university is viewed as a structured social space (field) wherein the actors are characterized by specific assets (capitals) that can be more or less valued in the field. The actors' respective position in terms of power in the field depends on the assets they possess and the extent to which those assets are valued by reference to the prevailing set of norms (legitimation principles). The actors are involved in an ongoing struggle over the distribution of assets among themselves and/or over the reproduction or change of the prevailing norms against which the assets can be valued, and which thereby determine the actors' respective positions in the field. According to Bourdieu, the university as a field operates along these lines. It is structured mainly by two antagonistic legitimation principles, namely, the *scientific* principle, which emphasizes scientific and intellectual capital, and the *academic* principle, which values social capital. Academic disciplines occupy different positions according to these principles. Typically, according to Bourdieu, science is in a higher position in terms of scientific capital and in a lower position in terms of social capital, whereas the position of law, medicine and humanities is the other way around. The other disciplines hold intermediate positions. It follows that academics will invest their time, energy and competence in those activities that are consistent with the legitimation principle prevailing in their respective faculties. For example, in the science faculty the academics will strive primarily to reach scholarly excellence through high-standing research and publications at the expense of other tasks, such as teaching or service to the community.

Therefore, it can be hypothesized that the development of adult participation and access provision will be the lowest in those faculties wherein the scientific principle predominates and highest in faculties where the academic principle prevails. The underpinning argument is that, in the former case, teaching adults can in no way be regarded as an avenue for scholarly excellence and therefore will not be given much attention. Conversely, in the latter case the actors will strive to strengthen their position in the field by increasing social resources, for example, through a greater investment in socially rewarding activities. To that extent, they might be particularly sensitive to specific demands from the civil society, including those for adult continuing education and training. In the other faculties, wherein both principles are more or less equally valued, the game will be more open. There would be multiple, competing avenues to power: excellence in research, teaching youngsters or adults, or else service to the internal or external communities could be equally valued in those faculties and the actors can opt for one or another, depending on their specific assets. Such a situation would be conducive to the development of new activities, such as teaching adults, in case of saturation of the other conventional markets such as teaching traditional students, doing research or performing community service.

Findings   The structural–functionalist hypotheses are partly verified by the empirical analysis of the Louvain case. The study shows that the scientifically dominant faculties (science, applied science and agronomics) have the lowest proportion of adult students (between 1.6 and 2.9 per cent) and the lowest adult-access provision. At the other end, faculties with the highest proportions of adult students and with the most developed adult-access provision are those which occupy an intermediate position in both the scientific and academic hierarchies. However, unexpectedly, the 'academically dominant' faculties of law, medicine, and humanities are not the most active in terms of adult access and participation. Analysis of the sociological characteristics of the academic body in the different faculties also confirms Bourdieu's hypothesis. More specifically, significantly higher age average, higher socio-economic and educational family background, and lower scholarly achievement level[19] were found in the academically dominant faculties rather than in the scientifically dominant ones.

Some of the findings that were examined in relation to the cultural and contingency approaches also support the structural–functionalist thesis. For example, significant differences were found among faculties as to the perceived institutional value of research and teaching activities. This finding is important, given the strong positive correlation between the perceived value of the teaching variable and adult participation. The perceived institutional value of research was shown to be highest in the science faculties and lowest in the social science faculties, whereas the opposite pattern is observed with regard to perceived value of teaching. This conforms to the structural–functionalist prediction. Likewise, it was found that social science faculties, except for philosophy and theology, are significantly more positive than others over widening university access to adults. Furthermore, the proportion of time devoted by faculty members to service to the external community appeared to be significantly higher in the typically academically dominant faculties of law and medicine than in others, and the perceived value of this type of activity is higher in social science than in other areas.

However, other observations presented above do *not* clearly support the structural–functionalist thesis. For example, no significant differences were found among faculties as to: the proportion of time actually spent on research and teaching respectively; the faculty members' individual attitudes and preferences regarding those tasks; or their attitudes towards various aspects of the university's mission vis-à-vis society, except for the issue of widening access to adults. Another part of the study focused on faculty attitudes and behaviours in the area of *internal* services, that is service to the academic community. Again, no significant differences were found, in terms either of time actually spent by academics on those tasks, individual preferences or perceived institutional value of such activities.

In conclusion, the structural–functionalist view of the university and interpretation of the differences in the faculties' behaviours and attitudes regarding adult access and participation is not clearly supported by the data. This could be partly explained by some methodological limitations of the study, but Bourdieu's thesis can also be questioned. Remember that the theory proposed by Bourdieu in 1984 was developed on the basis of research conducted in the late 1960s in France. It is highly probable that the situation has changed over the last 25 years. At the macro level the massification of HE in Western countries has surely affected the social position of the academic profession in society. The diversification of the cultural capital, its increasing accessibility and the growing importance of the role exerted by new social agents in the reproduction and distribution of this capital, in particular the media, alongside the development of research and knowledge production outside the university, may have weakened academics' social position and status. Internally, these societal trends may have modified the use of either academic or scientific assets as sources of power within the academe. It is also possible that the academically dominant faculties have gradually become more responsive to the scientific legitimation principle. Conversely, scientifically dominant faculties may have become more permeated with the academic legitimation principle, as suggested by Rothblatt (1985), Elzinga (1987), Barnett (1988) and Becher (1989). This evolution would imply less contrasted positions of all the faculties with respect to those principles. Moreover, Bourdieu's theory may fit peculiarities of the French context that do not necessarily apply to other countries. In particular, the French HE system appears to be far more centralized *and* hierarchized than any other in Europe.

Beyond those limitations, the structural–functionalist perspective remains particularly stimulating. One of the shortcomings of the original cultural and contingency approaches is their tendency to restrict focus to the scientific activity of the academics in explaining institutional and individual strategies and behaviours in the academy. These are explained only in reference to epistemological (the disciplines) and organizational (faculties, departments) categories. They do not account for the diversity of the competing logics on which academic behaviours and strategies are based. It is difficult to explain the hierarchy among disciplines underscored by the culturalist approach and its longstanding viability, without accounting for the competition between the academic and the scientific logics, in Bourdieu's sense. In contrast, the structural–functionalist perspective considers faculty members not only as members of a given epistemological area (the disciplines) and organizational unit (faculties and departments), but also as social actors who occupy specific positions in a given social field, struggling over the distribution of a variety of relevant assets and the conservation or change of the legitimation principles that determine their value and power in the field. In addition, Bourdieu's perspective underscores the fact that the criteria and logics on the basis of which the field is structured, and the actors' positions are defined, are not disconnected from those which operate in society at large.

An implication of this analysis and discussion may be that universities generally are becoming less closed, more vulnerable to those changes and challenges from within and without which are the theme of this book, and which herald the emergence of the adult university.

Notes

1. *Faculté ouverte en politique économique et sociale.*
2. MOC (Mouvement Ouvrier Chrétien) is a large organization federating various types of Christian labour organizations (trade unions, adult worker education institutions, worker health insurance companies, and so on).
3. In Belgian society, there is a long-standing tradition of close ties among institutions belonging to the same linguistic and confessional (lay v. Catholic) sphere of influence, even though they operate in remote segments of social life. In this sense, a Catholic and French university is closer to a Catholic and French labour organization than are a Flemish and a French university, or a Catholic and a state (lay) university, or a Catholic and a lay labour organization.
4. At that time, UCL was in the process of moving from its home town (Leuven, in Flanders) to Wallonia. This enterprise was not only costly (it implied the building

of a whole new campus town) but also politically sensitive (the Catholic party – and institutions – have traditionally been in a minority position in the socialist-dominated Wallonia).

5. The reader is referred to the original research report (Bourgeois, 1990) for a comprehensive account and analysis.
6. Another version of the discussion presented in the next three sections has been published by Bourgeois, 1993.
7. See in particular Baldridge, 1971 and Pfeffer, 1981.
8. *Commission Travail-Université* ('University-Labour Committee').
9. *Section Travail-Université* ('University-Labour Task Force').
10. For an extensive discussion of the typology, see Bourgeois, 1990; Bourgeois and Nizet, 1993; 1995.
11. This distinction was originally formalized by Bourgeois, 1990, on the basis of discussion of Pfeffer, 1981.
12. See in particular Bourdieu, 1984, and Bourdieu and de St Martin, 1978. Also see Maroy, 1988 for an application of the theory in the study of an adult education institution.
13. Strategic uses of the other resources are discussed and illustrated in Bourgeois, 1990 and Bourgeois and Nizet, 1993.
14. See Guyot, 1998 ch. 2 for a comprehensive presentation and bibliography on this approach.
15. The science division at UCL includes the agronomics, applied science and science faculties; the human science division includes the law school, the divinity school, the economic, social and political science faculty, the psychology and education faculty, the humanities faculty and the school of philosophy. The medical division includes the medical and some other health-related schools.
16. See Guyot, 1998 ch. 2 for a comprehensive presentation and bibliography on this approach.
17. The reader should refer to Guyot, 1998 (ch. 7) for more details on this approach.
18. A detailed presentation of this theoretical framework can be found in Guyot, 1998 (ch. 8).
19. For instance, post-doctoral research.

7

The Adult University: from Adult Education to Lifelong Learning?

Writing this book proved more complicated, more challenging, as well as slower than we had expected. We knew at the outset that it was not a simple task. Our publisher's referees, in commenting on the initial proposal, set an agenda of issues, dimensions and tensions which we would have to take into account if the venture was to succeed. What are the most important of these considerations, and what should this concluding chapter be expected to achieve?

The book is a kind of dialectic between the theoretical and the empirical. For us, because of our calling and practice as educators of adults and proponents of adults' access to higher education, it is also an encounter between the operational and the experiential on the one hand, and the conceptual, abstracted and generalizable, on the other, which is core business for the academic scholar. One reader of the proposal judged it, accurately, to be more theoretical in intent than Duke's *The Learning University* (1992). It was also, evidently, to be less polemical. Another saw it as too safe, not committed, polemical or ideological enough, and called for a more active, less dry and unengaging book than the proposal implied.

We are in no doubt about our commitment to equity in general, and to the access of adults to HE in particular. However, in pursuit of this quest we also wished, and needed, better to understand what comes between an intention to widen and facilitate access and the continuing inequalities and exclusions which study after study of the behaviour of universities and the experiences of aspiring and enrolled mature-age students has documented. We set out, therefore, to analyse our own experience of access and exclusion in our respective systems and universities in Belgium and the United Kingdom; and to revisit and reflect on the literature, the different theoretical perspectives which purport to explain the dynamics of organizational and human behaviour and their manifestations in the policies and practices of HE. By probing in depth and detail experiences in Belgium and the UK we sought to see what was new in the familiar, and mutually to force ourselves to re-examine and explain to each other what we were attempting to do, on the ground, in our different situations. We combined comparative study between systems with a 'deep slice' probe into the experience of policies-in-operations as they are felt and expressed by tutors and their students – students and their tutors. We required ourselves to look consciously at the different, broadly sociological schools and traditions which separately or severally we recognized, valued and practised, and to ask which threw light on the practice of access in HE.

The book thus attempts, notably in Chapters 3 and 6, to review, critique and extend the conceptual frameworks and perspectives used about access and about universities more generally. By bringing these together with empirical studies drawn upon in Chapters 4 and 5 we seek not only to juxtapose the theoretical and the empirical but also to use them to illuminate and critique each other. The task of the book, and particularly of this final chapter which draws several threads together, is to conclude whether these theoretical perspectives provide insight from which may derive clearer understanding and better informed practice, and to ask what these insights imply.

The core of this quest, and all our work, is a clearer understanding of disjunctions between policy-making and practice. Disjunctions, in showing where and why access policies fail to deliver what is hoped for, may also cast doubt on the utility of top–down strategic planning. Also central to our study and conclusions is the importance of connections across the three levels of analysis – macro or national policy, meso or institutional policy and planning, and micro or grassroots behaviour, where the voices and testimony of students affirm, or give the lie to, policy protestations of the institution and, indeed, of the society and its governmental administration.

Ambitious as this venture now appears in a context of collaboration across languages, systems and geographical as well as, at times, wider conceptual and cultural difference, it was further enriched, and made more complicated, by rapid changes in the policy context and consequential operating environment of universities in the 1990s. In Britain, in particular, there has been remarkably swift transition from élite to mass HE with minimal change to the core purposes and curriculum of the British (especially the English) university and its honours degree system (see Parry's preface to Williams (ed.), 1997). The system shifted gear from rapid growth, constantly outrunning planning and funding projections, to the capping and ending of growth in the early 1990s, and a continuing necessity to 'do more with less'. Then came the period of the Dearing review of HE, which was overtaken in turn, and the Dearing report largely thrust aside, by the epochal change of national leadership from Majorite post-Thatcherism to a new form of radical conservatism under Blair's New Labour. Meanwhile, the discourse of 'lifelong learning' shot from obscurity into prominence. Created and all but forgotten a quarter century before, it became the faddish expression in every speech and policy pronouncement (also 1996 was the European Year of Lifelong Learning), then in turn attracting critical scrutiny from the academic community as to its real meaning and implications.

We believe the deliberations and the conclusions of this study to be relatively timeless. However, in times of politicization and rapid transformation of the object of study there is a temptation to trade the position of scholar for that of journalist, and to write the kind of commentary on current affairs which dates rapidly. We believe, in taking account of policy changes and consequent uncertainty to inform our analysis, that we have nevertheless succeeded in addressing the more abiding and essential dynamics and dialectics of the university in its society, especially from an access perspective. The conclusions, if not timeless, since all such issues of policy and practice are necessarily context-specific, are widely sustainable as well as applicable to actual, highly specific and diverse institutional situations. The circumstances and behaviour of each university and its subsidiary systems are particular and unique. However, the broad cultural, political and economic context is generally shared, and the organizational behaviours display strong patterns of familiarity.

In short, this book is anchored in the behaviours and activities of two particular institutions in two particular countries, but the propositions deriving from these studies have broader currency. It is for the reader to judge whether the connections between 'adultification' and organization theory come together clearly enough. Are the specificities of Louvain and Warwick able to sustain but not be obscured by the universalities which have also been explored and proposed? Do the comparative dimensions and the empirical materials adequately protect against any charge of unfounded abstraction? It is proper, too, to ask critically whether, despite reference to high theory, the authors have succeeded in distancing themselves from their particular and possibly parochial adult education traditions so as to embrace the diversity of traditions, missions, histories and futures which comprise the modern university spectrum.

More importantly, does personal ideological commitment interfere with a capacity to study and discern? Or, if this appears unproblematic, do we, on the other hand, fall into the sterile pit of neutered scientistic 'objectivity' and lose the point of the study along with our passion for equity? Another possibility: are those old-fashioned modernists who still believe in the 'enlightenment project' now to be found only among our older and early retired readers? If the rest of the world is now agnostically and pluralistically postmodern, are we too dated in our ill-disguised, surviving commitment to access and equity – a passion but lightly masked?

Finally, for the practitioner, policy-maker, manager or chalk-face working tutor, is it all worth the effort anyway? One reader-reviewer asked about outcomes: whether the mature-age student coming to HE later in life has comparable or reasonable access to the labour market. If not, does access to HE have much real point and purpose, it is asked, however open and effective may be the adult admission process, and however congenial the subsequent learning process and student experience? No less important, our interest in adults and access was and should be questioned from a wide and lifelong perspective: what about class, gender and ethnicity for example? 'Access does not equal adults.' Many young people are categorically excluded from social and educational opportunity. Are we looking in the wrong place, wrestling with a gate after the horse has bolted? If, indeed, learners are born and not made by educational participation, as one recent research study claims, this suggests that policy-makers should concentrate on reducing inequalities in society rather than encourage adults' learning (Jarvis, 1998).

These, then, were the challenges with which we were confronted when we decided to go ahead with this collaborative writing project. In this final chapter we attempt to answer each of these questions and reservations in ways which, at the least, will in turn confront, challenge and, with good fortune, positively energize those readers who have persevered thus far and who, like us, wish to bring together the experiential with the theoretical, practice with policy, and aspiration with outcome.

Is there an 'essential university'?

Why is the access of 'non-traditional students', young and especially adult, such contested ground?

The idea and ideal of 'the university' is itself contested. Some models are defended loyally and not without self-interest. The university as an abstraction is also sharply criticized and sometimes vigorously attacked by government, the media and other stakeholder interests as being self-seeking and non-responsive to outside needs.

Research and teaching remain core university functions; that is, the creation and dissemination of knowledge. Onto these explicitly avowed purposes are added other functions, made more complicated as universities have grown in number and variety, and the university and HE sector has grown in total size and cost. The processes of social selection generally, and selection for particular high-status positions in society, are long established. Preparation as well as selection for high-status professions is also well-known and familiar, as is the reproduction of social class and status. Universities are more often attacked than commended for their part in the hegemonic process of reproduction.

However, universities also recruit talent from other social strata so that modern complex society can be stocked with people able to perform its many and different tasks. Preparation for a technologically and organizationally more complex society has thus been added to the core functions of the university. Demand for high-level skills and understandings across more and more diverse specializations has grown. Enabling access for bright individuals from lower social strata outside the traditional ruling élites added on and brought together new sociological as well as economic functions on the part of the modern university. In the process, at different times and rates in different societies, initial rates of participation (the APR or age participation rate) have risen. Also, more people of ability who by virtue of their particular age and cohort missed out on this process of rising APR found their way back into HE, whether full- or part-time, with the prospect of entering some professional or other better-paid and higher-status employment later in life. These processes and functions explain as well as describe the well-nigh universal change from élite to mass HE.

It is not surprising as the HE sector has so greatly expanded, and the social and economic expectations placed upon it as well as its sociological functions so greatly diversified, that the sector itself should diversify. Hierarchies and league tables are natural, whether open to continuous easy change or relatively fixed in character. From the perspective of access, whether of the young or of older students from or as traditionally excluded categories, the question then becomes one of access to which parts of HE, as well as on what terms and with what results. Our studies have shown the importance of this question within universities – access of adults to which faculties and disciplines – and its intersection with analyses of universities in terms of their internal cultures and characterizations (Chapters 3 and 6).

The meaning of the term university has been extended beyond recognition of Newman's oft-cited 'idea of a university', even though the university curriculum and most institutional behaviours have thus far proved remarkably resilient and often quite resistant to change in the face of other changes. As proportions of a third and approaching half the population graduating from school go on to university, 'going to university' (or 'college' in American terms) becomes a normal progression and a feature of social participation. Not only does this greatly increase the total cost of the sector, resulting in redistribution of costs away from public revenue to the individual as 'consumer', it also makes impossible the exclusivity and near-certain access to high-status positions and employment which went along with traditional participation in a small exclusive system.

This places new pressures on universities. A strategic response, amplifying older competitive tendencies, is to differentiate themselves to their respective advantage, such that some can continue to secure more privileged outcomes for their graduates. Moreover, the level of graduate employment has become an important public indicator of an institution's standing. Depending on its philosophical persuasion, the government at macro or system level may direct or induce the (re)differentiation of institutions between a high-status best-resourced 'international' group and the mass providers. Hence in different countries there are distinctions such as university and non-university sectors; research and 'teaching(-only)' groups of institutions; ivy or sandstone and regional leagues. Within the university, at micro level, there may be an equally fierce contest for rank and status (together with resources). At the level of institutional management (meso level) leaderships may decide to concentrate or to diversify the character and mission of the university as a whole. Warwick, for instance, through a process of continuing internal dialogue, has thus far chosen to sustain a broad community service mission alongside its mission of international research excellence.

From the point of view of access, then, it is clearly not enough to ask how open the 'HE system' is to adult or other non-traditional students. There is also the question 'access to what?' To which parts of a complex and still diversifying system do different groups of the traditionally excluded now gain access? And what is the market-value of the degree thus obtained? New information and learning technologies add to the uncertainty and sharpen the question: will traditionally excluded categories gain access only to do-it-yourself degrees at virtual universities, while the slightly better-placed get an increasingly self-directed part-time experience at a local university, and the well-positioned still enjoy the richer learning experience of full-time and maybe residential campus life? Equitable access to HE in the interest of social inclusion may prove an ever-receding target, as system differentiation cedes the name university but not the substance of the university experience and its benefits to newcomers. In Britain the Open University won credence over time, but in 1998 the 'University for Industry' faced a similar question. As the University of the Third Age (U3A) continues and private and company-owned universities spring up, the quest for full access and participation may become more and more confused by the postmodernist confusion which surrounds the meaning and the 'idea' of the contemporary 'university'.

Pause and reflect on the historic meanings and values embedded in 'adult education'; the later more affluent meaning often ascribed to its successor (professional) continuing education; and the new contest over the nature and real meaning of lifelong learning. This reminds us not only of an almost bi-polar dichotomy between underprivileged (first-time second-chance) adults and privileged (upgrading, updating culturally and economically advantaged) adults which this study recognized empirically, but also of the uselessness of campaigning for adults' access without being clear about which adults, and which places and opportunities for learning. If it is access to meanly resourced and essentially self-directed opportunities leading, after high attrition, to degrees of no market-value, then both the idea and the function of Newman's university has eluded the 'access community'.

Social exclusion and the university

Is there, then, an 'essential university'? If there is, how much does it have to do with the needs and wants of socially excluded categories and classes of people? Historically these have included women, and they still do to a probably diminishing extent in terms of certain areas of disciplinary study and practice. They continue to include the working classes, albeit a diminishing sector in any highly technical and increasingly electronically (IT) driven knowledge society. They include diverse minority ethnic groups, indigenous, refugee and other migratory and immigrant, as well as other historically repressed and socially marginalized groups, from country to country.

They also include an emergent 'underclass' produced in industrial societies by a new economic world order from the late 1970s, apparently recruiting from right across the old social spectrum. The new ambiguity of role and uncertainty in respect of employment, especially of young males, has made this a new source of community and political concern, related also to resurgent racism in many societies. Hence the appearance of 'social exclusion' on the European Community and many national agendas. To this can be added another new insecurity in the form of executive redundancy, and a new debate about the disappearance of the 'job for life'. The extent of this labour-market change is being challenged: it is possible that it will prove to be more a psychological than an objective, statistically demonstrable and sustained labour-market phenomenon, despite trends favouring casualization, 'outsourcing' and 'home-working'. Either way, it adds a new category of disadvantage to the long list known in the 'access community': the well-qualified, middle-class newly unemployed.

Does this really have much to do with the traditional university and access thereto? Is the essential university prescribed and described in terms of an essential (liberal) curriculum and learning environment? How widely may this be replaced by a more modern core curriculum prescribed through competencies for employment? If so, how far along the typological spectrum of 'universities' do the traditional and the modern respectively extend? Will there somehow be a synthesis between these two orientations, or will they divide HE into two largely discrete sectors – possibly three if a hybrid model emerges between the strictly liberal and the functional or vocational? Access to what?

Maybe the essential question, in times of liberal economics rather than liberal politics, is one of access to relatively secure and remunerative later employment, in a world where the 'professions' have multiplied and become more varied and less exclusive and the MBA a normal ticket to mid-career graduate employment and advancement. From a student (client or consumer) perspective, is it now a matter of pragmatic economics rather than pedagogical and social principle? Here are some of the reasons why we listened with keen interest, in our research, to the voices of non-traditional adult students and their immediate tutors. Is there in addition to the economic imperative also a search for social inclusion, in terms of personal development and access to 'cultural capital'?

If so, non-traditional students clamouring at the door represent no innate threat to an established university ideal. If, however, the quest is above all for reliable and good employment, then the implications are different. In a world of global economics, a shorter half-life to much knowledge, and high systemic unemployment and insecurity, expectations placed upon the university may be unattainable, its mission impossible for many of the more conventional, let alone its new non-traditional, students. The essential university may have to recede into the research laboratory and back to a more monastic tradition. In order to survive as an enclave in the mass system it may also need increasingly to go private in those systems where public universities are the norm, and attempt thereby to sustain a high-status niche position where exclusivity within HE continues to secure both institutional prestige and high-status employment for graduates from this part of the sector.

If the university system evolves in this way, the access movement of the future will still wish to monitor who gets in where. However, its agenda may become less ambitious, albeit yet more complicated, if there is acceptance that the more pure or 'liberal' recesses of a mass/universal HE system may not be those that the socially disadvantaged job-hungry expect, want or try to reach. On the other hand, to the extent that the excluded seek full social inclusion and cultural participation, these privileged and maybe more esoteric zones will remain the ultimate test and challenge, whether or not they manage to secure the privileged labour-market niche and associated social cachet that without question vice-chancellors and university councils in such institutions are playing for. So long as there are bastions of privilege, it is also unlikely that the more radical proponents of an equity agenda will wish to ignore them. So social exclusion and the disturbing new phenomenon of widening inequalities provide new energy and new challenges for those concerned about access to HE, irrespective of the direct relationship between new phenomena and old equations.

The changing world of employment, globalization and world economic perturbations impacting on local economies, along with an older debate about the impact of micro-electronics on labour-market needs, systemic unemployment and the 'leisure society', thus provides a further level or wrapping of uncertainty around access and the modern university. This is quite apart from the transformations, and continuities, within the system itself. It is unclear where globalization is taking universities and the world they inhabit, although we may be confident that universities will continue to reflect, be partly determined by, and try to adapt in order to survive in, this changing environment.

It also seems probable that the new social instability represented by an 'underclass' will keep social exclusion on the public agenda. It will reinvigorate arguments about the social functions of universities and about access to them. If awareness of 'cultural capital' continues to grow, as late 1990s professional literature suggests it will, then consideration of the relationship between the university, access, and education for social participation as well as employment will become more prominent and better focused.

It is not our task to speculate further about these alternative social futures or to suggest which large scenario will come to pass. However, as we return to the policies, processes and inner life of the university, we acknowledge that any conclusion for the future behaviour of universities in respect of access will be contingent upon the changing external context as well as these resilient internal dynamics. Within this environment universities will go on developing policy and modifying practice. The environment will set parameters and constraints. Within it there will remain room to manoeuvre and to exercise leadership and discretionary judgement. Universities through their managements will try to calculate, adapt and respond in order to survive.

Wider participation and purposeful change

For some institutions the judgement will be to restrict intake and concentrate identity and purposes, rather than to widen access. Within such universities there may be disciplinary areas, units, groups and individuals who would prefer to move the institution in a different direction. Conversely, a sense of mission and an instinct for survival may persuade a university to become a much wider – even an open – access institution. Again, there will most likely be tribes, sub-cultures and individuals who strongly object to this tendency and, whether openly or covertly, will subvert, delay or if possible ignore policy changes in such direction.

Conceivably there might be institutions where there is unanimity of purpose from the supreme governing body through executive and lower level managements, embracing every scholar and functionary to the lowest level of tutor or clerk. Here, policy and practice are owned and shared throughout the university. Theoretically a highly authoritarian, or more likely a highly participatory, form of management might achieve such a condition. In our experience, however, this is a strictly theoretical proposition, a purely hypothetical, ideal institutional type. Our empirical studies as well as our professional experience point to the actual impossibility of attaining such unanimity in any known university in the broad Western tradition. The logic of our organization theory also suggests the impossibility of attaining such a pure type. (The qualification 'Western tradition' is needed since the name 'university' can now be attached to quite different and alien forms of organizational life and legal form in Western as well as other societies.)

A further logical possibility is that a university may, either deliberately from belief in its character as a university community of peers or collegium and in the impropriety of having any such thing as leadership or a strategy, or on the other hand through neglectful oversight and what is usually called an ivory tower attitude, simply not have a policy and a strategy for changing or moving anywhere. Such institutions probably no longer exist in anything like pure form, though traces and legacies abound and they can be clearly recalled from recent times. The pressures for change and accountability in the expanded, visible mass system draw all universities into scrutiny and make such quiescence well-nigh impossible. Increasingly, a condition of attracting even reduced public subvention, and of avoiding direct interference from public authorities, is a kind of transparency at least of purpose, which takes the form of mission statements and strategies, business plans and audits of quality (teaching and research), and efficiency in the use of human and material resources including space, time, human and physical assets.

In practice there is no hiding place. Attempts to hide are likely to attract greater intrusion so that the practice of transparency as well as the adoption of politically acceptable discourse becomes normal and universal. The language of enterprise and the market, of efficiencies and economies, total quality, of inputs, throughput and output, trading balances, reserves, return on investment, opportunity cost, benchmarking, best practice and world-class, has invaded official discourse. Access and lifelong learning, at least as a means of utilizing rather than wasting 'human resources' and economic potential, find a place in this newer discourse, as well as in the older access, equity and adult education communities and value systems.

As this study has repeatedly shown, however, there remain worlds of discourse, subterranean tribes of academe as well as different cultures and customs within administration, beyond the direct reach of political scrutiny and the public eye. Periodic attempts by unsympathetic political admin-istrations to extirpate offensively radical sub-cultures among faculty and students are commonly frustrated. What seemed clear becomes fuzzy, black and white become grey. Usually the intervention (into a suspect faculty or a student union) runs out of energy and the intrusion withers away.

Similarly within, the capacity to absorb and deflect energy directed at inter-fering and bringing about changes imposed from outside is also available to turn or blunt policies designed to change practice from within the institution. Policy-making does not equal practice. We have seen many examples of absorption of energy and partial subversion of the intention of institutional, or meso-level, policies in the field of access. There are, then, very large steps to take between willing wider participation in HE as a matter of national policy in a ministry of education or a funding council, and seeing it actually happen in the law or biology school of a particular institution.

Purposeful change towards wider participation by changing the rules and practices of access, and by changing the behaviour of the university to those 'non-traditional' students whom it has admitted, will remain a policy plat-form in most societies for well-rehearsed economic, demographic, political and sociocultural reasons – reasons spelt out by the European community and before that by Unesco, OECD, the Council of Europe and national governments from Sweden and the former Soviet Union spreading south and west. The pressures from above and below will increase. Greater uncertainty about the global economy and the labour market, including the sense (at least) of the impermanence of any particular job or form of employment, and the greater mobility of labour across sectors and geographical regions, press towards ever higher rates of participation in HE. Graduate unemploy-ment seems unlikely ever to be so serious as to turn young school-leavers of modest ability and aspiration away from HE in any abiding sense. Pro-gression to HE will continue to become an encompassing middle-class norm. The decline of a blue-collar class to virtual extinction and the perception of labour-market disadvantage without a degree will encourage high rates of initial and later life second-chance HE. The issue will not be about rising rates of demand and participation, but about how these are funded: HE at what price through what paying mechanism for what kind of university experience.

Our meso- and micro-level studies of institutional and individual behavi-our at Louvain and Warwick, and applications of the theoretical insights as exercised in Chapters 3 and 6, conspire to suggest that a successful campaign to widen participation through purposeful change will need to be sustained, multi-pronged and multi-level. It will require continuous vigilance and renewal; there are institutional dynamics and tendencies which recur and reproduce themselves like new strains of the 'flu virus as fast as one is extirpated. National lobbying and well-rehearsed, well-informed arguments about the labour market, technological change and the obsolescence of knowledge and skills, statistical analyses and research reports which reach policy levels and the media, all have a part to play. Winning the minds of power-brokers (as on the face of it was achieved in the UK with the 1997 General Election) is important; but, as the UK experience within months of the change of political power again showed, this will almost certainly soon prove disappointing.

Even where policy is changed decisively and sweepingly – an unlikely prospect except towards free-market cost-shifting in times of contracting welfare politics – we have shown in this study how long and tenuous is the link to the experience of the FOPES or 2 + 2 student starting a programme as a non-traditional student; how hard it is, indeed, to start at all in many of the faculties at Louvain and departments at Warwick, for all the institutional rhetoric of access. The devil, it is said, is in the detail. For the wider access movement to see results there is a need at institutional level for the general statements of purpose about access to translate into resource terms. Incentives, rewards and penalties are needed for performance and under-performance according to clear, closely monitored criteria. University administrations require persistence, vigilance, and the capability to intrude into the tribal preserves of departments, schools and faculties where older ways persist, insulated from policy and the immediate outside environment. Not all administrators and administrations have the will, wit and courage for this. Nor do the theories of management imported from other sectors necessarily appear to favour such interventionism either.

Indeed, there is the need at this critical meso- or institutional-level of management for sociological awareness, an instinct and a sensitivity to the particular character of universities as probed by Baldridge, Bourdieu and others, and to the importance of interactivities and subjectivities as explored by Goffman and Becker, if institutional commitments to the widening of access are to be carried into effect. In reality it will be through a combination of political levering, persuasive pressure, rewards and penalties, and above all purposeful, albeit often covert, inducement of cultural change and change of values, priorities and attitudes, that the gap between access policies (easy and probable) and institution-wide and deep implementation (almost unattainably hard) will be narrowed. There are many bolt-holes to be blocked off; many stratagems to be countered in changing practices and creating a culture of openness and acceptance of the unfamiliar. This may mean welcoming students who are different by virtue of age, cultural orientation, linguistic and ethnic identity, and even, still, in terms of gender and certainly social class, in all the far reaches of the culturally diverse modern university.

One bolt-hole in particular will prove exceedingly hard to block up. Several interests combine to keep it open and it is clearly functional from a particular political and sociological perspective. This is the proposition favouring institutional diversity. HE serves to select, train, socialize for and reproduce an élite or meritocracy, and to enable society and employers to determine who gets which jobs and related social positions. The need for discrimination, in this functional rather than any pejorative ideological sense, is if anything stronger in modern complex societies. The competition for favoured positions becomes keener as unemployment persists and graduate numbers continue to rise. Meanwhile, the total cost of an expanding, publicly funded system rises and is capped by government. Old, high-status and privileged universities whose graduates include society's leaders, meanwhile protest the relative decline of resources. The shroud of national non-competitiveness is waived as research funds, in particular, are spread more thinly, or appear under threat of so being dispersed.

These factors, as well as the natural competitiveness of parents for their young, and of academics to protect established territory and habits, come together in unplanned support of diversification in HE. Any such institutional specialization is all but inevitably hierarchical. In Britain in the late 1980s it was tentatively proposed but not pressed, as R (research-only) X (mixed) and T (teaching-only) universities. In countries like Australia, which abolished the 'binary divide' within HE, there is talk of reintroducing binarism under another guise. Similarly with the distinction between university and non-university HE, and between higher and further education (noting too the complication of HE within FE) the same issues, the same temptations to stress difference and foster hierarchy, arise.

In short, purposeful change to bring about wider participation in HE can be achieved by the sleight of hand (as some would see it) or sensible rationalization (according to others) of differentiating institutions by mission, activities and resourcing. If resourcing at the highest levels of status within the HE system becomes private or partly private, the status differential may further widen, as it has in other sectors such as medicine, legal services and housing. Widening access – and this applies similarly to young and older non-traditional students – may thus occur in the system as a whole, but the most prestigious venues will become no more, and probably less, accessible. One indicator is the sensitivity of the most prestigious universities such as 'Oxbridge' to their proportions of private school admissions.

The middle-class selective, finishing school function of the UK tradition may be reaffirmed as most students under a new financial regime come to follow their Continental and Scottish counterparts in going to the local 'day' university and working part-time to pay their way, while the more privileged few go away into residence in a traditional university. Here their fellow-students and prospective friends (and future fellow power-brokers) for life will be the more wealthy, or upper-middle class, international students who can also afford to be sent away to study. The social reproduction of a governing élite which universities have traditionally effected at least from the nineteenth century may thus be translated to the international stage, in symmetry with the new global economy. Participation in HE would be increased and in one new sense widened thereby, although participation across the social spectrum may or may not change very much. The age cohort entering HE will meanwhile continue to rise, along with adult participation in HE. The character of this access will, however, then be more selective and exclusive. The proponents of wider access may see themselves as having won a battle but lost a war.

This is a reasonable rather than paranoid interpretation of several trends and tendencies. Such an outcome would be regarded by many stakeholders, though possibly not by readers of this volume in our culturally differentiated societies, as entirely sensible and desirable, to judge by the ease with which widening income, wealth and related social inequities have been accepted throughout the 1980s and 1990s worldwide, within and between societies. Such a scenario might even assist the inclusion of more of the quite poor and some of the very poor in the mainstream society and its culture, loosely understood, and may nurture the wider acquisition of cultural capital over two generations rather than one.

Rather than speculate further about these wider social matters, let us turn again to the character and inner life of the university itself.

Does 'adultification' change the university?

In some obvious senses the university is changed as adults come to constitute a rising proportion, now commonly more than 50 per cent, of an institution's total student population. This demographic reality flows on into many other features of its character and behaviour. These include the places from which and the means whereby older students are recruited, compared with school-leavers, and their relationship to the paid work-force to which many have belonged and of which they may as part-time students continue to be a part. The crude data can, however, mislead. In absolute numbers older students may outweigh those straight from school, even including those who have taken a break, perhaps enjoying a 'gap year' between school and further study to travel or earn money prior to studying again. If adult or continuing education students are included, the total number of older students may exceed that of full-time undergraduates by a factor of several. If, however, the full-time equivalent student load is calculated, the numerical advantage may disappear. Traditional young students studying for a first degree, or an initial graduate degree, may still constitute the majority in terms of load.

It is, however, not only or principally an objective matter. The young full-time undergraduate student may remain the archetype or model student around which the university's life gravitates even where they have become a minority. What is the extent of and the conditions for perpetuating this perceptual lag and behavioural inertia after the demographic change has occurred? When we ask whether 'adultification' changes the university we have to treat the question in several senses. Has it already done so? Yes demographically, but maybe not behaviourally and in self-concept? Will it come to do so as the force of inertia is exhausted and other forces for change are added to this fact of a new internal demography? How does it produce change? Through deliberate will, and by acts of policy? By evolving barely conscious changes of attitude and practices on the part of administrators and faculty? Or through the needs and purposes, by conscious acts and activities at microcosmic grassroots level, of individual students and their tutors?

Approached thus, it is easy to see why people contest the existence and extent of change in the modern university. Those of more conservative inclination may regret the changes. They warn of a decline in standards, the end of liberalism and free thought, the debasement of the university towards competency training. Some of reform persuasion regret how little the social intake and the social functions of the university have altered, how little the curriculum and degree structures have altered; how the resilient is the traditional university to avoid change, its capacity to bend without breaking. Is the bottle half full or half empty?

Most important, given the values-based nature of the university and the entrenchment of professional identities within and across disciplines which we have examined, a belief that things have, or have not, significantly changed becomes a major 'objective' factor in itself. If enough members of the academic community believe that significant change has taken place or is occurring, this becomes an important element. Specifically, a university may fill up with adults taking first and higher degrees as well as general or professional short courses, while the sense of the institution on the part of its more permanent members (faculty and administrative) continues undisturbed. The essential culture is unaltered and the dissonance which this produces in terms of attuning to the new clienteles is managed by ignoring the contradiction, or by treating new kinds of student in much the same way as the more familiar kinds of student have always been treated.

If, on the other hand, a new definition of the university takes root, either by governmental fiat or by a successfully promulgated institutional redefinition of identity and mission, then the staff of the university may compete to be first to adopt the new character and behaviour. More fundamental change may occur, subjectively instituted. One can cite examples where a reforming government signals an inclination. Some institutions excel in conforming, even exceeding, government intention and expectation. Others carry on, with little beyond token acknowledgement of the political event. Of course, an institution the leadership or membership of which is already aspiring to move in this direction may seize on the external change to catalyse and justify action. It needs an analysis of the receiving condition in each institution to understand why such events precipitate large responses in one place and tokenism in another. Recent examples include pressures and incentives to move faster into distant, self-directed and multimedia 'teaching delivery'; demands to behave in a more transparently efficient managerialist mode;

and in Australia the initiative by Minister Dawkins in the later 1980s to create a National Unified System which led to more and more ambitious mergers than the minister had expected or intended

Evidently 'adultification' as a form of institution change requires decomposing into its dimensions of subjectivity and objectivity; and into different aspects of the university and its behaviour throughout all aspects of its life: curriculum, assessment, teaching methods, learning environment and learning styles, as well as such characteristics as the attitudes, aptitudes and aspirations of its students. It is as much a matter of internal culture as one of demography. Nor is it restricted to students. Note the 'greying of the campus' in terms of academic staff in many places, and the concern to reshape this demography. In such cases rectors and vice-chancellors seek to remove the middle- and later middle-age bulge created by the expansion of the 1960s and 1970s, early-retire older staff and recruit novitiates through 'new blood' schemes such as the Warwick Research Fellowship scheme of the early 1990s.

Academic communities differ in age composition and consequently in culture and behaviour. Some are both older and all-age, although the institution may be young. An institution comprising predominantly very young adults in short-term full-time membership, for whom being a student is the overwhelmingly dominant social identity (whether the orientation by sporting or recreational, academic or cultural, or political in the mode of the late 1960s–early 1970s and *Les Miserables*) is very different from one in which most students also carry one or more other significant social identities (parent, carer, partner, paid worker, voluntary community leader). Here ages range from under twenty to over sixty; and the campus – assuming it is used at all, for not all students are on campus as universities become more 'open' if not 'virtual' – is only one significant location in life rather than the dominant one. Looking at people around some campuses, it is hard to know by casual observation which are the professors and which their students. In such universities, faculty no longer have the monopoly of either age or wisdom, though they continue to exercise authority as experts and assessors. In some universities, adultification has transformed most aspects of the university and its life. In others, the changes, even when demographically and statistically significant, have effected little if any cultural penetration. On the other hand, we may hypothesize, and the work reported in this book tends to support this, that where there has been no internal cultural transformation adults continue either not to gain entry as students at all, or where they do are made to adapt, to hide or suppress their difference, and probably to feel uncomfortable and unwanted.

As students, adults do change universities but there is no universal rule to this effect, and no guarantee of adaptation across schools and disciplines. We have shown *a priori* as well as empirically how differently disciplinary cultures and identities respond to new kinds of student. Our experience and studies also show, however, that in those fields where there is an in-principle orientation and willingness, or indeed a market necessity, to admit non-traditional adult students, the experience of such students is commonly highly favourable. They can quickly change the learning environment and the transactional culture of the seminar room. At least this opens the way for easier entry of subsequent adult cohorts; at best it may be transformational.

Change of this kind is unplanned and spontaneous, rather than a product of deliberate and direct intervention from the top of the university. This is not to say that it cannot enter into the calculations of administrators seeking to engineer a change of attitude to older (or other non-traditional) students, recognizing that such students may be their own best advocates. It is a common experience of adult educators and access personnel that departments become favourably inclined to a more mixed and older clientele, to 'adultification', on the basis of first-hand experience, as this study once again shows. This is not to deny that there is a mix of responses. Some adults are found to be too dominating and demanding. Some tutors feel themselves and their students cowed by a combination of life-experience and idiosyncrasy.

On balance, we conclude that one simple and clever way to foster a change of attitude towards adult students is simply to get them into the classroom. In practice it is a little less simple. Judgement about how far to go, how non-traditional to be, what risks to take, also enter into it. The result of such caution is summarized in the criticism that participation is increased, but not widened in sociocultural terms. A stronger approach is to seek to identify and recruit by focused positive action prospective students from the more marginalized and excluded communities, but also to prepare them and their receiving departments, by means of study skills and other orientation, and also by staff workshops, so that it is not just left to chance. This kind of chalk-face level planning characterizes more sophisticated approaches to access and return-to-learn, and informs the more advanced and thought-through strategies for adultification through micro-change. In principle this might also apply to students drawn at school-leaving age from the communities of the excluded. In practice the addition of maturation and some life-experience is seen as an important assurance, though not a complete guarantee, that the non-traditional will have the attitudes, qualities and motivations to overcome family, community and earlier educational deficits as seen from the perspective of the middle-class high school graduate moving almost effortlessly and naturally on to university.

Such gradualistic, experiential, 'bottom–up' change may be too slow to satisfy many people. It may also not be sufficiently cross-infectious. We have seen how well some academic disciplines are buffered by their identities, their standing and wider connections from peer influence at department or faculty level. The traditional (mythological?) collegial university is a non-hierarchical, non-directive, quasi-anarchic collectivity. Within there are distinct cultures and enclaves, the stronger aligned with socially privileged and/or high-income professions and other occupations (medicine, law, business, accountancy) in the world outside. Traditional status and market strength can both be used to resist pressures from the policy and strategy level of the institution, as well as from outside it, to change the purpose, character and behaviour of the institution. Pressure for change can come from government, loosely representing the broader community; from the media, also a very approximate *vox populis*; and from philosophically inspired (or, if you disagree with them, 'ideologically driven') groups who demand greater access on grounds of democracy, equity and, increasingly in the more economistic 1980s, efficient use and development of 'human resources'. It may result in a revision of mission statements to encompass access, equity, and most recently lifelong learning. (Mission statements are themselves a manifestation of new managerialism responding to the new intrusiveness that has followed the massive expansion of HE to become a big public-sector industry.) It may not, however, follow naturally, or with any logic derived from organizational dynamics, that adults will find their way into schools of, for example, physics or medicine.

We have several times noted another strategy for massifying HE and expanding access without changing the university heartland. Not only is there *de facto* internal differentiation of mission and response to demand manifested in disciplinary diversity within the one institution, it is in fact possible to encompass a very wide mission span without putting at risk the élite world-class brand image, as Warwick well displays. At meso level it can be an intelligent and successful strategy to differentiate internally, thereby playing to and satisfying the often diverse, ill-considered and mutually contradictory claims of government and the general community. Such a stratagem does not, however, satisfy the assiduous access proponent who has breadth of vision and ambition – who wants to see women in engineering, blue-collar workers becoming doctors, and outcast ethnic minorities (gypsies or Turks, Aborigines or Bosnian refugees) studying and remaking philosophy, literature and cultural studies as well as getting the MBA.

The other, macro-level response, another way to change without changing, is as we have seen to diversify at system level. Thus we have universities for adults (the Open University 30 years ago and the University for Industry most recently in the UK); mainly teaching (or new, or non-university) universities or HE institutions for the under-privileged, be they low school achievers or adult returners, where resources are scarcer and self-directed learning becomes perforce a valued innovation; and the well-established and better-resourced (international, world-class, élite, ivy league, or research) universities which celebrate excellence but in the process enjoy protection from the more disruptive aspects of massification.

The system may thus 'adultify' while the strongest quietly opt out, except where adultification is expressed as the further, advanced education of the highly qualified and well-privileged who add to their existing intellectual (and cultural) capital by means of advanced study and short courses – what a recent Australian report has called the 'profitable lifelong learning market' (Cunningham *et al.*, 1998). Thus adultification can be on a selective basis, bringing new private income which is attracted by quality, resources and prestige. There is, however, an inverse relationship with access, equity and social levelling, since these adults are not the disadvantaged but the highly educated who replenish the governing classes.

We cannot, therefore, assume that enrolling more adults necessarily changes the university. Adults can be enrolled, taught and granted credit without touching the core identity of the institution at all. Rather, they may underscore and strengthen its distinctiveness. Alternatively, adults may enter an institution but gain entry and win participation in significant numbers only in a few sociologically distinct, academically poorly established and socially low-status areas. Beyond if not within these areas, the adaptation will be all on one side: students must reshape themselves as square pegs in the prepared round holes. Their distinctive and unique qualities and life-experiences count as nothing. Worse, they are an impediment to be ignored or shoved away. Their very presence further lowers the status of an already low-status or marginal department and discipline.

On the other hand, adults may enter the institution in very large numbers, in the mainstream of its provision and not just on the periphery. In the process they change the total character, identity, public standing and internal culture of the institution, so that it becomes indeed a mature, all-age, normal rather than abnormal part of the wider community – less like an age-segregated school, more like the 'real world'. The crucial question for the future of HE may be the extent to which this more fundamental and total change of identity and state will spread from the less prestigious, mainly teaching, institutions to invade the heartland of traditional academe at system and institutional levels. Put it another way: what happens to 'the idea of a university' in the new era of lifelong learning which Europe entered in 1996?

The adult university in a learning society

A new discourse of lifelong learning was born recently. The earlier discourse originated in the late 1960s, mainly in Europe and through several European-based intergovernmental agencies. Significantly these included the Organisation for *Economic* Co-operation and Development which has done as much as any agency to promote analysis of the changing role of education including HE, in late advanced and post-industrial times of 'late modernity'. Interest had been lost in lifelong learning (together with recurrent education, *education permanente* and the learning society) during the 1970s outside a small group of scholars and lobbyists, until the 1990s. The vision of the Faure report faded. There were pressing concerns over the new economic realities as the oil crisis was followed by the unknown instabilities of 'globalization'. The new lifelong learning combines old and abiding concerns about equity, with emphasis upon HE as a means to equip for employment and for survival in conditions of uncertainty and loss of security in employment. Still more recently, scepticism has grown about official and political adoption of lifelong learning which, as the 1990s draw to a close, has become the official flavour of the decade. Following the European Year of Lifelong Learning, and publication of the Delors (1996) report as Faure's (1972) successor, Taiwan for example declared 1998 its Year of Lifelong Learning.

If lifelong learning is established as desirable and essential, the 'learning society', and at a lower level (what we have called the meso below the macro level) the 'learning organization' has also found its way into a burgeoning literature, especially of management. These terms have not been well articulated and it is little wonder that they are contested, hence, in part, the scholarly debate, underpinned by research groups in several countries, which is now growing up to 'unpack' and critique especially lifelong learning, often from quite traditional broadly sociological perspectives. Even so, most critics accept a reduced understanding of the learning society or organization in concentrating on equity and access policies and opportunities at individual and group levels.

The larger sense of a society or organization with the inbuilt capability to learn and adapt *its* behaviour (not merely the learning and life-chances of its individual members) slips away. Yet it is just this wider sense of the learning and adaptive organization – how an institution manages or subverts needs and pressures for change – which sits at the heart of the larger learning society concept and of this study. How far can strategic management – whether based in a vision and sense of mission or in a political survival instinct – exercise political means within the university to overcome deep cultural features and dynamics favouring continuity and conservatism at sub-system levels, which tend to restrict or frustrate attempts to change the university through 'leadership'?

It is not easy to stand back from the detail and discern what really matters. What are the big issues behind the clatter and buzz of daily discourse and piecemeal administration? We are not alone in considering social exclusion to be a major and long-term issue – for universities as their collective scale expands, as well as for society with its concerns about an underclass and weakening social fabric. Jarvis has recently suggested that the real battle is about the creeping semi-privatization of universities and its effect of excluding the poor and those of low aspiration from participating in the wider society. We have moved far beyond the old separatist 'extra-mural' and compensatory agenda of earlier adult education, but the future direction is less clear. It was being said in nominally egalitarian Australia in 1998 that university education is now beyond the financial reach of the poor, despite the deferred (HECS) mode of payment. Of the two broad types of adult in HE there is the prospect that the 'lucrative lifelong learning market' will expand and finance more universities as the state rolls back its support, but the kind of adult under study in this book, the educationally disadvantaged and socially excluded, will see at least the 'real university' recede further.

This perspective offers a sharp salient from which to critique the information technology-based 'virtual university' which has attracted the favour of governments seeking cost containment in HE. A negative scenario emerges from this perspective. It is of a marriage of 'lifelong' and 'virtual' as a response to the problems of resourcing mass HE in the early twenty-first century. Such a scenario would channel off much of the demand from adults for access to general HE into different kinds of new or quasi-universities. In this event, established universities might check and reverse the recruitment and admission of the non-traditional. Their burgeoning adult populations would then be increasingly restricted to the already highly educated and socially more advantaged. The fact of easy access to new or quasi-universities would further justify relying on a middle-class intake of young people to the 'real universities', on the grounds that

(a) other people can use other second-chance routes later in life when the will to succeed is there;
(b) it is not the job of (real) universities to remedy deficiencies and inequalities which reside deep in society and have not been remedied in the school system.

Without adopting this scenario we acknowledge where present tendencies may lead. In this scenario rising social exclusion, the despair and latent destruction of a persisting underclass, is none of universities' business, other than as an object of enquiry.

There are more optimistic alternatives. Our own preference places stress upon the capacity of individuals and groups, especially if their horizons are widened by some sense of history and sociology, to become actors in making their own and society's future. We value an understanding of organizational dynamics and of institutional capacity to sustain interests and subvert change; not to be deterministic and defeated by it, but the better to see where desirable influence and purpose can be exercised for wider common purpose while still recognizing and valuing inherited identities and qualities. A theme which runs all through this study, and is borne out even in the most 'objective' and statistical parts, is the importance of the subjective: the capacity to make the future by differently seeing and defining the present. The phenomenon was dramatically illustrated at the beginning of 1998 by the so-called Asian financial melt-down, when $200 bn of wealth was 'lost' without a factory or a farm having closed down. The fact of a crisis thus defined did then create real loss and promptly closed factories, farms and especially banks and finance houses.

Seeing the university as indeed an adult institution, peopled by students as well as staff of all ages, experiences, orientations and persuasions, changes actors' understanding of themselves, their roles and relationships, and of the nature of the university. From this can emerge a positive identity, a new sense of professional social purpose which changes the university in its role and actions as well as nominally. In this way universities – writing about which has been characterized for some years by terms like 'crisis' (Scott 1984 and later studies in this and other series) – also have the potential to regain a confident purpose, in societies themselves characterized as suffering from 'postmodern' ambiguity and drift, and a failure in economic direction.

From the early 1970s there has been a widely shared loss of confidence in what made universities special. First, it was thought they had lost their soul by being too close to the 'real world' (the academic–industrial–military complex). Student militancy in turn shook public confidence in what universities were about, and their utility. The propensity (especially by sociologists) to pronounce on public matters was deemed an impertinence exercised from the remoteness of an ivory tower. The research co-funded by industry was felt to be corrupting of academic independence. This makes the Gibbons *et al.* (1994) insight into new modes of knowledge production important. Finally, there was the threat of 'creeping corporatization' as the growth of the sector and its costs increased government interest and interference in management, budgets and even the curriculum. Collegiality was threatened by managerialism.

An adult university which is coterminous with and a microcosm of the 'real world' – if it is also both 'adult' and 'learning' in its being and behaviour, can spring free from this trap. By being less special it may again reassert its unique importance as one of the estates of the realm. Its stature may quickly grow in a knowledge society confused about its own destiny and management. The mature, adult university is a part of the world and is seen to be thus involved and immersed. Simultaneously it will be valued and supported for being somewhat apart from the short horizons and immediacies of daily discourse and politics.

Higher education may in this way win a more powerful and respected place as a counterbalance to other interest groups (economic, political, cultural). It may be seen to have a role analogous, for example, to the media and the judiciary at their best. Such a future, with adultification and greater assimilation or normalization, need not be a matter of high principle. It offers a pragmatic road to survival for an institution which again has the place and confidence to talk about the 'idea of a university'. At a lower but no less important level, the university may also become a leader in managing itself as a 'learning organization', nurturing new forms of collegiality and adaptive energy to be emulated in other sectors. Today it tends to pick up old 'how-to-manage' manuals and models which have been cast away by other sectors.

One further proposition, albeit speculative and subjective, is that universities will remain communities, places and events. They will not in general become just remotely accessed information sources – a job more efficiently done by the new forms of worldwide electronic data access. This is in effect what our student informants told us in our research, as reported in Chapter 4. The basis for such a proposition is slender, and trends can be cited to contradict it. However, we place confidence in the authority of our own databases, including collectively many years of working with older and non-traditional (as well as young and 'typical') university students in a number of societies.

This is at heart a tale of two universities. It uses a dipstick or deep slice approach. We have probed two cases, fully acknowledging the arbitrary nature of the selection. This, however, tells us more than can a purely theoretical or single-level policy study about the relationship between national levels of policy-making, the way institutions and their resident tribes behave, and what this means for the experience of students entering an alien and maybe not very hospitable environment.

We do not conclude that universities alone can transform society, overcoming social exclusion and inequality. They do, however, have a new and a continuing role to play in terms of access and social inclusion. Acts of purpose and will as well as shifts of perception are needed for this to occur. This road leads to a reaffirmed, strong and confident idea and role of the adult university of the twenty-first century. Other paths may seem tempting; but they lead to degradation and diminution of distinctiveness and pride for all but a few universities in the mass systems which the third millennium is to inherit.

References

Abrahamsson, K., Rubenson, K. and Slowey, M. (eds) (1988) *Adults in the Academy: International Trends in Adult and Higher Education.* Stockholm: Swedish Board of Education.

Abrahamsson, K. (1986) Adult participation in Swedish higher education. *Studies in Higher Education in Sweden,* No. 7. Stockholm: Almqvist and Wiksell International.

Acker, J. (1989) Making gender visible, in R. Wallace (ed.) *Feminism and Sociological Theory.* Beverley Hills, CA: Sage.

Ainley, P. (1994) *Degrees of Difference.* London: Lawrence and Wishart.

Baechler, J. (1978) *Le pouvoir pur.* Paris: Calmann-Levy.

Baldridge, J.V. (1971) *Power and Conflict in the University.* New York: J. Wiley.

Baldridge, J.V., Curtis, D.V., Ecker, G.P. and Riley, G.L. (1977) Alternative models of governance in higher education, in G.L. Riley, J.V. Baldridge (eds) *Governing Academic Organizations.* Berkeley, CA: McCutchan.

Barnett, R. (1988) Limits to academic freedom, in M. Tight (ed.) *Academic Freedom and Responsibility.* Milton Keynes: Open University Press.

Becher, T. (1981) Towards a definition of disciplinary cultures, *Studies in Higher Education,* 6: 109–22.

Becher, T. (1989) *Academic Tribes and Territories.* Buckingham: Society for Research into Higher Education/Open University Press.

Becher, T. and Kogan, M. (1980) *Process and Structure in Higher Education.* London: Heinemann.

Becker, H.S. (1971) Social class variations in the teacher–pupil relationship, in B. Cosin, I. Dale, G. Esland *et al.* (eds) *School and Society.* London: Routledge/Open University Press.

Becker, H.S. and Strauss, A. (1970) Careers, personality and adult socialization, in H.S. Becker, *Sociological Work.* Chicago: Aldine.

Becker, H.S., Geer, B., Strauss, A. and Hughes, E. (1961) *Boys in White: Student Culture in Medical School.* Chicago: University of Chicago Press.

Benn, R. (1995) Access and participation of adults in higher education in Austria, in P. Davies (ed.) *Adults in Higher Education: International Perspectives on Access and Participation.* London: Jessica Kingsley, pp. 38–60.

Berger, P. and Luckmann, T. (1966) *The Social Construction of Reality.* Harmondsworth: Penguin.

Biersted, R. (1950) An analysis of social power, *American Sociological Review,* 15.

Blau, P.M. (1964) *Exchange and Power in Social Life*. New York: J. Wiley.

Blaxter, L., Dodd, K. and Tight, M. (1996) Mature student markets: An institutional case study, *Higher Education*, 31, 2: 187–203.

Blume, S. (1985) After the darkest hour . . . integrity and engagement in the development of university research, in B. Wittrock and A. Elzinga (eds) *The University Research system*. Stockholm: Almqvist and Wiksell.

Blumer, H. (1964) Society as symbolic interaction, in A. Rose (ed.) *Human Behaviour and Social Processes*. Mifflin: Houghton.

Boudon, R. and Bourricaud, F. (1986) *Dictionnaire critique de la sociologie*. Paris: Presses Universitaires de France.

Bourdieu, P. (1984) *Homo Academicus*. Paris: Editions de Minuit.

Bourdieu, P. and de Saint Martin, M. (1978) Le patronat, *Actes de la recherche en Sciences Sociales*, 20–21: 3–82.

Bourgeois, E. (1990) University politics: adult education in a Belgian university. Unpublished PhD thesis, University of Chicago.

Bourgeois, E. (1991) Dependence, legitimation and power in academic decision-making, *Higher Education Policy*, 4 (4): 21–4.

Bourgeois, E. (1993) Organizational conditions and strategies for widening access to the university. A Belgian case study, *International Journal of University Adult Education*, 32 (1): 17–45.

Bourgeois, E., Duke, C., de Saint Georges, P., Guyot, J.-L. and Merrill, B. (1994) *Comparing Access Internationally. The Context of the Belgian and English Higher Education Systems*, working paper no. 13. Warwick: Continuing Education Research Centre Department of Continuing Education University of Warwick.

Bourgeois, E., Duke, C., Guyot, J.-L., Merrill, B., and de Saint Georges, P. (1995) *Admission; Provision and Adult Participation in Two Universities*, working paper no. 14. Warwick: Continuing Education Research Centre Department of Continuing Education University of Warwick.

Bourgeois, E. and Guyot, J.-L. (1995) Access and participation of adults in higher education in Belgium, in P. Davies (ed.) *Adults in Higher Education: International Perspectives on Access and Participation*. London: Jessica Kingsley, pp. 61–83.

Bourgeois, E. and Liénard, G. (1992) Developing adult education in universities: a political view, *Higher Education Management*, 4 (4): 80–90.

Bourgeois, E. and Nizet, J. (1993) Influence in academic decision making; towards a typology of strategies, *Higher Education*, 26 (4): 387–410.

Bourgeois, E. and Nizet, J. (1995) *Pression et légitimation*. Paris: Presses Universitaires de France.

Bourgeois, E. and Nizet, J. (1997) *Apprentissage et formation des adultes*. Paris: Presses Universitaires de France.

Bourner, T., Reynolds, A., Hamed, M. and Barnett, R. (1991) *Part-time Students and their Experience of Higher Education*. Buckingham: Open University Press/SRHE.

Brookfield, S. (1996) Breaking the code: engaging practitioners in critical analysis of adult education literature, in R. Edwards, A. Hanson and P. Raggatt (eds) *Boundaries of Adult Learning*. Open University/Routledge.

Brown, P. and Scase, R. (1995) *Higher Education and Corporate Realities: Class, Culture and the Decline of Graduate Careers*. London: UCL Press.

Bundesministerium für Wissenschaft und Forschung (1993) *Hochschul Bericht 1993: Band 1 Statistisches Porträt*. Vienna: BMWF.

Carp, A., Peterson, R. and Roelfs, P. (1976) Adult learning interests and experiences, in K.P. Cross and J.R. Valley (eds) *Planning Non-traditional Programs*. San Francisco: Jossey-Bass.

Cicourel, A.V. (1968) *The Social Organisation of Juvenile Justice*. New York: Wiley.
Cicourel, A.V. (1976) *The Social Organisation of Juvenile Justice*. London: Heinemann.
Cicourel, A.V. (1982) *Quantity and Quality in Social Research*. London: Routledge.
Clark, B.R. (1977) Faculty Organization and Authority, in G.L. Riley and J.V. Baldridge (eds) *Governing Academic Organizations*. Berkeley, CA: McCutchan.
Clark, B.R. (1983) *The Higher Education System: Academic Organization in Cross-National Perspective*. Berkeley: University of California Press.
Clarke, J., Hall, S., Jefferson, T. and Roberts, B. (eds) (1976) Subcultures, cultures and class, in S. Hall and T. Jefferson, *Resistance Through Rituals*. London: Hutchinson.
Cooke, A. (1995) Access and participation of adults in higher education in Denmark, in P. Davies (ed.) *Adults in Higher Education: International Perspectives on Access and Participation*. London: Jessica Kingsley, 84–101.
Cross, K.P. and Valley, J.R. (eds) *Planning Non-traditional Programs*. San Francisco: Jossey-Bass.
Crozier, M. (1963) *Le phénomène bureaucratique*. Paris: Seuil.
Crozier, M., Friedberg, E. (1977) *L'acteur et le système*. Paris: Seuil.
Cunningham, S. *et al.* (1998) *New Media and Borderless Education. A Review of the Convergence between Global Media Networks and Higher Education Provision*. Commonwealth of Australia, AGPS, Canberra.
Cyert, R.M. and March, J.G. (1963) *A Behavioral Theory of the Firms*. Englewood Cliffs, NJ: Prentice Hall.
Dal, L. and Dupierreux, J.M. (1996) *Analyse descriptive et modélisation de l'enseignement supérieur non universitaire de la Communauté Française de Belgique, rapport de recherche final*, working paper. Brussels-Louvain-la-Neuve: Institut de Démographie, Université Catholique de Louvain; Laboratoire de Méthodologie du Traitement des Données, Université Libre de Bruxelles.
Dal, L., Dupierreux, J.M., Guyot, J.-L., Kita-Phambu, P. and Tille, Y. (1994) *Etude prospective de la population étudiante des universités de la Communauté Française de Belgiquée, rapport de recherche final, Vols I and II*, working paper. Brussels-Louvain-la-Neuve: Institut de Démographie, Université Catholique de Louvain; Laboratoire de Méthodologie du Traitement des Données, Université Libre de Bruxelles.
Davies, P. (1995a) Access and participation of adults in higher education in France, in P. Davies (ed.) *Adults in Higher Education: International Perspectives on Access and Participation*. London: Jessica Kingsley, 134–58.
Davies, P. (1995b) Themes and trends, in P. Davies (ed.) *Adults in Higher Education: International Perspectives on Access and Participation*. London: Jessica Kingsley, 278–92.
Davies, P. and Reisinger, E. (1995) Access and participation of adults in higher education in Germany, in P. Davies (ed.) *Adults in Higher Education: International Perspectives on Access and Participation*. London: Jessica Kingsley, 159–80.
Deem, R. (1978) *Women and Schooling*. London: Routledge, Kegan and Paul.
Delors, J. (1996) *Learning: the Treasure Within*. Paris: Unesco.
Duke, C. (1992) *The Learning University*. Buckingham: Open University Press.
Department for Education and Employment (1997) *Higher Education for the 21st Century*. London: HMSO.
Department of Education and Science, Education Statistics for the United Kingdom (1992), *Statistical Bulletin 18/92*. London: DfE.
Edwards, R. (1993) *Mature Women Students. Separating or Connecting Family and Education*. London: Taylor and Francis.

Elzinga, A. (1987) Internal and external regulatives in research and higher education systems, in R. Premfors (ed.) *Disciplinary Perspectives on Higher Education and Research, Report No. 37*. Stockholm: University of Stockholm GSHR.

Emerson, R.M. (1962) Power–dependence relations, *American Sociological Review*, 27: 31–41.

Etzioni, A. (1961) *A Comparative Analysis of Complex Organizations. On Power, Involvement, and Their Correlates*. Glencoe, Ill.: The Free Press.

Faure, E. (1972) *Learning To Be*. Paris: Unesco.

Fondation Universitaire (1970–1990) *Rapports Annuels du Bureau de Statistiques*, Brussels.

French, J.R.P. and Raven, B. (1968) The basis of social power, in D. Cartwright (ed.) *Studies in Social Power*. Ann Arbor: University of Michigan Press.

Freynet, P. (1991) The training of adult educators in France, in P. Jarvis and A. Chadwick (eds) *Training Adult Educators in Western Europe*. London: Routledge.

Friedberg, E. and Musselin, C. (1989) *En quête d'universités*. Paris: L'Harmattan.

Friedberg, E. and Musselin, C. (eds) (1992) *Le gouvernement des universités. Perspectives comparatives*. Paris: L'Harmattan.

Gaff, J.G. and Wilson, R.C. (1971) Faculty cultures and interdisciplinary studies, *Journal of Higher Education*, 42 (3): 186–201.

Gellert, C. (ed.) (1993) *Higher Education in Europe*. London: Jessica Kingsley.

Gergen, K.J. and Gergen, M.M. (1984) *Psychologie sociale*. Saint-Laurent: Etudes Vivantes.

Gibbons, M. *et al.* (1994) *The New Production of Knowledge*. London: Sage.

Goedegebuure, L., Kaiser, F., Maassen, P., Meek, L., van Vught F. and de Weert E. (eds) (1994) *Higher Education Policy. An International Comparative Perspective*. Oxford: Pergamon Press.

Goffman, E. (1959) *The Presentation of Self in Everyday Life*. Harmondsworth: Penguin.

Goffman, E. (1961) *Asylums*. Harmondsworth: Penguin.

Goffman, E. (1974) *Frame Analysis: An Essay on the Organization of Experience*. New York: Harper and Row.

Groupe de Travail sous l'égide de la Conférence des Directeurs de Services Universitaires de Formation continue et le Ministère de l'Education Nationale (1990) *Adultes en Formation Initiale dans l'Enseignement Supérieur – Guide pratique à l'usage des établissements d'enseignement supérieur*. Toulouse: Université de Toulouse-Le Mirail.

Guyot, J.-L. (1991) *Micro-populations et perspectives: présentation de la méthodologie développée dans l'étude de la population étudiante de l'Université Catholique de Louvain*, working paper no. 158. Louvain-la-Neuve: Institut de Démographie, Université Catholique de Louvain.

Guyot, J.-L. (1995) Vieilles marmites et meilleures soupes – ou – quand le démographe se doit de faire mentir l'adage populaire, *Actes de la Chaire Quetelet 1995*. Louvain-la-Neuve: Institut de Démographie de l'U.C.L.

Guyot, J.-L. (1996) *Méthodes pour l'analyse des sous-populations scolaires – Accès et accessibilité à un système d'enseignement donné*, working paper no. 181. Louvain-la-Neuve: Institut de Démographie de l'U.C.L.

Guyot, J.-L. (1997) *Accès d'adultes à l'université en Communauté Française de Belgique. Etude comparative avec le Royaume-Uni. Etude de cas Final Research Report*. Louvain-la-Neuve: Department of Education, Université Catholique de Louvain.

Guyot, J.-L. (1998) Particularismes disciplinaires et formation des adultes à l'université. Analyse des facteurs sociologiques des politiques de formation d'adultes à l'université. Unpublished PhD thesis, Université Catholique de Louvain.

Halsey, A.H. (1992) *The Decline of Donnish Dominion*. Oxford: Clarendon Press.

Harman, K.M. (1989) Professional versus academic values: cultural ambivalence in university professional school in Austria, *Higher Education*, 18: 491–509.

Harries-Jenkins, G. (1982) The role of the adult student, *International Journal of Lifelong Education*, 1 (1): 19–39.

Hickson, D.J., Hinings, C.R., Lee, C.A., Schneck, R.H. and Pennings, J.M. (1971) A 'strategic contingencies' theory of intraorganizational power, *Administrative Science Quarterly*, 16: 216–29.

Hore, T. and West, L.H.T. (eds) (1980) *Mature Age Students in Australian Higher Education*. Blackburn: Acacia Press.

Jarvis, P. (1998) Paradoxes of the Learning Society, in J. Holford, C. Griffin and P. Jarvis (eds) *Lifelong Learning: Reality, Rhetoric and Public Policy*. Guildford: DES, University of Surrey.

Jencks, J. and Riesman, D. (1968) *The Academic Revolution*. New York: Doubleday.

Jenkins, R. (1996) *Social Identity*. London: Routledge.

Kasworm, C.E. (1993) Adult higher education from an international perspective, *Higher Education*, 25 (4): 411–24.

Kerr, C. (1963) *The Uses of the University*. Cambridge, Mass: Harvard University Press.

Knowles, M. (1984) *The Adult Learner, a Neglected Species*. London: Gulf Publishing Group.

Kolb, D.A. (1981) Learning styles and disciplinary differences, in A. Chickering (ed.) *The Modern American College*. San Francisco: Jossey-Bass.

Leonard, M. (1994) Transforming the household: mature women students and access to higher education, in S. Davies, C. Lubelska and J. Quinn, *Changing the Subject: Women in HE*. London: Taylor and Francis.

McGivney, V. (1993) Participation and non-participation: a review of the literature, in R. Edwards, S. Sieminiski and D. Zeldin (eds) *Adult Learners, Education and Training*. London: Routledge.

McGivney, V. (1996) *Staying or Leaving the Course; Non-Completion and Retention of Mature Students in Further and Higher Education*. Leicester: NIACE.

McLaren, A. (1985) *Ambitions and Realizations – Women in Adult Education*. London: Peter Owen.

McLuhan, M. and Fisra, Q. (1967) *The Medium is the Message*. Rickmansworth: Penguin.

McPherson, J., Hadfield, M. and Day, C. (1994) Student perspectives and the effectiveness of continuing education, in S. Haselgrove (ed.) *The Student Experience*. Buckingham: SRHE/OUP.

Manning, P. (1992) *Erving Goffman and Modern Sociology*. Cambridge: Polity Press.

Marchand, L. (1983) *Introduction à l'éducation des adultes*. Montreal: Préfontaine.

Maroy, C. (1988) Formation professionnelle et professionnels de la formation. Unpublished PhD thesis, Université Catholique de Louvain.

Maynard, E. and Pearsall, S. (1994) What about male adult students? A comparison of men and women students, *Journal of Access Studies*, 9: 229–40.

MEC (1990) *Development of Education – National Report on Spain*, International Conference in Education, 42nd Meeting, Geneva, Ministerio de Education y Ciencia.

Merrill, B. (1999) *Gender, Change and Identity: Mature Women Students in Universities*. Aldershot: Ashgate.

Merton, R.K. (1973) *The Sociology of Science*. Chicago: University of Chicago Press.

Millett, J.D. (1962) *The Academic Community. An Essay on Organization*. New York: McGraw-Hill.

Ministère de l'Education Francophone (1972–1988) *Etudes et Documents*. Brussels.

Ministère de l'Education Nationale (1961–1971) *Annuaires Statistiques de l'Enseignement.* Brussels.

Ministère de l'Education Nationale (1991) *La formation continue dans les établissements d'enseignement supérieur au cours de l'année civile 1989 (Note d'information 91–17).* Paris: MEN.

Ministerie van Onderwijs (1972–1988) *Statistische Jaarboeken van het Onderwijs.* Brussels.

Ministry of Education and Science (1992) *Education policy in the Netherlands: 1990– 1992.* Zoetemeer: Ministerie van Onderwijs en Wetenschappen.

Mintzberg, H. (1979) *The Structuring of Organizations: A Synthesis of the Research.* Englewood Cliffs, NJ: Prentice Hall.

Mintzberg, H. (1983a) *Power In and Around Organizations.* Engelwood Cliffs, NJ: Prentice-Hall.

Mintzberg, H. (1983b) *Structure in Fives: Designing Effective Organizations.* Englewood Cliffs, NJ: Prentice Hall.

Mintzberg, H. (1989) *Mintzberg on Management. Inside Our Strange World of Organizations.* New York: The Free Press.

Moore, W.L. (1979) Determinants and outcomes of departmental power: a two campus study. Unpublished PhD dissertation, University of California, Berkeley.

Newman, J.H. (1976) *The Idea of a University.* Oxford: Oxford University Press, originally published 1853.

Nizet, J. and Pichault, F. (1995) *Comprendre les organisations: Mintzberg à l'épreuve des faits.* Paris: Gaëtan Morin Editeur.

O' Shea, J. and Corrigan, P. (1979) Surviving adult education, *Adult Education,* 52 (4): 229–35.

OECD (1992) *Les systèmes éducatifs en Belgique: similitudes et divergences.* Paris: OECD.

OECD (1996) *Lifelong Learning for All.* Paris: OECD.

OECD/CERI (1987) *Adults in Higher Education.* Paris: OECD.

Osborne, M. (1995) Access and participation of adults in higher education in Spain, in P. Davies (ed.) *Adults in Higher Education: International Perspectives on Access and Participation.* London: Jessica Kingsley, 252–78.

Osborne, M. and Gallacher, J. (1995) Access and participation of adults in higher education in Scotland, in P. Davies (ed.) *Adults in Higher Education: International Perspectives on Access and Participation.* London: Jessica Kingsley, 224–51.

Parker, S. (1995) Access and participation of adults in higher education in Italy, in P. Davies (ed.) *Adults in Higher Education: International Perspectives on Access and Participation.* London: Jessica Kingsley, 181–202.

Parry, G. (1995) Access and participation of adults in higher education in England, Wales and Northern Ireland, in P. Davies (ed.) *Adults in Higher Education: International Perspectives on Access and Participation.* London: Jessica Kingsley, 102–33.

Parry, G. (1997) Foreword, in J. Williams (ed.) *Negotiating Access to Higher Education.* Buckingham: SRHE/Open University Press.

Pascall, G. and Cox, R. (1993) *Women Returning to Higher Education.* Buckingham: SRHE/Open University Press.

Pfeffer, J. (1981) *Power in Organizations.* Marshfield, MA: Pitman.

Postle, G. (1995) Access and participation of adults in higher education in Australia, in P. Davies (ed.) *Adults in Higher Education: International Perspectives on Access and Participation.* London: Jessica Kingsley, 6–37.

Rasmussen, T.K. (1992) Equality, in B. Marchine and M. Giuberti (eds) *Proceedings of the Conference on Access to Higher Education in Europe, Parma 13–16 October 1992.* Parma: Università degli Studi di Parma.

Reitter, R. and Ramanantsoa, B. (1985) *Pouvoir et Politique.* Paris: McGraw Hill.

Riley, G.L. and Baldridge, J.V. (eds) (1977) *Governing Academic Organizations.* Berkeley, CA: McCutchan.

Rothblatt, S. (1985) The notion of an open scientific community in scientific perspective, in M. Gibbons and B. Wittrock (eds) *Science as a Commodity.* Harlow: Longman.

Salancik, G.R. and Pfeffer, J. (1974a) Organizational decision making as a political process: the case of a university budget, *Administrative Science Quarterly,* 19: 135–51.

Salancik, G.R. and Pfeffer, J. (1974b) The bases and uses of power in organizational decision making: the case of a university, *Administrative Science Quarterly,* 19: 453–73.

Schutze, H.G. (1988) The context of adult participation in higher education: an overview of the CERI/OCDE project, in K. Abrahamsson, K. Rubenson and M. Slowey (eds) *Adults in the Academy: International Trends in Adult Higher Education.* Stockholm: Swedish National Board of Education.

Scott, P. (1984) *The Crisis of the University.* London: Croom Helm.

Scott, P. (1995) *The Meanings of Mass Higher Education.* Buckingham: SRHE/Open University Press.

Scott, P. (1996) The idea of the university in the 21st century: a British perspective in P. Raggatt, R. Edwards and N. Small (eds) *The learning society: challenges and trends.* London: Routledge/Open University Press.

Scottish Office Education Department (1992) *Adults in Schools and Colleges,* Statistical Bulletin K1/1992/2. Edinburgh: SOED.

Scottish Office Education Department (1994) *Adults' Participation in Schools, Colleges and Universities – Provisional Data for 1991.* Edinburgh: SOED.

Simon, H.A. (1979) Rational decision making in business organizations, *American Economic Review,* 69: 493–513.

Slowey, M. (1987) Adults in higher education: the situation in the United Kingdom, in H.G. Schutze (ed.) *Adults in Higher Education,* report for CERI/OCDE. Stockholm: Almqvist and Wiksell.

Slowey, M. (ed.) (1995) *Implementing Change from within Universities and Colleges.* London: Kogan Page.

Spackman, A. and Owen, M. (1995) Access and participation of adults in higher education in The Netherlands, in P. Davies (ed.) *Adults in Higher Education: International Perspectives on Access and Participation.* London: Jessica Kingsley, 203–23.

Spender, D. (1982) *Invisible Women, The Schooling Scandal.* Reading: The Women's Press.

Sporn, B. (1996) Managing university culture: an analysis of the relationship between institutional culture and management approaches, *Higher Education,* 32 (1): 41–61.

Thompson, A. (1997) Gatekeeping: inclusionary and exclusionary discourses and practices, in J. Williams (ed.) *Negotiating Access to Higher Education.* Buckingham: SRHE/Open University Press.

Thompson, J. (1997) *Words in Edgeways, Radical Learning for Social Change.* Leicester: NIACE.

Tight, M. (1991) *Higher Education: A Part-time Perspective.* Buckingham: SRHE/Open University Press.

Toffler, A. (1970) *Future Shock.* London: Bodley Head.

Tuijnman, A. (1990) Dilemmas of open admissions policy: quality and efficiency in Swedish higher education, *Higher Education,* 20 (4): 443–457.

Webb, S. (1997) Alternative Students? Conceptualizations of Difference, in J. Williams (ed.) *Negotiating Access to Higher Education, The Discourse of Selectivity and Equity.* Buckingham: SRHE/Open University Press.

Webb, S., Davies, P., Green, P., Thompson, A. and Williams, J. (1993) Alternative Entry to Higher Education. Summary Report, Employment Dept./FEU.

Weil, S. (1986) Non-traditional learners within higher education institutions: discovery and disappointment, *Studies in Higher Education,* 11 (3): 219–35.

Weil, S. (1989) From a language of observation to a language of experience: studying the prospectives of diverse adults in higher education, *Journal of Access Studies,* (1): 17–43.

West, L. (1996) *Beyond Fragments.* London: Taylor and Francis.

West, L. and Hore, T. (1989) The impact of higher education on adult students in Australia, *Higher Education,* 18: 473–83.

West, L., Hore, T., Eaton, E. and Kennard, B. (1986) *The Impact of Higher Education on Mature Age Students.* Melbourne: Monash University, Higher Education Advisory and Research Unit.

Williams, J. (ed.) (1997) *Negotiating Access to Higher Education: The Discourse of Selectivity and Equity.* Buckingham: SRHE/Open University Press.

Willis, P. (1977) *Learning to Labour.* Westmead: Saxon House.

Woodley, A., Wagner, L., Slowey, M., Fulton, O. and Bourner, T. (1987) *Choosing to Learn.* Buckingham: SRHE/Open University Press.

Woodrow, M. (1996) *Access, Adults and Under-representation in European Higher Education,* European Conference on 'Lifelong Learning and its Impact on Social and Regional Development'. Bremen: Bremen University.

Young, M. (ed.) (1971) *Knowledge and Control.* London: Macmillan.

Index

The Society for Research into Higher Education

The Society for Research into Higher Education exists to stimulate and coordinate research into all aspects of higher education. It aims to improve the quality of higher education through the encouragement of debate and publication on issues of policy, on the organization and management of higher education institutions, and on the curriculum and teaching methods.

The Society's income is derived from subscriptions, sales of its books and journals, conference fees and grants. It receives no subsidies, and is wholly independent. Its individual members include teachers, researchers, managers and students. Its corporate members are institutions of higher education, research institutes, professional, industrial and governmental bodies. Members are not only from the UK, but from elsewhere in Europe, from America, Canada and Australasia, and it regards its international work as among its most important activities.

Under the imprint *SRHE & Open University Press*, the Society is a specialist publisher of research, having over 70 titles in print. The Editorial Board of the Society's Imprint seeks authoritative research or study in the above fields. It offers competitive royalties, a highly recognizable format in both hardback and paperback and the worldwide reputation of the Open University Press.

The Society also publishes *Studies in Higher Education* (three times a year), which is mainly concerned with academic issues, *Higher Education Quarterly* (formerly *Universities Quarterly*), mainly concerned with policy issues, *Research into Higher Education Abstracts* (three times a year), and *SRHE News* (four times a year).

The society holds a major annual conference in December, jointly with an institution of higher education. In 1996 the topic was 'Working in Higher Education' at University of Wales, Cardiff. In 1997 it was 'Beyond the First Degree' at the University of Warwick and in 1998 it was 'The Globalization of Higher Education' at the University of Lancaster. The 1999 conference will be on the topic of higher education and its communities at UMIST.

The Society's committees, study groups and networks are run by the members. The networks at present include:

Access	Mentoring
Curriculum Development	Postgraduate Issues
Disability	Quality
Eastern European	Quantitative Studies
Funding	Student Development
Legal Education	Vocational Qualifications

Benefits to members

Individual

Individual members receive:

- *SRHE News*, the Society's publications list, conference details and other material included in mailings.
- Greatly reduced rates for *Studies in Higher Education* and *Higher Education Quarterly*.
- A 35 per cent discount on all SRHE & Open University Press publications.
- Free copies of the Procedings – commissioned papers on the theme of the Annual Conference.
- Free copies of *Research into Higher Education Abstracts*.
- Reduced rates for the annual conference.
- Extensive contacts and scope for facilitating initiatives.
- Free copies of the *Register of Members' Research Interests*.
- Membership of the Society's networks.

Corporate

Corporate members receive:

- Benefits of individual members, plus:
- Free copies of *Studies in Higher Education*.
- Unlimited copies of the Society's publications at reduced rates.
- Reduced rates for the annual conference.
- The right to submit applications for the Society's research grants.
- The right to use the Society's facility for supplying statistical HESA data for purposes of research.

Membership details: SRHE, 3 Devonshire Street, London W1N 2BA, UK. Tel: 0171 637 2766. Fax: 0171 637 2781. email: srhe@mailbox.ulcc.ac.uk
World Wide Web: http://www.srhe.ac.uk./srhe/
Catalogue: SRHE & Open University Press, Celtic Court, 22 Ballmoor, Buckingham MK18 1XW. Tel: 01280 823388. Fax: 01280 823233. email: enquiries@openup.co.uk

THE LEARNING UNIVERSITY
TOWARDS A NEW PARADIGM?

Chris Duke

Chris Duke addresses issues central to the evolution and future of higher education. He examines assumptions by and about universities, their changing environments, the new terminologies and their adaptation to new circumstances. He explores how far universities *are* learning, changing and adapting; and whether they are becoming different kinds of institutions or whether only the rhetoric is altering. He is particularly concerned with how far universities, as key teaching and learning organizations, are adopting the new paradigm of lifelong learning. He discusses how far the concepts and requirements for institution-wide continuing education have been identified and internalized in institutional planning; are they, for instance, reflected in programmes of staff development (in the continuing education of staff in higher education)? *Is* a new paradigm of university education and organization really emerging?

Contents
Old assumptions and new practices – Change and higher education: the new discourse – Mission, aims and objectives – What may be new? – Out of the box: continuing education university-wide – Finishing school or service station: what mix? – Access, quality and success: old and new criteria – Staff development and organizational learning – The fallacy of the ivory tower – Appendix – Bibliography – Index.

160pp   0 335 15653 3   (Paperback)

THE MEANINGS OF MASS HIGHER EDUCATION

Peter Scott

This book is the first systematic attempt to analyse the growth of mass higher education in a specifically British context, while seeking to develop more theoretical perspectives on this transformation of élite university systems into open post-secondary education systems. It is divided into three main sections. The first examines the evolution of British higher education and the development of universities and other institutions. The second explores the political, social and economic context within which mass systems are developing. What are the links between post-industrial society, a post-Fordist economy and the mass university? The third section discusses the links between massification and wider currents in intellectual and scientific culture.

Contents
Preface – Introduction – Structure and institutions – State and society – Science and culture – Understanding mass higher education – Notes – Index.

208pp   0 335 19442 7   (Paperback)   0 335 19443 5   (Hardback)

NEGOTIATING ACCESS TO HIGHER EDUCATION
THE DISCOURSE OF SELECTIVITY AND EQUITY

Edited by Jenny Williams

Who has access to higher education and how are students selected? How is access discussed and whose voices are heard? As we move toward a mass higher education system who are the 'new' students, and why and how are they so labelled?

Negotiating Access to Higher Education uses a discourse approach as a framework for making sense of recent changes in access to higher education. It analyses these changes and the debates surrounding them across several levels of policy, practice and experience within the higher education system: the state, higher education agencies, research, institutions, admissions tutors, and students. It examines how discursive struggles over entitlement, selectivity and equity determine who can be a student; what varying understandings inform admissions policies and practices; and the relationship between those policies (and practices) and student needs in a changing system.

Contents
Foreword – Preface – Acknowledgements – List of Abbreviations – Access to Higher Education in the late Twentieth Century: Policy, Power and Discourse – The Discourse of Access: The Legitimation of Selectivity – Number Crunching: The Discourse of Statistics – Alternative Students? Conceptualizations of Difference – Institutional Rhetorics and Realities – Gatekeeping: Inclusionary and Exclusionary Discourses and Practices – Student Voices: Alternative Routes, Alternative Identities – Conclusions – Appendices – References – Index.

208pp   0 335 19678 0   (pbk)   0 335 19679 9   (hbk)